Fundamentalism and Gender

Fundamentalism and Gender

Edited by

JOHN STRATTON HAWLEY

New York   Oxford

OXFORD UNIVERSITY PRESS

1994

Oxford University Press

Oxford   New York   Toronto
Delhi   Bombay   Calcutta   Madras   Karachi
Kuala Lumpur   Singapore   Hong Kong   Tokyo
Nairobi   Dar es Salaam   Cape Town
Melbourne   Auckland   Madrid

and associated companies in
Berlin   Ibadan

Copyright © 1994 by Oxford University Press, Inc.

Published by Oxford University Press, Inc.
200 Madison Avenue, New York, New York 10016

Oxford is a registered trademark of Oxford University Press, Inc.

Library of Congress Cataloging-in-Publication Data
Fundamentalism and gender / edited by John Stratton Hawley.
p. cm.   Includes bibliographical references and index.
Contents: American Protestantism / Randall Balmer — Indian Islam
/ Peter J. Awn — Hinduism / John S. Hawley — Japanese new
religions / Helen Hardacre — "Fundamentalism," objections from a modern
Jewish historian / Jay M. Harris — Fundamentalism and the control
of women / Karen McCarthy Brown.
ISBN 0-19-508261-3   — ISBN 0-19-508262-1 (pbk.)
1. Women and religion.   2. Fundamentalism.
I. Hawley, John Stratton, 1941–
BL458.F86   1994
200'.82—dc20   92-42298

2 4 6 8 9 7 5 3 1

Printed in the United States of America
on acid-free paper

Acknowledgments

The discussion recorded here began as a two-year faculty seminar based in the associated Religion Departments at Barnard College and Columbia University. Those of us who have contributed essays wish to thank our colleagues in the seminar, whose observations greatly benefited this volume: Celia Deutsch, David Weiss Halivni, Robert Somerville, and Alan Segal; as well as Holland Hendrix, now of Union Theological Seminary; Brian Smith, now of the University of California, Riverside; and Paul Watt, now of DePauw University. Thanks are also due to Marjorie Lehman, our seminar rapporteur, and to Kristie Contardi and Tara Susman, who helped with secretarial and bibliographical tasks farther along the way. Tara Susman's labors have greatly improved the index.

The editor is grateful to Ainslie Embree and Kevin Reinhart for their wise and forthright comments on the content of the introduction, and to Laura Shapiro, as ever, for suggestions as to style. Cynthia Read, Peter Ohlin, and others at Oxford University Press, as well as Steven Gray, have been kind friends and good critics, and we owe a debt of thanks as well to Lauren Bryant of Beacon Press for her astute reading of the manuscript. Paul Courtright and an anonymous reader at Oxford have also made very helpful appraisals of the book. We appreciate assistance provided by the University Seminars at Columbia University in the last stages of preparing the manuscript for publication. Certain of the ideas presented in these pages have benefitted from discussions in the University Seminar on Tradition and Change in South and Southeast Asia. Finally, we thank the Fundamentalism Project of the American Academy of Arts and Sciences and the University of Chicago Press, its publisher, for permission to reprint the essay by Helen Hardacre, which appears in substantially the same form in the Fundamentalism Project's volume *Fundamentalisms and Society: Reclaiming the Sciences, the Family, and Education* (1992), edited by Martin A. Marty and R. Scott Appleby. While she was professor in the Department of Religion at Princeton University, Professor Hardacre was simultaneously active in both the AAAS project and ours. All rights to portions of Professor Hardacre's essay that are printed in *Fundamentalisms and Society* are reserved. Reprinted sections appear here courtesy of the University of Chicago Press.

Contents

Fundamentalism and Gender

Fundamentalism & Gender
ed. J. S. Hawley. NY:
Oxford, 1994.

1

Introduction

JOHN S. HAWLEY AND WAYNE PROUDFOOT

Fundamentalism, the dictionaries tell us, is something that has to do with texts. In the most basic use of the term, fundamentalists are American Protestants with a militant desire to defend religion against the onslaughts of modern, secular culture; their principal weapon is their insistence on the inerrancy of scripture. As for the enemy—the world view propagated by secular naturalism or "scientific humanism," as fundamentalists often call it—its most invidious manifestations are the theory of evolution and the methods of "higher" textual criticism, as applied to sacred texts. Both raise questions about the inherent correctness of the Bible.

The inviolability of a text may be crucial to fundamentalists, but a quick reflection on the history of American fundamentalism in the 1980s and 1990s shows that much more is involved than that. It is true that the controversy about "creationism" concerns biblical inerrancy, and the debate about prayer in the public schools is also obliquely related. Yet the other issues that fundamentalists have most hotly contested—the Equal Rights Amendment and the legality of abortion—have nothing to do with inerrancy of scripture. One can search the Bible forever without finding any pronouncement on these subjects, at least in the plain, unvarnished biblical terms that fundamentalists themselves insist on. In the abortion debate certain pas-

3

sages are sometimes marshalled as relevant—"Be fruitful and multiply," for example—but the primary thrust of the effort is not to defend the correctness of the biblical text: it is not under attack. What does it mean, then, that these issues have come to hold center stage in the drama of American fundamentalism?

Admittedly certain echoes of the creationist debate ring in the anti-abortion campaign: what God hath done, let no mortal rend asunder. Creation concerns the macrocosm; the "right to life," the microcosm. Yet the creationist analogy has been at best a minor force in rallying fundamentalists to the "pro-life" cause. Far more important is the conviction of many American evangelicals that the family is the natural home of religion, and that the woman in the family is its pivotal personality and principal guardian. As Randall Balmer shows in his essay here, fundamentalist religion idealizes woman: she is the self-sacrificing wife and mother whose hands are little sullied by the business of running the external world. When "secular humanism" and those who struggle for women's rights assert that a woman's deepest identity may be found in something other than her connection to her family, as the possibility of abortion seems to guarantee, the challenge to fundamentalism is profound. As American fundamentalism has prospered over the last two decades, its most powerful message has been one of social, not scriptural, inerrancy.

The purpose of this book is to set out a range of materials that will enable readers to understand the strength of the tie between fundamentalism and a conservative ideology of gender—not just in American culture, but in other places where fundamentalists are active. Why, in 1979, did the leaders of the Islamic revolution in Iran insist that women be covered in public, and why did militant Muslims demanding an independent Kashmir do the same thing ten years later?[1] Why, in 1981, did the Akali Dal, the most influential Sikh party, demand a code of personal law that would bar Sikh women from using cosmetics, jewelry, or clothing that exposed their bodies?[2] Think also of Vishva Hindu Parishad—the group primarily responsible for the bloody agitations aimed at building a temple to Rama to mark his supposed birthplace, on a site where a mosque stood until Hindu militants destroyed it in 1992. Why did the VHP's general secretary, in 1989, list three points of Hindu honor that he held to be nonnegotiable: the building of the temple, to be sure; but also the veneration of woman and the defense of "mother cow"?[3] Why has women's wearing of the sari, not Western dresses or pants, recently become an aspect of Vishva Hindu Parishad teaching? Is there a connection between demands like these and the behavior of Hasidic Jews who in the same year stoned a group of women who were defying tradition by carrying the Torah as they went to pray at the Wailing Wall in Jerusalem?[4] Finally, in the "New Religions" of Japan, even in sects where women often hold important positions of leadership, why has there been a great emphasis on returning to ideals of the family that would remove women from the workplace and define their identities entirely through the service they render to their husbands, in-laws, and children?

We hope that this book will provide the means for working out answers to such questions. We do not, however, have a single explanation to propose. When the volume was in its germinating stage, in a series of faculty seminars undertaken by the Departments of Religion at Barnard College and Columbia University in 1988–1989, we hashed things out on a fortnightly basis; even so, we found ourselves unable to come to a consensus. Issues of definition and approach loomed large—the question of what a fundamentalist is, comparatively speaking, and whether indeed one can speak comparatively about such a thing. Yet it is safe to say that most contributors to the seminar felt the cumulative force of a series of "family resemblances" as we moved from one militantly antimodern religious group to another, tradition by tradition and culture by culture.

Plan of the Book

As a way of allowing readers to recapitulate our discussion in this volume, we begin with a series of case studies, rather than with a single, unitive theory. These case studies—Christian, Islamic, Hindu, and Japanese—occupy the first four chapters of the book. All concern fundamentalist groups active in the present day; the major events under discussion occurred in the course of the last decade. At the end, we move on to two more theoretical essays that respond to these case studies and to major issues in the discussion at large.

Randall Balmer leads off by taking an extended look at the ideal of femininity that functions in contemporary American fundamentalism. He approaches current convictions, however, from a historical point of view. Balmer points to the Second Great Awakening, in the first part of the nineteenth century, as the source of "the traditional ideal of femininity" so confidently espoused as a timeless truth by contemporary fundamentalists, and he draws attention to the economic context that made that vision of femininity possible. The coming of the Industrial Revolution gave women an autonomous domain—the home—that they had not previously had, while at the same time making them more dependent on their husbands (for their wages) than they had ever been before. Balmer then describes the shock to this view of the "evangelical household" that was caused by the social forces unleashed in the latter half of the twentieth century, when a renewed adulation of the nuclear family, during the 1950s and 1960s, gave way before a rising divorce rate and floods of women returning to the workforce. He lays out the several ways in which the issue of abortion served to crystallize fundamentalists' understanding of secular culture as "antifamily," and suggests that the fetus itself plays an important symbolic role, representing both the purity and the helpless vulnerability that figure so prominently in fundamentalists' understanding of their own position in relation to the modern world.

It was a Supreme Court case—the decision to legalize abortion in *Roe* v. *Wade*—that jolted Jerry Falwell out of the apolitical slumber he called typical for American evangelicals well into the 1970s; and it was a Supreme Court case in India that drew Muslims, especially the more conservative among them, into a new form of political activism in the mid-1980s. In his essay on the political use of religion in Indian Islam, Peter Awn describes the affair that swirled around Shah Bano, an elderly woman who appealed to the courts for state intervention when her husband left her indigent by divorcing her to marry a younger woman. The English-speaking middle classes, who think of themselves as the primary guarantors of secular democracy in India, tended to see Shah Bano's case as an issue of individual justice. Certainly most feminists took this approach. Most Muslims, however, viewed the matter differently, seeing it as an attempt on the part of the secular government to interfere in the domain of Islamic family law. This India's constitution had somewhat reluctantly delegated to the Islamic *shari'ah*, where Muslims were concerned. Ultimately this case was perceived by Muslims to pose such a threat to their cultural identity that it propelled them to unified action even as many individual Muslims expressed their sympathy for the justice of Shah Bano's complaint. Was it because the Shah Bano case had so directly to do with the definition of woman's place?

John Hawley's essay, which follows, deals with another incident that occurred in North India—this time in 1987, only a year or so after the Shah Bano affair subsided. In this instance, however, the ambience was Hindu, not Muslim. The controversy began when a young Rajput woman named Roop Kanwar committed suttee (or "became *satī*," as Hindi speakers would say), in contravention of the law of the land. When secularists and feminists expressed shock that this could have been allowed to happen, various conservative Hindu groups vociferously defended Roop Kanwar's right to have acted as she did. The state, they said, had no business interfering in matters of religion. Theirs became the next cause célèbre to follow Shah Bano's in the national press.

To secularists, the Hindus who rallied to defend the cause of *sati* were fundamentalists, just like the Muslims who worked to keep Shah Bano within the confines of *shari'ah*. Interestingly, the Hindu fundamentalists also saw an analogy (albeit an adversarial one) between the two cases: the government had ultimately backed away from an attempt to "legislate religion" in the Shah Bano case — indeed, it had created new legislation specifically mandating that the matter be left exclusively in Muslim hands — while the reverse happened in the case of Roop Kanwar. Hindus' perception of an imbalance between the way in which they and Muslims are treated under the Indian constitution continues to provide grist for the mill of interreligious strife in India. It may not be accidental that the two incidents that managed to bring this issue so forcefully before the public eye both concerned the religious construction of gender.

The fourth and final case study, which explores fundamentalist gender ideology in the New Religions of Japan, is laid out by Helen Hardacre. Unlike the instances of Christian, Muslim, and Hindu fundamentalism previously presented, where the principal religious activists are overwhelmingly male, many of these religions are led by women. Even so, one of the hallmarks of these religions is their view that women ought to be subservient to men in ways that were institutionalized in the multigenerational, male-dominated *ie* household, which was forced aside when the Allied Forces recast the basis of Japanese law in 1947. On the whole, Japan's New Religions extol a return to this "golden age," when women entirely depended on men and habitually displayed the humility and self-sacrifice appropriate to their position. As a way of making a specific comparison to fundamentalist Protestantism in the United States, Hardacre describes the anti-abortion postures taken by two of these New Religions in particular: Seichō no Ie and Reiyūkai. She also describes a social background that invites other analogies between fundamentalist movements in these two countries that superficially look so disparate.

Clearly four case studies cannot set out all the significant motifs one would need to consider in evaluating the relation between fundamentalism and the construction of gender, either on a global scale or in relation to any particular setting. We hope, however, that they offer a certain balance that may prove helpful. Two involve religions that belong to the Abrahamic tradition (Balmer, Awn) and two in-

volve religions that do not (Hawley, Hardacre). Two concern fundamentalist groups in advanced industrial societies (Balmer, Hardacre),
while two describe fundamentalists active in postcolonial "Third-
World" societies (Awn, Hawley). All four take fundamentalism not
just as a doctrinal phenomenon but as a political and social reality as
well. Nonetheless, they can only suggest the range of issues one
would need to think about in determining the relation between fundamentalism and gender.

For that reason, in part, we include two additional essays that
have a more explicitly theoretical thrust. The first, by Jay Harris,
attacks the notion that "fundamentalism" provides a good rubric for
drawing comparative conclusions about religious groups and traditions. Harris, a scholar of post-Enlightenment Judaism, surveys Jewish responses to modernity from the early eighteenth century onward, to determine whether there ever was anything comparable to
Christian antimodernist fundamentalism among Jews. His answer is
in the negative. For Harris, the Jews' encounter with modernity, their
characteristic understanding of sacred texts, and their sense of besetment were all so radically different from what Protestants experienced that in each area a close comparison to Protestant fundamentalism is ruled out. As for the groups in modern-day Israel and
elsewhere that have been identified as fundamentalist in the current
literature, Harris is again suspicious. He perceives the use of this
label as implicitly pejorative: rather than rendering such groups intelligible, he thinks, it merely condemns them as fanatical. Similarly in
regard to women: Harris fails to find a distinctive attitude toward
gender in the branches of Judaism that have sometimes been called
fundamentalist.

Three conclusions might be drawn from Harris's essay. The first
is that the Jewish tradition is an exceptional case, from a comparative
point of view. It has been argued that this is true in other realms – in
regard to saints, for example[5] – although Harris explicitly rejects the
idea that the Jewish tradition may be irreducibly special here, too. A
second possible conclusion is that the category "fundamentalism" itself proves too blunt an instrument to guide comparative study in
the field of modern religion – a possibility we will shortly take up. A
third conclusion might ask whether Harris is mistaken in some of
his judgments, a response that would surely be given by such scholars
as Bruce Lawrence, Hava Lazarus-Yafeh, and others who have used
the term *fundamentalism* to refer to Jewish groups active on the
modern scene.[6]

Such writers would doubtless stress that—for all the obvious differences that brand the Neturei Karta ("Guardians of the City") as conservative, while the Gush Emunim ("Bloc of the Faithful") are innovative, to use words adopted by Menachem Friedman[7]—these groups are nonetheless drawn together by their strident opposition to secular Zionism, by the fact of their encompassment by the State of Israel, and by their common reliance on "the same halakhic-midrashic-kabalistic literature." The Neturei Karta and Gush Emunim also share the conviction that they represent the faithful "remnant" within modern Israel, even though they differ over whether they are operating within the time of exile or that of redemption.[8] To such considerations one might add the fact that these groups' zeal in preserving conservative attitudes toward gender in the context of modern Israel also pulls them into alignment, although one would have to concede that in this respect the Neturei Karta, with their very strict segregation of the sexes, are somewhat to the "right" of the Gush Emunim.

But even if one grants that a response can be made to Harris along these lines, one must acknowledge the force of his argument. At the very least, Harris sounds a profound (if witty) note of caution to anyone who would define *fundamentalism* primarily in relation to modernity—and in that sense see it as a phenomenon with international, interreligious resonance—without also appreciating that it always derives strength and character from the particular religious tradition within which it develops. To gloss over this fact and suggest that fundamentalism itself is a unitive religious tradition that variously infects or manifests itself in other, older religions such as Judaism or Islam is to use a desperate shorthand. Harris puts a much needed question mark next to the sort of perspective that speaks of the Neturei Karta and Gush Emunim as if they were, in Bruce Lawrence's words, "the two most compelling exponents of Jewish fundamentalism in Israel."[9]

In this book's concluding essay, Karen McCarthy Brown adopts an approach that is in spirit almost diametrically opposed to the one put forward by Jay Harris. Precisely by undertaking a close analysis of the gender component in modern American fundamentalism, she develops a perspective that enables her to see "fundamentalisms" elsewhere in the world as representing the same basic constellation of responses to the stresses of post-Enlightenment modernity. She accomplishes this task by moving beyond the specific historical stimuli that caused the "pro-life" movement to flower in the United States from the 1970s onward, and by bringing to light a complex of deeper, less clearly defined factors that moved abortion to the forefront of American religious politics.

Brown takes American fundamentalism to be essentially reactive, and she makes the argument that societies under considerable stress almost inevitably seek to allay their anxiety by firming up boundaries having to do with women and children. The reason for this behavior is that these groups are closely keyed to the first, most basic categories of order that children universally learn—adult versus child, male versus female—and therefore serve as fine raw material for producing symbolic order when the world seems dangerously chaotic. Brown suggests that the "pro-life" urge to affirm one's own effectiveness and virtue by rescuing the innocent is to be understood in the context of other symbolic actions that have emerged in recent American history—efforts like Operation Babylift, which was launched as popular support for the Vietnam War disintegrated, or the Soviet–American campaign to save whales, which took on life as the reference points of the Cold War began to evaporate. All these represent symbolic attempts to deal both with cognitive befuddlement and with the loss of conviction about one's own moral purity.

Brown points out that this overlap between the realms of "is" and "ought" has traditionally been at the core of religion. Similarly, the strong combination of rational and prerational aspects that one finds in religion contributes substantially to this domain's special power in dealing with deeply disorienting stress. When the Enlightenment attempted to replace religion with reason, it inevitably disappointed modern people with what Brown calls "the failed promise of Enlightenment rationalism." She depicts fundamentalist religion as both an instrument of protest against this failed promise and an example of the failure itself, in that fundamentalist religion displays the same horror of embodiment and of nonrational interaction with the world that one finds in the Enlightenment perspective more generally. The resulting desire to repress the realities of appetite, bodily finitude, and sexuality finds its object, once again, in the "other." From a male point of view particularly, this other is woman; but at some level both men and women feel safer when women are kept within bounds. Working primarily from the examples set forth in this volume, Brown shows how this recognizably generic fundamentalist ideology of gender can appear in a variety of historical contexts. She then concludes with some observations about why Western scholarship has typically scapegoated fundamentalism in much the same way that fundamentalists themselves have scapegoated (or at least targeted) women. On this point—that current discourse about fundamentalism has a disturbingly myopic component—Harris and Brown agree.[10]

Fundamentalism in Its American Context

The term *fundamentalism* came into common usage in the second decade of this century, with the publication of a series of pamphlets called *The Fundamentals*, which appeared between 1910 and 1915, and through a set of conferences of the World's Christian Fundamentals Association in 1919.[11] Historians of American religion agree that fundamentalism's classic period followed, in the 1920s, but they have used different criteria to identify and account for it. The fundamentalist movement has been described in at least three very different ways: (1) chiefly in sociological and political terms as a last-ditch defense of a way of life that was rapidly being superseded; (2) by reference to its roots in revivalism and pietism; (3) by its nineteenth-century intellectual antecedents in millenarianism and the Princeton theology.[12] The utility of each approach depends on what is being studied, but none seems entirely satisfactory for comparative use.

The most helpful point of general departure is provided by George Marsden, who shows that the fundamentalist movement of the 1920s went considerably beyond millenarian circles and who goes on to define *fundamentalism* in its heyday as "militantly anti-modernist Protestant evangelicalism." "Militant opposition to modernism," he says, "was what most clearly set off fundamentalism from a number of closely related traditions, such as evangelicalism, revivalism, pietism, the holiness movements, millenarianism, Reformed confessionalism, Baptist traditionalism, and other denominational orthodoxies."[13]

The emergence of fundamentalism in opposition to modernism—or to what it apprehended to be liberal modernism—is the crucial point, but we must be clear about what this means. In the American case, we do not normally think of the Amish, the Mennonites, the Hasidim, or other orthodox groups as fundamentalist, although in different ways they resist change and what we might call modernity. On the other hand, fundamentalist groups have proved themselves to be masters of some of the technology and the organizational sophistication that we identify with modernity, as well as showing an interest in science and its relation to religion that often exceeds that of religious liberals.[14] Unlike the Amish or (in some respects) the Hasids, fundamentalists do not reject the technological trappings of modern life—indeed, sometimes they eagerly embrace them—but they do define themselves in opposition to certain aspects of modern culture, especially scientific naturalism, higher criticism of the Bible, and perceived changes in moral values.

The reactive character of Christian fundamentalism in America — its militant opposition to modern*ism*, if not to all modernity — is important. This militancy signals that the oppositional posture is what actually defines fundamentalism. Fundamentalists do not merely detach themselves from certain trends in modern culture; they commit themselves to battle against those trends. They are defined by that opposition and that battle. Clearly the Amish and Hasidim are also shaped by their twentieth-century context more than might appear at first glance. Their claims to be carrying on a traditional life of piety as it was lived in the seventeenth or eighteenth centuries, unaffected by the intervening years and by the rest of the world, are specious; and close study would show how their "traditional" lives bear the marks of the contemporary world and of an idealized and selectively remembered past. But they are identified by their claim to be continuing a traditional way of life and piety rather than by their campaign against modernism.

Christian fundamentalism in the 1920s, by contrast, began and flourished as a campaign against liberal theology, higher criticism of the Bible, and changes in culture and society. Now that their numbers and influence have increased, many fundamentalist groups inside and outside the traditional denominations have moved from sect to church, in Ernst Troeltsch's famous typology — from a voluntary association separate from and defiant of general society to an established organization with a bureaucratic structure that operates within existing society and its institutions.[15] Marsden reports that, even in the 1920s, fundamentalists sometimes identified themselves with the establishment and sometimes played the role of being a beleaguered minority of outsiders.[16] In either case, though, it was a position defined by its opposition to what they considered the corrosive effects of modern liberal thought and culture. They understood themselves to be going back to the fundamentals.

The history of religions, of course, is full of such movements. Martin Luther is among the historically most prominent of many Christian reformers who have urged their followers to throw off the Babylonian captivity of the churches and return to the authentic religion of New Testament Christianity. There are parallels in all religious traditions, from local reformers whose influence is limited, to those who give rise to new religious institutions and traditions. And in all cases the golden age to which reformers claim to return is very much an artifact of their own time, reflecting contemporary problems and assumptions that cause them to interpret the texts of earlier periods in a certain way. Yet we do not and should not refer to Luther, the citizens of Calvin's Geneva, or even the followers of Thomas Muentzer or others within the radical wing of the Reformation as fundamentalists, because fundamentalism is a modern phenomenon—both a reaction to modernity and a creature of it. Fundamentalism is defined not only by its oppositional stance, but also by its opponent, and that makes it a post-Enlightenment phenomenon in every respect, a twentieth-century event.

The development of modern science and the possibility it afforded, both as promise and as threat, of explaining the world in naturalistic terms, have played an important role in the development of religious thought and thought about religion during the past two centuries. Fundamentalism in its American setting is a product of and a response to this particular development. Like the dogma of papal infallibility, promulgated in 1870, it responds to a crisis of authority by asserting a "traditional" authority in a way that could not be understood without reference to the Enlightenment critique of religion. Even though the groups that constituted the radical Reformation would be classified by historians as early modern and were responding to the effects of science and technology, the differentiation of religious practices and institutions from other domains, and the political and social changes against which fundamentalists later set themselves, had not yet taken place.

Three examples may serve to illustrate the point that Christian fundamentalism is a response to and a product of the process of modernization and the rise of modern science. First, fundamentalists do not typically insist on a literal interpretation of the Bible, as their counterparts might have done in a premodern era. Rather, they defend the inerrancy of the Bible. This leads them to oscillate between literal and nonliteral readings in ways that often appear arbitrary to observers from outside the system.[17] Literal readings turn up contradictions and discrepancies in the text (for example, Exodus 6:16–20 gives three generations from Levi to Moses and Exodus 12:40 represents the intervening time as 430 years) that are among the motivations for higher criticism and for the postulation of different sources. Fundamentalists typically deal with such problems by postulating and rationalizing gaps in the biblical account. The creation stories found in the first chapters of Genesis present similar problems, and many—probably most—contemporary fundamentalists do not interpret them in an entirely literal way. The evidence for the length of elapsed geological time is so strong that the word *day* in the reference to six days is interpreted to mean not a twenty-four-hour period, but a geological age.

These readings, and the oscillation between literal and nonliteral interpretation, are not arbitrary. They are controlled by the principle that the Bible must be shown to be without error. If a literal meaning of the six days of creation would contradict what we know about geological time, then *day* must be reinterpreted. The result is that in these passages the Bible is not being read on its own terms at all (if, indeed, it ever is). Rather, current popular knowledge about the world is taken as the reference criterion, and the Bible is interpreted so as to prove it inerrant with respect to that knowledge. Fundamentalist interpretation of the Bible, then, is parasitic on modern science, even though the popularized conception of the results of that science often differs considerably from what scientists themselves say. The mode of interpretation is varied so as to permit no "error," and the criteria for determining error are taken from popular science.

Second, the nineteenth-century "Princeton theology" of Charles Hodge and Benjamin Warfield, which informs fundamentalist thought, is a form of eighteenth-century rationalism that makes much of the analogy between religion and Newtonian natural science.[18] The world of Hodge and Warfield is far removed from that of John Calvin, although he is cited as their chief theological authority. Hodge and Warfield were writing in response to the Darwinian controversy, the development of "higher criticism" of the Bible by German scholars, and the notion of Romantic liberals such as Schleiermacher, Coleridge, and Bushnell that biblical inspiration resides in the spirit of the biblical text rather than in the literal meaning of the individual words. Coleridge, for example, argued that the Bible, like Shakespeare, ought to be read for the spirit that infused it, rather than as a compilation of divinely inspired verses. "Does not the universally admitted canon—that each part of Scripture must be interpreted by the spirit of the whole—lead to the same practical conclusion as that for which I am now contending; namely, that it is the spirit of the Bible, and not the detached words and sentences, that is infallible and absolute?"[19] Hodge's statement, "The thoughts are the words. The two are inseparable," and Warfield's claim that each word "was at one and the same time the consciously self-chosen word of the writer and the divinely-inspired word of the Spirit," were refutational answers to Romantic theories of inspiration of the sort Coleridge put forth.[20]

They were also, of course, responses to the claims of recent biblical criticism — a distinctly post-Enlightenment phenomenon. Although Hodge and Warfield and the fundamentalist thinkers who followed them conceived of themselves as working within the limits of Calvin's doctrine of biblical inspiration, they were actually removed from Calvin's sixteenth-century argumentation. Scholars still debate whether Calvin's doctrine is best described as one of verbal inerrancy. His critical exegeses reflected his training in the methods of scholarship of the Renaissance humanists, but as a theologian he defended a doctrine of verbal inspiration. For Calvin, those two approaches did not conflict. By the late nineteenth century, after two centuries of conflict between science and religion, things looked quite different. Post-Enlightenment defenders of the verbal inerrancy of the Bible thought that the very possibility of revelation was at stake in the defense of that doctrine.[21]

Third, the fundamentalist emphasis on personal religious experience — whether of conversion or of other experiences of the power of the spirit — which is set in virtuous contrast to the formal, external, hypocritical character of liberal Christianity, is also a post-Enlightenment understanding of religious experience. While this emphasis is derived in part from the Puritan conception of the church as a gathering of visible saints and from the morphology of conversion experience and narrative that developed in England and America, Billy Sunday and Billy Graham differ significantly from Jonathan Edwards. The appeal to personal experience to provide conviction and authority for religious belief in the face of modern science and increasingly secular domains of thought and practice differentiates fundamentalism from the evangelical Christianity of Edwards's Northampton, where the justification of belief in God or of the Christian view of the world was never in question. For fundamentalists, personal experience and biblical inerrancy prove the truth of the Christian doctrinal scheme in the face of modern doubt, and one message of the revivalist is that personal salvation can reform the society and restore the civility that has been lost.

Billy Sunday diagnosed the problems of industrial society, unemployment, poverty, immigration, and urban crime as being consequences of the evil tendencies in human nature.[22] As solutions, he offered the personal acceptance of Jesus Christ as one's Savior, temperance, reform of one's personal moral life, and the anticipation of the imminent Second Coming. Personal salvation was offered as a solution to society's ills — a solution that Sunday contrasted to the economic and political reforms advocated by proponents of the Social Gospel and to such liberal pieties as the universal fatherhood of God and brotherhood of man.

Edwards preached to a congregation whose cosmos was defined by Puritan theology. Conflict between science and religion was not an issue, although Edwards himself was well read in Locke and Newton, and drew on their work for his philosophical theology. While the question of personal morality was an issue in the community, there was nothing analogous to the problems of modernity, industrialization, and urban poverty that were so salient for Billy Sunday's constituents. The social and economic causes and consequences of the Great Awakening were important in Edwards' time, but revivalists and parishioners alike were ensconced in a world described in theological terms. Early twentieth-century revivalists and their converts, by contrast, viewed personal conversion and a Christian life as answers to social, political, and economic ills.

William McGloughlin says of Billy Sunday that he "offered Americans of the twentieth century the ideology of the nineteenth century. He told them that the problems with which they struggled in an industrial society were based on the same evil tendencies inherent in human nature since Adam's fall. . . . The nation was crying out for reform, and Sunday cried with it; but he offered an old-fashioned diagnosis and an overly facile remedy for disturbingly new and complex problems."[23] The same could be said of the fundamentalist movement more generally. It defined itself against the threatening backdrop of the social and economic problems that beset a modern industrial society, and it was rooted in nostalgia for an earlier way of life. That earlier life, however, was not the life of Jesus and of primitive Christianity, as it was often portrayed, but an idealized version of home and community life in the small towns of rural, nineteenth-century America. As Randall Balmer shows, the social institutions that fundamentalists view as the backbone of Christianity were themselves only made possible by the Industrial Revolution.

The Comparative Use of the Term Fundamentalism

American fundamentalism, then, is a form of militant religion that opposes the modernist, liberal forces unleashed in Western society since the Enlightenment, in favor of a return to a notional past in which people are held to have experienced no tension between secular and religious loyalties, and in which the authority of scripture defined a community where truth was undiluted by the relativity of knowledge. Thus, in its classic phase, following World War I, fundamentalism was a fervent appeal to return not only to doctrinal basics but to the community in which these were supposed to have been fostered. This combination was suggested by a charter verse that fundamentalists cited over and over again. Their campaign, they said, was to return to "the faith once delivered to the saints" (Jude 1:3). American evangelicals have had considerable success advancing such an agenda since the 1970s; and that vigor, together with the nature of the causes for which they plead, has increasingly made fundamentalism seem the natural point of reference for describing religious resurgency around the world. This tendency has been especially strong among the "modernists" against whom fundamentalists define themselves. The usage took hold first in the press and in relation to Islam, and it has expanded in widening circles ever since—not just in English but in French, German, Norwegian, Spanish, and so forth.

Not surprisingly, this broad, implicitly comparative use of the term *fundamentalism* raises serious questions. Consider, for example, an article that appeared in the *New York Times* in 1989 under the title "Soviet Muslims Seek Leader's Ouster." This article, written from Tashkent, Uzbekistan, in Soviet Central Asia, concerned efforts by local Muslims to remove from power Shamsidin Babakhanov ibn Zeyudin, the head of the Muslim council for Central Asia and Kazakhstan, on charges of "drinking, womanizing, and excessive subservience to secular authorities."[24] According to the *Times*, the group making these charges called itself "Islam and Democracy" and was dedicated to the task of "cleans[ing] Islam in the Soviet Union." Subsequent events have demonstrated that Babakhanov was criticized because "he is not his own man, he is their man. He is illiterate. He hardly speaks Arabic."

In describing the situation, the *Times* saw fit to characterize Babakhanov's opponents as "fundamentalists" or "religious fundamentalists." But as nearly as one can tell from what is printed, the most compelling evidence for the accuracy of this label in relation to Soviet Muslim groups comes from the fact that, in disturbances in Azerbaijan the preceding fall, placards of Ayatollah Khomeini were displayed. In Khomeini's revolution, undoubtedly, many of the principal traits of American fundamentalism were visible: antimodernism, antiliberalism, the intent to return to a religious golden age when scripture held sway, and a social base composed of people who felt alienated and displaced by the groups they deemed responsible for the Western-style secular reconstruction of society. It is not at all obvious, however, that these elements were present among Babakhanov's critics—certainly not in their Iranian form. For as the *Times* itself pointed out, whereas Azerbaijani Muslims are (like Iranians) mostly Shiite, Uzbekistani Muslims (presumably including the "Islam and Democracy" group) are predominantly Sunni. And in general the information presented in the *Times* gave little hint of fundamentalism; rather, it seemed to describe a group of people concerned abut official corruption that sullied the name and institutions of their religion. It was perhaps telling that the *Times* found it natural to speak of Muslims as "fundamentalists," while in the same article it referred to Christians and Jews merely as "religious groups."[25]

Fundamentalism is a loaded word. In the present context of discussion, it is rarely used by people who want to describe themselves. This was not always so, either in the period after *The Fundamentals* were published—although a positive use of the term was rare—or during Jerry Falwell's heyday. Even in recent years one occasionally finds a nonpejorative usage of the term by members of groups it serves to designate. Since the late 1980s certain Muslims have identified themselves as *'usuli* ("fundamentalists"), transposing the concept from English via the Arabic word *asl*, meaning "fundamental."[26]

Yet the overall pattern is clear. Most people who speak of fundamentalists mean someone else—some *them* who crudely contrast to the evenhanded, pluralist, liberal approach *we* would prefer to take. This pejorative connotation is not confined to Western countries, either. In India, for example, a recently published book carries the title *Fundamentalism, A Weapon Against Human Aspirations*,[27] and numerous newspaper articles are written from the same perspective. In such a situation, Jay Harris is surely right to wonder how one can hope to use the term *fundamentalism* as a tool for serious comparative analysis. Is there not an overwhelming temptation to use it simply to refer to forms of vibrant religion that Western academics find distasteful?

The temptation is undeniably great. Because the word *fundamentalism* emerges from a particular battleground of ideas, it necessarily carries with it some of the emotions brought to the surface by that battle within American culture—to its detriment. The issues agitating other cultures are rarely precisely the same, and even in America the meaning and emphasis of fundamentalism have changed somewhat over the years. The 1970s, 1980s, and 1990s, with their focus on the ERA and—enduringly—abortion, are not the 1920s.[28] Moreover, as this contrast within American fundamentalism suggests, the placement of would-be fundamentalists elsewhere within the larger religious cultures to which they belong varies greatly. This may account for part of the confusion underlying the article in the *Times*. Finally, secularists may make use of fundamentalist sentiment and fundamentalist organizations to achieve their own political aims — either publicly or behind the scenes. If violence results, secularists may tend to ascribe blame to the fundamentalists involved, rather than to recognize the extent of secular involvement.[29]

There is, however, another side to the coin. At least in the case of the Iranian Revolution, if not in the protests of Muslims in Uzbekistan, a number of "family resemblances" to American fundamentalism do appear. Not the least of these is the high emotion involved, and use of the term *fundamentalism* calls this to mind. At the same time, unfortunately, it tends toward pejorative usage, so there is an obvious advantage in choosing a more neutral term to refer to the resemblances — "militant antimodern religious activism," let us say, a phrase that would seem even more neutral once it was displaced by the inevitable acronym: MAMRA! Many such designations have been proposed.[30]

Yet there is also a problem in blunting the emotional connection to suggest something more scientific. Every term of comparative analysis, even the most abstract sounding, has a cultural base. A term that has an obvious history in a particular culture thus offers a twofold advantage: it suggests the depth of the emotions involved, and the weight of history; and it highlights the danger of its own bias, as has clearly happened in relation to the word *fundamentalism*. Jay Harris is not alone in his protests.[31] Moreover, working with a term that is prominent in popular discussions, rather than retreating to the arcane subtleties of the ivory tower, acknowledges the broader public concern about fundamentalism that has made it matter so much to scholars.

During the last decade, fundamentalism has emerged as a major feature in Western conversation about the world because it points to cracks in the walls of an edifice Westerners had thought was secure and ever-expanding. This edifice is the nation-state, rooted in (among other things) a differentiation between secular and religious authority that interprets the latter as occupying a realm accessible to individuals through voluntary ascription. Religion, on this understanding, is in principle irrelevant to the general operation of society. In some "Second World" societies, in fact, it was actually banished, and with a high degree of success that only recent events have shown was apparent rather than real.

To secularists, the surprise has been that many societies — not just in the "Second World," but in the "Third World" especially — now reject their understanding of the social contract in either its "Second World" or "First World" form. Important elements within these "Third World" and formerly "Second World" nations find it natural to think of society, even when organized into a nation-state, as having intrinsically religious associations. Proponents of such a view have no use for the godlessness of the modern Western world, even in the limited sense in which it separates religion from other social processes. Some even charge that this bifurcated vision of society, far from being neutral, is actually the product of a particular religious tradition—Western Christianity, especially in its Protestant form.[32]

When such people and groups come to grips with modern, Western society, often through its postcolonial legacy, they seem to share many of the prominent traits of American fundamentalism, even when the terms they use to describe themselves can be more directly translated into other English words.[33] These traits have been variously enumerated in recent scholarship. Lionel Caplan, for example, describes fundamentalists as being committed to the authority of scripture in some form, desirous of rescuing the whole person from the fragmentations of modern society, suspicious of historicism, hopeful of restoring a pristine morality (which would include a rectification of proper relations between the sexes), and in some cases convinced that they are engaged in a cosmic struggle between good and evil, quite possibly one that heralds the end of the world.[34]

Martin Marty and R. Scott Appleby, who have organized the project on fundamentalism undertaken by the American Academy of Arts and Sciences, use the rubric of militancy to draw together various aspects of fundamentalism. They speak of fundamentalism as fighting back (it is reactive); fighting for (it has a vision of social renewal); fighting with (its weapons especially include "real or presumed pasts"); fighting against (it battles an external other and apostates closer to home); and fighting under (it defines itself in relation to God or some other "transcendent reference").[35] It seems hardly accidental that, numerous caveats notwithstanding, they offer "radical Sikhism" as the epitome of the sort of movement they have in mind. Perhaps no major religious tradition has a more vivid military dimension than the Sikh.[36]

Bruce Lawrence, restricting his scope to Christianity, Judaism, and Islam,[37] lays out still another constellation of factors that characterize fundamentalism as a religious ideology. Some elements he identifies are the same ones highlighted by others: fundamentalism is a distinctively modern phenomenon, despite its historical precursors; it appeals in a direct way to scripture; it is oppositional; it unites a group whose members see themselves as the holy remnant of an idealized past and as the vanguard of a future yet to be revealed. Other items in Lawrence's list add new dimensions to the discussion. He emphasizes that fundamentalists generate their own technical vocabulary (though this in itself does not distinguish them from other groups), and he draws attention to the fact that their leaders come from "secondary-level male elites."[38]

Additional Definitional Characteristics

Although we have tried here to draw particular attention to the cultural roots of the concept of *fundamentalism*, the set of definitional characteristics we stress is not substantially different from any of the foregoing. We would not insist that our thumbnail sketch is more definitive than any of the others: so much depends on the use to which such a description is being put. We do, however, note that our discussions of fundamentalism gravitated toward several aspects of the phenomenon that have not come to the fore in other treatments of the subject. We focused on a shared sense of besetment; on the issue of historical connections and mutual awareness that exist between disparate fundamentalist groups; and, of course, on the gender dimension in fundamentalists' self-understanding.

Besetment—of the Majority or of the Minority?

Comparative studies of fundamentalism to date have devoted considerable attention to fundamentalist militancy, and for obvious reasons this element is often stressed by the press. We found ourselves rather more interested in the sense of beleaguerment that gives it rise, for fundamentalist groups typically see themselves as victims of someone else's violence, physically or otherwise. They feel battered by the onslaughts of the modern world—not technologically, perhaps, but from a moral and communitarian point of view. An intriguing question about this feeling is whether it is to be associated primarily with groups who conceive themselves to be majorities or with those who operate as a minority. From an external vantage point, one often wants to designate groups that seem to be extremist fringe elements in relation to a larger society as "fundamentalist." The conception is that these are minorities at work in a host society where most people do not share their views. Frequently their own rhetoric of persecution and their estimation of the mammoth strength of their enemy make it easy to draw such a profile. And sometimes the sense of being an "unsullied minority" is stated explicitly.[39]

Yet with surprising regularity, fundamentalists talk as though they represent a majority—not a minority—point of view. One sees this in Jerry Falwell's case, where the majority might (he conceded) be silent, but it was a majority nonetheless. Sometimes this position has a desiderative or moral force: if fundamentalists are not the actual majority, they should be—or were, when times were better. Outsiders sometimes marvel at the fact that this wounded majority harbors what appears to be a "minority complex." Yet part of what is involved, from the inside, is a commanding (if somewhat prescriptive) sense of one's own ordinariness.[40]

Much of the literature on radical religious groups in the West is shaped by attention to secessionist sects of various sorts—the kind Troeltsch was thinking of when he elaborated his well-known typology. From the inside of many fundamentalist groups, however, the sense of being a tiny remnant is not so prominent as one might think. In many instances the perception of being a beleaguered majority predominates, as in the case of Anglo-Saxon American fundamentalists thrown on the defensive by an increasingly plural society but feeling themselves still to represent the majority position—the core of Americanness. Hindu fundamentalists protesting special advantages enjoyed by minority groups in India share this perspective,[41] as do Sikh fundamentalists, who see their identity as forming the essence of Punjabi culture, however many Muslims and Hindus crowd in at the sides.[42] Millennial groups are usually somewhat different, of course, but in them, too, one frequently finds a sense of "us" as an implicit majority—one whose hegemony has not yet been achieved. This true majority will be revealed in eschatological time, when outsiders and backsliders have been converted or destroyed.

What strikes outsiders as a strange oscillation of minority and majority perspectives sometimes has a strong basis in fact. For one thing, fundamentalist groups are apt to articulate points of view and exhibit forms of interaction for which there is considerable sympathy in a wider spectrum of society than they themselves embrace. The Gush Emunim provide an interesting example in this regard, not only because they have relied so heavily on the wider "knitted skullcap" element in modern Israel and see themselves as its vanguard,[43] but because they have dedicated themselves to achieving what one might call a "geographical majority"—the restitution of Israel to its supposed biblical mass.

Another situation in which the majority/minority issue becomes central to fundamentalist consciousness involves religious radicals finding themselves a minority in reference to the political groups that immediately surround them, but a majority when viewed more broadly, as is the case with Indian Muslims. Conversely, Hindus in India may lay great stress on their being the majority religion in their own domain, but at the same time they feel hemmed in at the edges— politically, economically, and socially. Hindus find themselves surrounded on many sides by Muslim nations, and they are often unhappily affected by political events in the Middle East.[44] A similar pattern obtains with Buddhists in Sri Lanka, but this time, of course, the encompassing alien is Hindu. In any of these settings, the sense of being a rightful but persecuted majority may easily emerge—not in willful disregard of the exact demographics and their relativity, but in part because of these very imponderables.[45]

In such instances, the secular modernism of the perceived other is not always its most salient trait. Yet because the secular state (as in India or Sri Lanka) or a secular network of nation-states (in some measure a legacy of "secular" colonalism) seems responsible for having created the present structure, it becomes a natural target for attack. In fact, simply to attack the religious other—Muslim, Hindu, Buddhist, whatever—often does not work to advantage in a situation where fundamentalists want to apply the rubric of a secular nation-state while at the same time opposing it, perhaps with the purpose of eventually displacing it. Moreover, the rhetoric of religion frequently makes it easier to oppose godlessness than to denigrate another form of faith. Hence fundamentalism at times becomes in part a language for venting historical and/or ethnic grievances—a secondary rather than a primary phenomenon. Once it makes its entry, however, the language of religion may well establish its own primacy. The large symbols it employs are notoriously capable of effecting this transformation.

Historical Connection and Mutual Awareness

A second aspect that loomed large in our discussions of fundamentalism was the matter of dialectic and historical connection. Since fundamentalist groups are by nature reactive or oppositional, the nature of the opponent, both in reality and in conception, has a considerable effect on the nature and intentions of the fundamentalist group struggling against it. To some extent, then, we can only expect a series of "family resemblances" to connect movements and groups we might wish to designate as fundamentalist, even if the enemy is universally associated with the sort of modernist vision first propagated in Western societies. Yet this sense of having a shared enemy—and sometimes of having shared ideals—often makes allies of fundamentalist groups, even when their conceptions of themselves diverge sharply. Of course, resurgent Islam in one part of the world (especially Iran) has clearly had a "demonstration effect" in other parts of the Muslim world, even when the constellation of events and institutions to be dealt with elsewhere is quite different;[46] and various militant groups in disparate parts of the Islamic world actively cooperate with one another.[47] But it is also true that Christian groups have rallied to defend Jewish "fundamentalists" such as the Gush Emunim, who are dedicated to aligning the State of Israel with the boundaries they believe were assigned to the "Land of Israel" in the Bible.[48] The biblical (as against Qur'ānic) warrant for a Jewish Jerusalem has also led some Christians to be sympathetic to the aims of the Temple Mount Faithful, a group of Israeli Jews who are trying to destroy Islamic shrines on the Haram ash-Sharif.[49]

These fundamentalist groups share at least portions of a common scriptural tradition, so in a certain respect such alliances are not unexpected. But it does seem surprising that Sikh militants in the Punjab can work in parallel and in consort with Muslim militants in Kashmir, and that those same Kashmiri militants proudly call themselves "tigers"—adopting a name made famous in South Asia by Tamil Hindu insurgents in Sri Lanka—despite emphasizing the Hindu (rather than secular) identity of their own opponent, the government of India. In another example of the same phenomenon, Hindus battling the secular state in the Roop Kanwar episode saw their position as paralleling that of Muslims disputing the government's judgment in the Shah Bano case, although at the same time they characterized the secularist enemy common to both of them in crypto-Muslim terms. And resurgent Muslim fundamentalism, often so-called, is clearly a factor in the rhetoric of militant Hindus, Jews, and Christians: if Muslims want to structure their states along religious lines, they themselves should feel free to do the same.

One may wonder, therefore, whether Emmanuel Sivan is right in saying that "only rarely are the extremists of one religion even interested in extremists of another."[50] Sivan saw the sympathy expressed by ultra-Orthodox *haredi* Jews for Muslims offended by Salman Rushdie as the exception that proved the rule of insularity. We would tend to see it much more as consonant with a general tendency, as would seem to be indicated by the fact that conservative Christian groups, even the Vatican, also expressed their solidarity with Muslims against

Rushdie.[51] To view fundamentalist groups as being all the same is clearly an uninformed oversimplification, but even divergent groups sometimes perceive that they have a shared lot. In a time of rapid international communication, groups whose members intensely resent the fact of pluralism and are repelled by any effort to accommodate their world view to it, find themselves in the odd position of sharing meaningfully in the very plurality they despise. That this is so demonstrates once again that fundamentalists are defined not only by their opposition to the modern world but by their participation in it.

Fundamentalist Ideologies of Gender

The third focus that emerged in our discussions is the one at the heart of this book: the question of whether fundamentalists have a characteristic perspective on gender. It surprised us that the matter of gender ideology had received so little attention in the nascent literature on comparative fundamentalism. Emmanuel Sivan and Menachem Friedman, in their edited volume on "religious radicalism and politics in the Middle East," ignore it, as does James Bjorkman in introducing a series of essays on "fundamentalism, revivalists, and violence in South Asia."[52] The same can be said for the essays collected in *The Fundamentalist Phenomenon*, edited by Norman J. Cohen, and for Thomas Meyer's extended essay, *Fundamentalismus: Aufstand gegen die Moderne*.[53] The large American Academy of Arts and Sciences project on fundamentalism includes a section on "fundamentalism and the family" in its third volume, but this accords the issue a secondary or even tertiary place in the overall scheme, hardly suggesting that gender ideology is fundamental to fundamentalism.[54] In their essay summarizing the first, most basic stage of the AAAS project, Martin Marty and Scott Appleby do make a gesture in the direction of gender: they speak of "charismatic and authoritarian male leaders" as being an important feature in what they call "'the ideal typical impulse' of fundamentalism."[55] But in the paragraphs describing these leaders, we hear much about charisma and authority and nothing about maleness. Lionel Caplan, in his excellent comparative essay, takes a different tack by raising the gender issue in the context of morality, not leadership. He speaks of women assuming a "symbolic poignancy" in fundamentalism.[56] This is surely not wrong, but it does seem once again to underplay the critical role of gender in the larger complex.

Bruce Lawrence makes explicit room for gender in his core description of fundamentalism, by noting that the fundamentalist causes he describes are championed by "secondary-level male elites." Yet he gives only limited attention to the prominent position of women in the rhetoric of fundamentalism.[57] Lawrence urges that it would be a mistake to isolate gender from other aspects of social reality—"the day-to-day experience of its subjects"[58]—and one can hardly disagree. Given the actual preoccupations of many fundamentalists, one might turn the matter upside down and ask whether considerations of gender should not be more pervasive in discussions of fundamentalism as a social reality, and often in treatments of fundamentalist doctrine as well.

Not surprisingly, it is a woman, Hava Lazarus-Yafeh, whose general typology of comparative fundamentalism (again, limited to Judaism, Islam, and Christianity) accords the highest profile to fundamentalist attitudes toward women.[59] In relation to Karen Brown's argument that women express the "other," it is interesting to note that Lazarus-Yafeh sees fundamentalist views on women as being comparable to their perspectives on other religious traditions. She speaks of "the general Fundamentalist attitude towards women and members of other religions."[60] Lazarus-Yafeh is struck by the fact that fundamentalists of various kinds reject legal steps taken to ensure equality between the sexes. She also draws attention to their typically excluding women from the higher ranks of their own leadership, if not advocating a general separation between the sexes.[61]

Lazarus-Yafeh's work has been nicely complemented and in many ways deepened by that of Martin Riesebrodt, whose comparative study of American Protestant fundamentalism in the 1910s and 1920s and of Shiite Iranian fundamentalism in the 1960s and 1970s uses sociological categories to cast fundamentalism as a "patriarchal protest movement."[62] Although Riesebrodt's primary theoretical interest is in the societal conditions that make fundamentalism a vibrant religious idiom in dialogue with modernity, his observations about the nature and rhetoric of fundamentalism often explore themes similar to those laid out by Lazarus-Yafeh. In both the American and the Iranian cases, his description of the moral decline decried by fundamentalists shifts with relative ease between laments about fallen women and denunciations of outsiders; and he pays considerable attention to fundamentalists' insistence on the separation of the sexes—if not physically, then conceptually.[63]

In this volume we hope to pick up the thread where Lazarus-Yafeh and Riesebrodt left off, testing their ideas against groups they themselves did not consider and amplifying these ideas with concepts of our own. It seems to us that the construction of gender is an important part of the meaning of fundamentalism, not just within the Abrahamic religions but elsewhere. In fact, we would argue, fundamentalist perspectives on gender cast a uniquely revealing light on the nature of fundamentalism as a whole.

Otherness   There are several ways to think about why the identity of woman often figures so critically in the discourse of fundamentalism; and, as one would expect, they interlock. First is the line of argument advanced by Karen Brown in the Columbia seminar and taken up in part in her essay here—namely, that in groups led by men whose identity is constructed in important ways by their confrontation with an external "other," great weight falls on the need to control the other "others" in their midst. Fundamentalists are often preoccupied with matters of boundary definition. They direct considerable attention to purifying their ranks of backsliders and apostates, and they spend many hours distinguishing themselves from groups whose perspectives are similar to theirs but not similar enough. Yet even while this kind of "internal enemy"[64] is being addressed, another other remains: the ever available yet ever alien "opposite sex." By its nature, fundamentalism considers that its primary other—secular naturalism and the forces that emanate from the post-Enlightenment West—has eluded its control. Small wonder, then, that great efforts are made to assert control over the more accessible other in its midst: woman.

In his chapter on Hindu fundamentalism, John Hawley quotes a telling passage from the *Bhagavad Gītā*, in which Arjuna laments that a world in chaos leads to the corruption of "women of the family," and this in turn leads to general social chaos.[65] Arjuna's point seems to be that if one wants to intervene in the spiral of chaos, one should begin with women. Often, however, the men at the helm of fundamentalist groups see things ever more starkly. Women's behavior is regarded not only as being symptomatic of cosmic dislocation but as being its cause. Embodying the other that is at once intimate and ubiquitous, women serve as a fine canvas on which to project feelings of general besetment. They are close enough to serve as targets, yet pervasive enough to symbolize the cosmic dimensions of the challenge. For every text that places well-domesticated womanhood on a religious pedestal, another one announces that, if uncontrolled, women are the root of all evil; and to the perception of many fundamentalists, the loosening of women is a prominent feature of modern Western secularism. Thus the focus of chaos is transferred from an external other to a familiar one, where it can effectively be counteracted with stringent measures of simultaneous denial and control: on the one hand, women are seen as exemplars of religion; on the other, they are confined to a sphere of activity that makes them as dependent as possible on men.

On some occasions, "projection of the other" is too delicate a rubric for describing the relation between the threat of modernism and the perceived need to control women. The critique that Christian missionaries made of the treatment of women in Hindu and Islamic societies has paved the way for a particularly virulent fundamentalist rejection of the degradation that has come with "loosening" women's roles in the societies that unleashed those missionaries on the world. According to this line of thinking, divorce, prostitution, open homosexuality, flagrant exhibitionism in women's dress, and pornography clearly expose the moral destitution of Western-style modernism—the same culture (it is alleged) that missionaries were so eager to export. Many Muslims have held that the purpose of such "Crusader imperialism," lately in collusion with Zionism, was to visit these effects on Islam. They believe that, as with Tokyo Rose, women were often selected as the best way to undermine a healthy society.[66] The chain reaction proceeds as follows, according to what Yvonne Haddad calls an "Islamist domino theory." First "female public exposure" is condoned, and this leads—via such horrors as dating and homosexual marriages—to "deep dissatisfaction, a criminal climate, a disquieting sense of insecurity," and ultimately "uncontrolled inflation, more frequent cases of rape, and the threat of depression and bankruptcy."[67] The defense? One must make woman "a queen crowned in her kingdom and her home," where she will be responsible for the transmission of Islamic values to her children, and not allow her to stray from that role.[68]

Of course, this vision of domesticity is not universally shared. It works better in urban, industrialized parts of Egypt than in rural Egyptian society, where women participate in a shared economy with men and function more freely in public space.[69] Hence the spearhead of Muslim fundamentalism in Egypt comes from the cities, not the countryside. And other contexts vary the pattern. As William Darrow has pointed out, the constitution of revolutionary Iran allows for the relatively full participation by women in public life, a condition made possible by segregating the sexes.[70] Yet in fact, as he also shows, the effect of the Islamic revolution has been to curtail radically the number of women who venture into the public realm, as if to confirm the view of one of its most prominent theorists that "women are inevitably a source of discord in areas where men and women interact."[71] The sense of woman as other is inevitably projected in the Iranian constitution, because it depicts womanhood as a profession, implicitly similar in its contours to the clergy or the army; these are discussed in the sections of the document that precede and follow the discussion of sexual segregation in public. It is also expressed in a perspective that regards women as intrinsically more vulnerable to consumerism and exploitation—as was experienced, the constitution says, "under the despotic regime" of prerevolutionary Iran.[72]

Karen Brown postulates that in great measure the strength of the image of woman as symbol of the other goes back to childhood experience: it is almost a universal inevitability that the mother becomes that against which a child must first define itself as it strives for independent identity. This is particularly true for boys, since their socialization depends in a double way on their recognition of mother as other. Not only must the boy move away from his mother's nurturing power and develop—sometimes through rage—the ability to cope with the occasional absence of that nurturing, but he must define himself as a male in contradistinction to her femininity.[73] Thus, in adults, especially adult males, a major means of denying childlike vulnerability is to project it onto the mother, as in the Egyptian and Iranian cases to which we have just referred. Yet men are by no means the only adults involved in this process, and a major theme in several chapters of this book is the complicity of fundamentalist women in confining the female "other," especially as mother, to her proper place.

In an arresting passage of his chapter in this book, Jay Harris throws out a pointed challenge to any such interpretation of woman's centrality in fundamentalist thinking (a centrality he also challenges) as having to do with her otherness. Harris doubts that there is a need for so-called fundamentalists to redirect rage toward an "other" internal to their own society, since they feel free to vilify the "real" devils that threaten from outside. He charges that the real purpose his colleagues and other liberal academics have in postulating the "otherness" dimension is their unconscious desire to deflect attention from their own unexamined ethnocentrism—a particular perspective on women that they would prefer to regard as universal truth. By resorting to a psychological profile of people who do not share their own feminist perceptions about the equivalency of women and men, they—that is, we—seek to transform a simple difference of perspective into a pathology. It is "smug and self-satisfied," he says, to do so.

These are important challenges since, as all agree, talk of fundamentalism so often masks cultural myopia. In response, however, one might ask whether the ability to rail against an outsider necessarily removes a felt need to bring the "inside other" under control. Several Islamic, Hindu, and Christian cases strongly suggest that it does not, even if the evidence is not so clear for Judaism. And as for the accusation about dubious psychologizing, why do parts of Harris's own analysis escape the charge?

Nostalgia   Whatever one decides, Harris's question is worth keeping in mind, since images of women are closely related to another trait that figures prominently in any collective portrait of fundamentalism: nostalgia. Here, too, one is tempted to argue that a matrix of childhood forces has had a deep effect. We have seen that an almost invariant component of fundamentalism is devotion to the cause of restoring an idealized past, a mythical age that never quite was, or in any case never quite was what it is claimed now to have been. Visions of such a past typically lay strong emphasis on the role women played in infusing that bygone time with perfection. Why?

One answer, for men and women alike, is that in every society the disparity between the sexes is a source of social and cognitive tension. In any account of the golden age, that tension must be wiped away if the past is to seem ideal. Since men primarily control the construction of this idealized past, their solution is to portray the women who inhabit it as self-sacrificing and generous: they yield before men to produce the greater harmony. Not only do they acknowledge the limits of their place in the social fabric, they glorify it. Hence, a special place is reserved in fundamentalist movements for women who articulate the virtues of this attitude in the present day, depicting it as a healthy alternative to the futile and ultimately demeaning struggles that come with trying to be a "modern woman."

But there is more. The felt need to recover a religious past that is dangerously far gone naturally echoes the frustrations we experience in other areas of life where we confront the vast distance between childhood and maturity. Each of our childhoods is truly gone, yet we confront them, it seems, on an almost daily basis, not only in the children we meet, but in the children within us. As the literature of psychoanalysis has shown, these inner children, none too successfully tucked away from sight in the unconscious strata of our personalities, manifest themselves in dreams, in slips of the tongue, in inner voices that are hard to suppress, and in situations that elicit spontaneous response. In the realm of religion we are free to acknowledge feelings of dependency that are inappropriate in most arenas of the adult world, and other aspects of childhood experience loom large there as well: a delight in ritual (even among those who criticize it in forms they themselves eschew), the desire for words to control facts, and the luxury of shared pretending that we usually associate with play.

Fundamentalist religion, more than most, capitalizes on the strength of the connection between religion and childhood. In its devotion to restoring a golden age—a time better structured and more innocent than the present—it pulls toward the center of religious experience the more broadly felt adult need to solidify ties with a nurturing childhood. Not surprisingly, the figure massively responsible for nurturance in childhood—mother—is often given a prominent symbolic position in religious groups for whom this act of reconnection is a very substantial concern. And not just the nurturant quality of this constructed past but its characteristic simplicity evokes remembrances of the mother, because in individual recollections one's mother often plays the role of the undifferentiated ground against which a person's subsequent complexity is defined. Such complexity is largely an inner phenomenon, something that happens inside as each person ages, but it is easily projected outward onto events in the present-day world, which are sufficiently complicated in their own right—too complicated, as so much of the rhetoric of fundamentalism avers.

When the present day is experienced as being intrinsically alien, as happens among fundamentalists, one sees a very strong version of this pattern of mutual reinforcement between the unwanted inner complexity and its outer counterpart. By the same token, it becomes all the more necessary, psychically, to preserve—or rather, to reconstruct—the dimension of the lost past most deeply identified with coherence and simplicity. For all fundamentalists (indeed, for all adults), this retrojected simplicity summons the remembrance of mother, but for males the connection is even stronger. In men, the otherness of the female sex makes it a natural ground, as terra incognita, on which to project the sense of simplicity and nondifferentiation that one experiences only with difficulty in one's own person. Once this task is shared with others, as it almost always is, the sense of simplicity is not just inchoately projected but genuinely constructed. It becomes an aspect of an ideology of gender.

For men, two seemingly contradictory processes are at work when this happens. On the one hand, a positive appropriation is made of the undemanding amorphousness that serves as a grounding for childhood. This is represented in the soft contours of Home and

Mother. On the other hand, the same amorphousness elicits fear, since it is associated with the ill-understood opposite sex. Such fear is often expressed as horror when traditionalists contemplate modern societies where women have a fair degree of independence. In compensation, the past, always more closely associated with Mother than the present in any case, is apt to be imagined as a domain where femininity is a comfort, not a threat: Mother Church, Mother India, Mother Cow.[74]

The vulnerability of this past to a ravaging present often associates it, at least in the minds of fundamentalists, with women. As William Darrow says in characterizing the rhetoric of revolutionary Iran, "[t]he nation is like a woman at the mercy of more powerful outside forces."[75] Similarly, much of the old-time element in Jerry Falwell's Old Time Gospel Hour is supplied by evocations of the "traditional family and moral values on which our nation was built"[76]—a family and a set of values that pivot on chaste, maternal womanhood. For men, the motifs of otherness and nostalgia, both prominent features of fundamentalist consciousness, reinforce each other and meet in a conservative ideology of gender that reconstructs an idealized past and attempts to reshape the present along the same lines.

Religious Machismo   Finally, a third element, which might be called "religious machismo," further compounds the connection between otherness and nostalgia. Many fundamentalist groups—that is, their leaders, fundamentalist men—believe that there is a necessity for maleness to reassert itself in the face of manifest threat. Sikh fundamentalists tout the martial heroism of Guru Gobind Singh and Maharaja Ranjit Singh, and the fearless martyrdom of Baba Dip Singh and Sant Bhindranwale. Bhindranwale himself rallied his followers with calls to abandon their weakness in the face of a vaguely identified enemy who had "dishonored our sisters" or "insult[ed] a Sikh girl"; they must be "prepared to die" to repel such insults.[77] Similarly, in Shiite Iran, where the holy figure of the fallen Husain is so vividly imprinted in the public consciousness, the grand cemetery for soldiers killed in the recent war with Iraq has become a major place of pilgrimage. In India, the core ritual of the Rashtriya Svayamsevak Sangh has for decades been a series of military drills,[78] and a comparable Hindu-nationalist group chooses to call itself "The Army of Shiva" (*shiv senā*). Among fundamentalist Christians in the United States, the exhortation "Onward Christian Soldiers" implies taking a hard line in the fight against Communism, a readiness to engage in nuclear war that sometimes borders on eagerness, and an unyielding stance on the necessity of using the death penalty against convicted murderers.

Many other examples of fundamentalist machismo could quickly to added to the list—instances where an attitude of militant opposition to secular modernism is amplified with an evident assertion of masculine pride. The behavior of men who belong to the Gush Emunim contributes an unusual example, because they take particular pleasure in using their dress and language to contradict the "wimp" image of religious Jews that is often held by secular Israelis. They wear commando boots and flight jackets as a complement to skullcaps and long fringed garments, and they talk about how "an AK-47 assault rifle and hammer make a perfect match with a book of Talmud and tefillin."[79] The late Meir Kahane's barrage of insults directed against "Hellenists" who were really no more than "Hebrew-speaking *goyyim*" crippled by self-hatred expressed machismo in another, even more strident vein, but the target of these insults was the same group that the Gush Emunim opposes: modern secular Israelis.[80] Finally, the fundamentalist rhetoric of both Christians and Muslims is often tinged with the suggestion that homosexuality is an inevitable consequence of modernism—a sign of the dishonor and downright emasculation that the collapse of traditional values visits on secular societies.[81]

For the rhetoric of religious machismo to succeed, its proponents often find it very helpful to feel the presence of women who require defense. Often these are real women: mothers and wives who need to be shielded from too much contact with the corrupt outside world. For example, in describing the activities of "the pursing Satan" evidently at work in the Shah's attack on Qum in 1963, Ayatollah Khomeini spoke of the archetypally evil Yezid, who had displayed "savage, inhuman behavior towards the helpless women and the innocent children of Husain."[82] Such helpless women may also be symbolic: territory, culture, and history that have been desecrated by the attacks of modernity are frequently depicted by fundamentalists as female. In Iran, again, sermons preached at the time of the revolution represented onslaughts against the Muslim community (*ummah*) through the metaphor of violations against women, as Muslim men were urged to cast off their weakness in the defense of their "women"—that is, their community.[83] These two kinds of women, the symbolic and the real, reinforce one another. Symbols of endangered womanhood can be more easily sustained if they are nourished in an environment where real women must depend on men to defend them; and the converse is also true. Hence, the characteristic militancy of fundamentalist groups is not, after all, just a metalanguage for a stance of opposition to modernity. It is an active force that helps make "traditional" gender roles second nature in fundamentalist religion.

Of course, a conservative construction of gender also comes as second nature to a much wider spectrum of "backward-looking" religious groups, because such attitudes to gender were in fact more prevalent in pre-Enlightenment societies than they are in the modern West. Yet the conservative attitudes toward gender so prominent in fundamentalist religion are "traditional" not primarily in the sense that they retain usages that were common in earlier times (although this is sometimes also true), but in the sense that they participate in an actively constructed past. As suggested by Eric Hobsbawm in his introduction to *The Invention of Tradition*, such usages are intended to reflect unchanging archetypes, rather than emerging in an organic way from processes that would properly be called "custom."[84] Recent scholarship has shown that the tradition of *sati*, as now understood in Shekhavati Rajasthan, is only a product of the last half-century (although, again, it builds on earlier conceptions).[85] Similarly, the *ie* family as understood since World War II in the New Religions of Japan differs in essential ways from that same institution as known in Meiji times. And as the Shah Bano case showed, Muslims living in India after it became an independent nation imagine quite a different Qur'ân in relation to divorce legislation than is typically assumed in predominantly Muslim societies; and the working out of a "pro-life" theology in American fundamentalism dates back only twenty years or so. Ideologies of gender that seem conservative to modern, Western eyes undoubtedly exist in religious settings that have nothing to do with fundamentalism, but here they matter especially and are objects of active construction.

In suggesting, as we have, how and why such constructions of gender often emerge in fundamentalist religion, we are merely making the roughest sketch. All symbols are capable of multiple meanings, including those that have to do with gender—indeed, perhaps especially those, since gender is such a basic and universal principle of binary organization in human societies.[86] Thus many important questions remain to be asked, not just in relation to particular fundamentalist cultures—both those explored here and others—but systematically, as well. Most obviously, one ought to ask what differences of perspective are apt to ensue when women, not men, speak the language of fundamentalism. A certain amount of information relevant to that question is presented here, especially in the chapter by Helen Hardacre, but much more detailed work must be done before the existence of characteristic differences can be affirmed with confidence. Might one find, for example, "symbols and myths . . . that build from social and biological experiences" rather than inverting them, or that "are given to the muting of opposition" even in an ambience where men (at least) define themselves precisely by their shared opposition to modernism? An important essay by Caroline Bynum suggests that one might.[87]

We repeat: such work still needs to be done. What we hope to have established here, even in the presence of an argument that questions the enterprise, is that the ideology of gender does indeed matter greatly in the shared world view of many fundamentalist groups. And we hope to have provided a set of materials that will help readers work out why that might be so.

Notes

Wayne Proudfoot contributed the section on "Fundamentalism in Its American Context." All other portions are by John S. Hawley.

1. In Kashmir, an organization called Hezb-i-Islami has threatened Muslim women with punishment if they fail to wear purdah, and a women's group called Dukhtaran-e-Millat has mounted a similar campaign (*India Abroad*, July 7, 1989, p. 21; cf. *India Abroad*, February 22, 1991, p. 13). A push for more conservative women's dress is also a prominent feature of the program of Bangladesh's Jamaat-e-Islami, a political party described as fundamentalist by the *New York Times* (*New York Times*, March 6, 1991, p. A11). The Jamaat has scored sufficiently significant gains in recent parliamentary elections to become a serious force in national policy-making. In the Sudan, efforts to enforce an Islamic dress code for women have recently succeeded (*New York Times*, January 29, 1992, p. A3); and an unlegislated movement in this direction has gained momentum in Palestine (Sabra Chartrand, "The Veiled Look: It's Enforced with a Vengeance," *New York Times*, August 22, 1991, p. A4).

2. Harjot Singh Oberoi, "Sikh Fundamentalism: Translating History into Theory," in Martin E. Marty and R. Scott Appleby, eds., *Fundamentalisms and the State: Remaking Politics, Economies, and Militance* (Chicago: University of Chicago Press, 1993), p. 272.

3. Bakunth Lal Sharma, interview, *India Abroad*, November 17, 1989, p. 15.

4. *New York Times*, March 21, 1989, p. A3.

5. Robert L. Cohn, "Sainthood on the Periphery: The Case of Judaism," in J. S. Hawley, ed., *Saints and Virtues* (Berkeley: University of California Press, 1987), pp. 87–108.

6. Bruce B. Lawrence, *Defenders of God: The Fundamentalist Revolt Against the Modern Age* (San Francisco: Harper & Row, 1989); Hava Lazarus-Yafeh, "Contemporary Fundamentalism—Judaism, Christianity, Islam," *The*

Jerusalem Quarterly 47 (1988): 27–39; Ian S. Lustick, "Israel's Dangerous Fundamentalists," *Foreign Policy* 68 (1987): 118–39.

7. Menachem Friedman, "Jewish Zealots: Conservative versus Innovative," in Emmanuel Sivan and M. Friedman, eds., *Religious Radicalism and Politics in the Middle East* (Albany: SUNY Press, 1990), pp. 127–41.

8. Lawrence, *Defenders of God*, pp. 139–41, 150–51; Friedman, "Jewish Zealots," pp. 139–40.

9. Lawrence, *Defenders of God*, p. 144.

10. Much has been written about the misguidedly hegemonic assumptions embedded in Enlightenment rationalism. In a recent contribution to the literature, Richard A. Shweder takes as his point of departure the following statement: "One of the central myths of the modern period in the West is the idea that the opposition between religion-superstition-revelation and logic-science-rationality divided the world into then and now, them and us." See Richard A. Shweder, *Thinking Through Cultures: Expeditions in Cultural Psychology* (Cambridge, Mass.: Harvard University Press, 1991), p. 2.

11. George Marsden, *Fundamentalism and American Culture* (New York: Oxford University Press, 1980), pp. 118–23, 153–64.

12. Cf. Marsden, *Fundamentalism*, pp. 1–8, 199–228.

13. Marsden, *Fundamentalism*, p. 4.

14. Cf. Jonathan Webber, "Rethinking Fundamentalism: The Readjustment of Jewish Society in the Modern World," in Lionel Caplan, ed., *Studies in Religious Fundamentalism* (Albany: SUNY Press, 1987), pp. 113–16; and Yvonne Y. Haddad, "Islam, Women, and Revolution in Twentieth-Century Arab Thought," in Y. Haddad and Ellison Banks Findly, eds., *Women, Religion, and Social Change* (Albany: SUNY Press, 1985), p. 297 note 1. The special relationship of modern technology to the preservation and propagation of true religion is a special topic within this general field; fundamentalist groups worldwide tend to welcome the adaptation of new technologies for this purpose. An example from American Christianity is a computerized King James Bible that enables the reader to call up any word, verse, or book in the Bible. This makes it possible for believers to avail themselves fully of the inerrancy of scripture. As two of the blurbs in the advertising copy distributed by ComSpec of Everett, Washington, say, "Have a problem . . . check the word of God first," and "God's Word 100% truth not 99.9%." Quite a different example is provided by the "technocratic" methods adopted by the Gush Emunim in the course of implementing their goal of territorial expansion. David Newman has seen these developments as being intrinsically alien to the group's original fundamentalist impetus, but comparisons with other fundamentalist groups make one wonder whether this is necessarily so. See David Newman, "Gush Emunim Between Fundamentalism and Pragmatism," *Jerusalem Quarterly* 39 (1986), pp. 33–34.

15. Ernst Troeltsch, *The Social Teachings of the Christian Churches*, trans. O. Wyon (London: George Allen & Unwin, 1932), vol. 2. There is an extensive literature elaborating, applying, and criticizing this typology.

16. Marsden, *Fundamentalism*, pp. 6–7.

17. See James Barr, *Fundamentalism* (London: SCM Press, 1977), especially chapters 3 and 5.

18. See Barr, *Fundamentalism*, especially pp. 270–79.

19. Samuel T. Coleridge, *Confessions of an Inquiring Spirit*, H. S. Hart, ed. (Stanford: Stanford University Press, 1957), p. 70.

20. Hodge, *Systematic Theology*, vol. 1, and Warfield, "Inspiration and Criticism," quoted in Kathleen Boone, *The Bible Tells Them So* (Albany: SUNY Press, 1989), p. 31.

21. For a discussion of the debate, see Edward A. Dowey, Jr., *The Knowledge of God in Calvin's Theology* (New York: Columbia University Press, 1952), pp. 90–105.

22. See William McGloughlin, Jr., *Billy Sunday Was His Real Name* (Chicago: University of Chicago Press, 1955), especially chapters 2, 6, and 7.

23. McGloughlin, *Billy Sunday*, p. 35.

24. Bill Keller, "Soviet Muslims Seek Leader's Ouster," *New York Times*, February 6, 1989, p. A3.

25. More recent examples of the *Times*'s use of the concept "Muslim fundamentalism" to replace "Islam" include, for example, a portrait of Hassan al-Turabi by Jane Perlez entitled "A Fundamentalist Finds a Fulcrum in Sudan" (*New York Times*, January 29, 1992, p. A3). Perlez reports that "Mr. Turabi describes the march of fundamentalism as inevitable," but the quotation she uses to support her point reveals that Turabi had in actuality been speaking not of fundamentalism but of Islam. She records his words as follows: "Islam is the only force that remains in this part of the world." Not surprisingly, this use of language has occasioned some protest on the part of Muslim readers. See, for example, the letter to the editor by Ahmed Sheikh, President of the Kashmir Association of North America, published on January 29, 1992. In a more scholarly vein and at a more general level, see C. M. Naim, "The Outrage of Bernard Lewis," *Social Text* 30 (1992): 114–20.

26. A. Kevin Reinhart, personal communication, April 15, 1991.

27. Shashi Bhushan, *Fundamentalism, A Weapon Against Human Aspirations* (New Delhi: National Convention on Secularism, 1986).

28. However, cf. James Barr, *Fundamentalism*, p. 2.

29. A cogent analysis of such a set of circumstances, which operated in the killing of Sikhs living in Delhi after Indira Gandhi was assassinated in 1984, is provided by Ashis Nandy in "An Anti-Secularist Manifesto," *Seminar* 314 (October, 1985): 14–24. It is characteristic for Nandy to emphasize the role played by groups and institutions representing secular, Western-style culture in manipulating, deforming, or even newly creating expressions of "traditional" and sometimes explicitly antimodern religion. See his "Sati: A Nineteenth Century Tale of Women, Violence, and Protest," in V. C. Joshi, ed., *Rammohun Roy and the Process of Modernization in India* (Delhi: Vikas, 1975), pp. 168–94; and "Sati as Profit versus Sati as Spectacle: The Public

Debate on Roop Kanwar's Death," in J. S. Hawley, ed., *Sati: The Blessing and the Curse* (New York: Oxford University Press, in press).

30. Emmanuel Sivan speaks of "religious radicalism" in his "Introduction" to E. Sivan and M. Friedman, eds., *Religious Radicalism*, p. 1. In a book on "religious nationalism," Mark Juergensmeyer speaks of the frequent linkage of religion and violence in the rejection of the secular state; see *The New Cold War? Religious Nationalism Confronts the Secular State* (Berkeley: University of California Press, 1993), pp. 153–70. Said Amir Arjomand uses the term "revolutionary traditionalism" in connection with "moral rigorism" ("Iran's Islamic Revolution in Comparative Perspective," *World Politics* 38(3) (1986): 402–3, 406, 408–10); while Yvonne Haddad, in a Muslim context, speaks of "Islamic revolutionism" ("Islam, Women, and Revolution," p. 292). Certain scholars seem to emphasize only one cluster of factors that figure within the wider phenomenon, as when Menachem Friedman defines *fundamentalism* in terms of a "belief in an ideal religious-political reality that has existed in the past or is expected to emerge in the future" (Friedman, "Jewish Zealots," p. 127). And of course, there is widespread use of phrases like "extremism," "ultra-orthodoxy," "neotraditionalism," and "religious resurgence" to characterize such groups. See, e.g., Jonathan Webber, "Rethinking Fundamentalism," p. 106; Menachem Friedman, "Jewish Zealots," p. 131; or Emile Sahliyeh, ed., *Religious Resurgence and Politics in the Contemporary World* (Albany: SUNY Press, 1990).

31. To date, these seem to have been most clearly articulated in relation to Islam and Judaism. See, e.g., Patrick J. Ryan, "Islamic Fundamentalism: A Questionable Category," in *America* 151(21) (December 29, 1984): 437–40; Riffat Hassan, "The Burgeoning of Islamic Fundamentalism: Toward an Understanding of the Phenomenon," in Norman J. Cohen, ed., *The Fundamentalist Phenomenon* (Grand Rapids, Mich.: Eerdmans, 1990), pp. 157–71; and Leon Wieseltier, "The Jewish Face of Fundamentalism," in Cohen, ed., *The Fundamentalist Phenomenon*, pp. 192–96. Other criticisms of the term have been more muted than those offered by Harris. See, e.g., Robert Frykenberg, "Fundamentalism and Revivalism in South Asia," in James Warner Bjorkman, ed., *Fundamentalism, Revivalists, and Violence in South Asia* (Riverdale, Md.: Riverdale, 1988), pp. 20–22; Jonathan Webber, "Rethinking Fundamentalism," pp. 95–121; Ainslie T. Embree, "The Function of the Rashtriya Swayamsevak Sangh: To Define the Hindu Nation," in Martin E. Marty and R. Scott Appleby, eds., *Accounting for Fundamentalisms: The Dynamic Character of Movements* (Chicago: University of Chicago Press, forthcoming). Martin Marty and Scott Appleby, the architects of the mammoth American Academy of Arts and Sciences "fundamentalism project," have implicitly bowed in the direction of these protests by retreating from the singular to an awkward, neologist plural. The cornerstone volume in their series is entitled *Fundmentalisms Observed* (Chicago: University of Chicago Press, 1991), and subsequent volumes follow suit.

32. Cf. Ibrahim Dasuqi Shitta of Cairo University, as quoted from an

interview with Mark Juergensmeyer on January 10, 1989. See Juergensmeyer, *The New Cold War?* p. 18. An influential precursor to Professor Shitta in his analysis of the Christian impulse behind Western-style secularism was Sayyid Qutb (1906–1966). See Yvonne Haddad, "Sayyid Qutb: Ideologue of Islamic Revival," in John L. Esposito, ed., *Voices of Resurgent Islam* (New York: Oxford University Press, 1983), especially p. 91.

33. E.g., Hindi/Sanskrit *jāgaraṇ*, a familiar term in the Vishva Hindu Parishad and Rashtriya Svayamsevak Sangh, translates more easily as "awakening," although its precise meaning is "keeping awake," as in an all-night vigil. A Hindi/Sanskrit term with somewhat different connotations and a hundred-year history in neo-Hindu causes is *śuddhi*, which is sometimes translated "conversion" or "reconversion" but actually means "cleansing." On the absence of a Hebrew term corresponding closely to *fundamentalism*, see Webber, "Rethinking Fundamentalism," pp. 101–2. Webber considers *kenai* ("zealot") to be the best approximation, but he urges that the proper force of the word *fundamentalism* comes precisely from its anchorage in relation to "modern ideological structures"—a situation that rarely obtains with words genuinely indigenous to non-Western languages. Harjot Singh Oberoi argues that the Punjabi word *mūlvād* corresponds exactly to *fundamentalism*, but concedes that it is "of recent coinage, resulting from the need to have a Punjabi counterpart of fundamentalism" ("Sikh Fundamentalism," p. 257). The word bears the same derivative stamp one would expect on the basis of Webber's observations, and it has for this reason been questioned as a proper analogue to *fundamentalism* by other scholars of Sikhism such as Gurinder Singh Mann. Mann notes that the term *mulvad* is very infrequent in current usage, being confined apparently to leftist journals and almost never being used in more general contexts such as newspapers; certainly religious militants would never so characterize themselves (Mann, personal communication, January 29, 1991). As to the array of relevant Arabic terms (*tajdīd, iṣlāḥ, nahḍa*: renewal, reform, renaissance), see John O. Voll, "Renewal and Reform in Islamic History: *Tajdid* and *Islah,*" in Esposito, ed., *Voices of Resurgent Islam*, pp. 32–47. Each of these suggests something different from *fundamentalism*, as do the concepts used to designate that against which they are aimed: *jāhiliyyah* ([an era of] ignorance), *lā dīnī* (secularists), and, of course, Satan (in the Muslim conception). For various usages of these, see Esposito, ed., *Voices of Resurgent Islam*, pp. 85–86, 101, 103, 154–55. On Persian *ṭāqat* (earthly ungodly power), similarly, see Arjomand, "Iran's Islamic Revolution," pp. 407–8.

34. Caplan, *Studies in Religious Fundamentalism*, pp. 14–20.

35. "The Fundamentalism Project: A User's Guide," in M. Marty and R. Appleby, eds., *Fundamentalisms Observed*, pp. ix–x.

36. Marty and Appleby, eds., *Fundamentalisms Observed*, pp. 833–35. The editors' apparent focus is on Sant Jarnail Singh Bhindranwale and his contemporary following, but they situate these extremists, as does T. N. Madan, against the background of the Singh Sabha movement in the early

twentieth century. (Cf. Madan, "The Double-Edged Sword: Fundamentalism and the Sikh Religious Tradition," in Marty and Appleby, eds., *Fundamentalisms Observed*, pp. 602–6.) The Singh Sabha's definition of Sikhism, which included the injunction not to cut one's hair, succeeded in becoming largely normative within the tradition. Hence one may wonder whether Marty and Appleby were right to designate Bhindranwale's emphasis on remaining unshorn as endorsing "a scandalous appearance." Suspiciously, scandal plays a role in Marty's and Appleby's group portrait of "fundamentalisms." (Marty and Appleby, eds., *Fundamentalisms Observed*, pp. 818, 834). From a typological standpoint the conflation of extremes and norms is apt to cause uncomfortable fits. On this issue, see the discussion of majority and minority that follows.

37. Apparently on principle (!), since in his opinion, "the foundational idea for fundamentalists is monotheism . . ." (Lawrence, *Defenders of God*, p. 106; cf. pp. 106–19).

38. Lawrence, *Defenders of God*, pp. 100–101. The phrase "secondary-level male elites" is never explicitly defined, but it seems to refer to groups of people who are "marginalized" by the institutions of modern society (pp. 236, 242).

39. Lawrence, *Defenders of God*, p. 230. Says James Barr, "one suspects that, even where conservative evangelicals have a great numerical dominance, it is still a rhetorical necessity for them to depict their views as if they formed a minority position" (*Fundamentalism*, p. 104). During the period in which the Muslim Brotherhood was suppressed in Egypt, it used the concept of *jamā'ah* ("party," "cell") with a distinctly "minority" sense, but the role of the *jamā'ah* was to usher in a society in which the majority would share. See Haddad, "Sayyid Qutb," pp. 87–88.

40. Cf. Caplan, *Studies in Religious Fundamentalism*, pp. 7, 157–59, 173–74. This feature emerges, for example, in the hagiography of Ayatollah Khomeini (see Michael M. J. Fischer, "Imam Khomeini: Four Levels of Understanding," in Esposito, ed., *Voices of Resurgent Islam*, p. 162).

41. They also, on occasion, make specific reference to their great numbers. In 1989 the general secretary of the Vishva Hindu Parishad stated, "Although our nationwide membership is one million, we have been able to mobilize 60 percent of the Hindus on the Ayodhya issue" (*India Abroad*, November 17, 1989, p. 15). Indian intellectuals who are critics of "Hindu fundamentalism" as represented by the Vishva Hindu Parishad frequently take the view that in reality Hinduism is a complex network of interrelated groups and that "the notion of a majority community . . . is alien to Hinduism (Rajni Kothari, "Fundamentalism Is Not the Essence of Hinduism," *Illustrated Weekly of India*, December 7–13, 1986, p. 16).

42. Sant Bhindranwale was explicit on this point: "We have a minority complex. But don't consider yourselves a minority. We are not the losers. A loser is the man whose Father is weak but the one whose Father is powerful

he can never be the loser." The translation is provided in Joyce Pettigrew, "In Search of a New Kingdom of Lahore," *Asian Affairs* 60:1 (1987): 15.

43. Ehud Sprinzak, "*Gush Emunim*: The Tip of the Iceberg," *Jerusalem Quarterly* 21 (1981): 28–47.

44. The conversion of large numbers of lower-caste people to Islam in the South Indian town of Meenakshipuram in 1981 and 1982 was believed to have been made possible by large infusions of Muslim money from countries bordering the Persian Gulf. Subsequent research seems to show that such funds were not in fact involved, but the Hindu perception that they must have been is very important (see Abdul Malik Mujahid, *Conversion to Islam: Untouchables' Strategy for Protest in India* [Chambersburg, Pa.: Anima, 1989], pp. 87–91). The new mood of fundamentalist militancy among Hindus in India, particularly as expressed in the Vishva Hindu Parishad, is sometimes dated to efforts that were undertaken to attract these Untouchables back into the Hindu fold, so as to prevent similar groups from departing and to combat the insidious effects of "petro-dollars" (see Peter van der Veer, "Hindu Nationalism and the Discourse of 'Modernity': The Vishva Hindu Parishad," in Martin and Appleby, eds., *Accounting for Fundamentalisms*, forthcoming; cf. *India Today*, May 31, 1986, p. 76).

45. On the idea of "majority" as a relatively recent concept in South Asia, see Frykenberg, "Fundamentalism and Revivalism in South Asia," pp. 38–39.

46. Sami Zubaida, "The Quest for the Islamic State: Fundamentalism in Egypt and Iran," in Caplan, ed., *Studies in Religious Fundamentalism*, pp. 27–28.

47. See, e.g., Daniel Pipes, "Oil Wealth and Islamic Resurgence," in Ali E. Dessouki, ed., *Islamic Resurgence in the Arab World* (New York: Praeger, 1982), pp. 45–51.

48. In this connection, see also Jonathan Webber's observations about the reappearance of biblical language among secular Zionists in the wake of dramatic political developments in 1967 (Webber, "Rethinking Fundamentalism," p. 116).

49. On the Temple Mount Faithful (Ne'emanei Har ha-Bait), led by Gershom Saloman, see *New York Times*, October 15, 1990, pp. A1, A12; and *Washington Post*, October 9, 1990, p. A15. On its background in relation to Yehuda Etzion, see Ehud Sprinzak, "From Messianism Pioneering to Vigilante Terrorism: The Case of the Gush Emunim," in David C. Rapoport, ed., *Inside Terrorist Organizations* (New York: Columbia University Press, 1988), pp. 204–14.

50. Sivan, "Introduction," in *Religious Radicalism*, p. 2.

51. Support for the Muslim cause against Rushdie was voiced in the Vatican newspaper *L'Osservatore Romano* on March 5, 1989 (see *New York Times*, March 7, 1989, p. A3).

52. James Bjorkman, "The Dark Side of the Force," in J. Bjorkman, ed.,

Fundamentalism, Revivalists, pp. 1–19. This is in some ways more striking because one article in the book, though it does not concern the contemporary period, is indeed directed at a discussion of gender issues: Kenneth W. Jones, "Socio-Religious Movements and Changing Gender Relationships Amongst Hindus of British India," pp. 40–56 (see especially pp. 49–50, 54).

53. Thomas Meyer, *Fundamentalismus* (Hamburg: Rowohlt, 1989). Meyer takes passing notice of the opposition to the ERA on the part of American fundamentalists (pp. 76–77), but his analysis of the global phenomenon of which he believes it to be a part makes no reference to gender ideology.

54. The family dimension of the AAAS "Fundamentalism Project" is published as part of Martin E. Marty and R. Scott Appleby, eds., *Fundamentalisms and Society: Reclaiming the Sciences, the Family, and Education* (Chicago: University of Chicago Press, 1993). Apparently gender questions will figure more prominently in much later volumes only recently planned.

55. Marty and Appleby, *Fundamentalisms Observed,* pp. 817, 826.

56. Caplan, ed., *Studies in Religious Fundamentalism,* p. 19.

57. Lawrence, *Defenders of God,* pp. 203–4 (Muslims), 230 (Christians). At times he seems to suggest that this element is only truly prominent in American Christian fundamentalism (p. 230), though his own discussion of fundamentalism in the American context ignores it almost altogether (pp. 153–88, despite the disclaimer on p. 186). At other times Lawrence claims that "marginalized male elites, coopting women by claiming to protect them as custodians of domestic space" are a general feature of fundamentalist groups (p. 236). Still again, he notes that "gender asymmetry" is more to be expected among Muslims than elsewhere, because of their location, for the most part, in Third World countries (p. 237).

58. Lawrence, *Defenders of God,* p. 203.

59. Hava Lazarus-Yafeh, "Contemporary Fundamentalism," p. 37.

60. Ibid.

61. Ibid.

62. Martin Riesebrodt, *Fundamentalismus als patriarchalische Protestbewegung* (Tubingen: J. C. B. Mohr [Paul Siebeck], 1990).

63. Ibid., pp. 75–80, 154–60, 247–48.

64. Bjorkman, "The Dark Side of the Force," p. 3. Cf. Lawrence, *Defenders of God,* p. 121; Aviezer Ravitsky, "Religious Radicalism and Political Messianism in Israel," in E. Sivan and M. Friedman, eds., *Religious Radicalism,* p. 34.

65. *Bhagavad Gītā* 1.41.

66. Cf. Haddad, "Islam, Women, and Revolution," pp. 276, 288–90.

67. Haddad, "Islam, Women, and Revolution," pp. 287, 302–3.

68. Ibid., p. 287.

69. Ibid., pp. 293–94. Similarly, in relation to the nontraditional assumption of a nuclear family—a recent, urban phenomenon—as standard in the

1979 constitution of Iran, see William R. Darrow, "Women's Place and the Place of Women in the Iranian Revolution," in Y. Haddad and E. Findly, eds., *Women, Religion, and Social Change*, p. 310.

70. In this respect, the Iranian pattern is comparable to the one at work with the Neturei Karta. There, as in the European *shtetl*, women are actually the breadwinners in the family, while the men devote themselves to a life of collective study. In neither case does the fact that women can be active in public — with appropriate covering and at an appropriate distance from men — mean that a woman ceases being the "custodian of domestic space," as Bruce Lawrence puts it (*Defenders of God*, p. 236); indeed, quite the contrary is true.

71. Darrow, "Women's Place," pp. 313–15. The reference is to Murteza Mutahhari.

72. Darrow, "Women's Place," pp. 308–9.

73. Cf. Nancy Chodorow, *The Reproduction of Mothering: Psychoanalysis and the Sociology of Gender* (Berkeley: University of California Press, 1978), pp. 180–97.

74. The motif of protecting the cow against slaughter is certainly not the exclusive property of Hindu groups that could be called fundamentalist, but in recent years it seems to have become most prominent there. On cow-protection societies (Gaurakshini Sabhas) as rallying points for diverse Hindu groups in the late nineteenth and early twentieth centuries, see Gyan Pandey, "Rallying Round the Cow: Sectarian Strife in the Bhojpuri Region, c. 1888–1917," in Ranajit Guha, ed., *Subaltern Studies II* (Delhi: Oxford University Press, 1983), pp. 60–129. On cow protection in the Ram Rajya Parishad, a Hindu political party formed at the time of India's independence, see Philip Lutgendorf, *The Life of a Text* (Berkeley: University of California Press, 1991), pp. 386–87. A ban on cow slaughter continues to be a plank in the platform of the Vishva Hindu Parishad and other militantly Hindu groups, such as the ones brought together at the most recent Allahabad *kumbha melā* by the Shankaracharya of Puri (*India Today*, May 31, 1986, p. 79). As to the general proliferation of images of Mother in recently influential Hindu groups such as the Vishva Hindu Parishad, see Peter van der Veer, "Hindu Nationalism and the Discourse of 'Modernity'," in Martin and Appleby, eds., *Accounting for Fundamentalisms*, forthcoming. Van der Veer takes note of the fact that the water pot (*kalaśa*) emerges as especially important in the ritual life of the Vishva Hindu Parishad; its associations with what he calls "the Mother Goddess" are strong.

75. Darrow, "Women's Place," p. 310.

76. Quoted by Steve Bruce from an unnamed Moral Majority brochure dating to about 1983, in "The Moral Majority: The Politics of Fundamentalism in Secular Society," in Caplan, ed., *Studies in Religious Fundamentalism*, p. 184.

77. Quotations from the sermons of Bhindranwale are analyzed in Mark Juergensmeyer, "The Logic of Religious Violence," in D. Rapoport, ed., *Inside Terrorist Organizations*, pp. 175–76. Two of these quotations are drawn from

Joyce Pettigrew, "In Search of a New Kingdom of Lahore," pp. 16–17, and she also gives others relevant to the subject at hand.

78. Interestingly, an all-female RSS drill corps has now been established in New Delhi, but it is so much the exception to a long established all-male rule that it attracted news coverage (*India Today*, July 16–31, 1978, pp. 48–49).

79. Gideon Aran, "Redemption as a Catastrophe: The Gospel of Gush Emunim," in E. Sivan and M. Friedman, eds., *Religious Radicalism*, p. 172. A typographical error in the original ("a K-47 . . . ") has been corrected in quotation.

80. Aviezer Ravitzky, "Religious Radicalism and Political Messianism in Israel," p. 34.

81. Examples are to be found in Haddad, "Islam, Women, and Revolution," pp. 302, 303; and Bruce, "The Moral Majority," p. 184. One Egyptian Muslim quoted by Haddad asserts that birth control, too, has the effect of sapping courage (Haddad, "Islam, Women, and Revolution," p. 302).

82. From Mehdi Abedi, tr., *Zendigi-Nameh Imam Khomeini* (Tehran: Fifteenth of Khordad Publishers, n.d.), vol. 2, pp. 38–43, as quoted by Fischer, "Imam Khomeini," p. 154.

83. Gustav Thaiss, "The Conceptualization of Social Change Through Metaphor," *Journal of Asian and African Studies* 13(1–2) (1978): 6–8. Thaiss notes that the Arabic word *ummah* "refers etymologically" to the word *umm*, "mother" (Thaiss, "Conceptualization," p. 7).

84. Hobsbawm, "Introduction: Inventing Traditions," in E. Hobsbawm and Terence Ranger, eds., *The Invention of Tradition* (Cambridge: Cambridge University Press, 1983), pp. 2–3.

85. Sudesh Vaid and Kumkum Sangari, "Institutions, Beliefs, Ideologies: Widow Immolation in Contemporary Rajasthan," *Economic and Political Weekly* 26 (17), April 27, 1991, p. WS-3; cf. Veena Talwar Oldenburg, "The Continuing Invention of the Sati Tradition," in J. S. Hawley, ed., *Sati, The Blessing and the Curse* (in press).

86. Cf. Thomas Laqueur, *Making Sex: Body and Gender from the Greeks Through Freud* (Cambridge, Mass.: Harvard University Press, 1990).

87. Bynum, "Introduction: The Complexity of Symbols," in C. Bynum, Stevan Harrell, and Paula Richman, eds., *Gender and Religion: On the Complexity of Symbols* (Boston: Beacon Press, 1986), p. 12.

Four
Case Studies

2

American Fundamentalism: The Ideal of Femininity

RANDALL BALMER

During a 1989 television interview, Bailey Smith, a fundamentalist and an official in the Southern Baptist Convention, offered his views of women. "The highest form of God's creation," he said, "is womankind."[1]

Such pronouncements are so commonplace among American fundamentalists that it is easy to gloss over their significance. Those who purport to be the twentieth-century guardians of Christian orthodoxy—a tradition that, more often than not, has blamed Eve for Adam's downfall—now trumpet the unique purity of women, the "highest form of God's creation."

These encomiums permeate fundamentalist piety. If you page through a fundamentalist songbook, you will find all sorts of examples of women alternately praying and weeping for their children, waiting for wayward, sometimes drunken, sons to come home. "Tell Mother I'll Be There," for instance, is a forlorn, anguished cry from one such son who wants desperately to assure his mother, now "home with Jesus," that her prayers have been answered. These paeans to female piety intensify as Mother's Day approaches each year:

> Mother is the sweetest word
> You and I have ever heard!
> Mother, oh how dear the thought,
> A bit of heaven you have brought![2]

Or consider the rather unpoetic chorus from a song entitled "Praying Mothers" by Tammy Deville:

> Praying mothers, Christian homes,
> Keeping families together where they belong;
> Teaching trust, respect, faith and love,
> Reverence to our God above.
> With love to godly mothers,
> We sing this song.[3]

All of this might be dismissed merely as vulgar sentimentality, the Protestant counterpart to popular Catholic pinings for the Virgin Mary, but the celebration of female piety by fundamentalists has a particular focus in the home. If the Blessed Virgin ever sorted socks, scrubbed the kitchen floor, or worried about ring around the collar, we seldom hear about it, even from her most devoted followers.

Not so for fundamentalist women, who are overwhelmingly white and middle-class. Their identity is tied almost exclusively to motherhood and to what one fundamentalist writer has called "the oft-maligned delights of homemaking."[4] You do not have to look very far in fundamentalist literature to find celebrations of motherhood and female domesticity. "Raising children is a blessing from the Lord, and I can't imagine a home without the mother being there," Nancy Tucker, a "stay-at-home mother," wrote in a fundamentalist magazine.[5] "Being a mother, and filling mother's place, is one of the greatest responsibilities there is in this . . . world," an editorial in *The Way of Truth* proclaimed. "Those who feel that a woman is wasting her time, and burying her talents, in being a wife and mother in the home, are simply blinded by the 'gods' of this world." Such domestic duties, the editorial continued, must not be taken lightly:

> What a grave and sacred responsibility this is. To provide food, clothing, and shelter, may be the easiest part for many couples. To be a true *mother* goes far beyond supplying these temporal needs. The love, the nurturing, the careful guiding, the moral example, the moral teaching, the training, is the most important of all.[6]

An article in *Kindred Spirit*, a magazine published by Dallas Theological Seminary, echoes this theme. "In many ways God measures a woman's success by her relationship with her husband and children," the author, a woman, writes. "Many women ache to learn how to be truly successful in marriage and motherhood."[7]

This ideology, of course, is cloaked in biblical literalism. Paul, the apostle, is not usually regarded as a feminist, and fundamentalists generally refuse to see his proscriptions as culturally conditioned. While most fundamentalists have maneuvered around Paul's insistence that women keep their heads covered in church, they cannot see—or have elected *not* to see—his commands to keep silence and to be submissive as similarly culture-bound. Consequently, fundamentalist women are expected to be submissive, to demand no voice of authority in the church or in the home. As the article in *Kindred Spirit* puts it, "Young women need to be taught a biblical view of their roles and relationships with their husbands in order to truly liberate them to be all that God intended them to be and to experience the best that He has for them."[8] Paradoxically, then, fundamentalist women are supposed to feel a kind of liberation in this submission to their husbands. "In seeking to recognize the crucial role of the husband and father as head of the household," the argument goes, "perhaps we have lost sight of the ways that family warmth is generated by the love and security given by a godly wife and mother."[9]

It was not always thus in American history, even in the evangelical tradition.[10] I have already alluded to the discrepancies between historic Christian theology and the contemporary lionization of women by fundamentalists. Through the centuries, Christian theology has often portrayed women as temptresses, the descendants of Eve, the inheritors of a wicked, seductive sensuality that could only be tempered through subordination to men. John Robinson, pastor of the Pilgrims in Plymouth, Massachusetts, for instance, enjoined a "reverend subjection" of the wife to her husband, adding that she must not "shake off the bond of submission, but must bear patiently the burden, which God hath laid upon the daughters of Eve."[11] The Puritans of New England also imbibed traditional suspicions about women; consider their treatment of Anne Hutchinson, their contempt for the Quakers' egalitarian views of women, and the evident misogyny of the Salem witch hysteria. More important, the Puritans regarded the man as both the head of the household and the person responsible for the spiritual nurture and welfare of his children.

Around the turn of the eighteenth century, however, the sermonic rhetoric in New England betrays a shift in sentiment. Women, who joined the churches in far greater numbers than men, began to be extolled as uniquely tender and loving and, hence, as spiritually superior to their husbands, who were increasingly involved in commercial pursuits.[12] Although during the interregnum of the revolutionary era *virtue* was chiefly a political term applied to the fusion of civic humanism with evangelical ardor, by the end of the eighteenth century *virtue* had become synonymous with femininity.[13]

The nineteenth century witnessed a domestic revolution in American life, with the romanticization of the home, changes in gender roles, and, finally, the idealization of female piety. While there is some evidence that the republican ideals of the revolutionary era permeated family life and led, at least for a time, to the relative equality of husbands and wives, the real changes occurred during the Second Great Awakening early in the nineteenth century, when women were freed from institutional restraints in the enthusiasm of the revival.[14] The Second Awakening taught that everyone was equal before God, a notion that combined roughly equal parts of republican ideology and Arminian theology. Charles Grandison Finney's "new measures," moreover, encouraged women's participation in revival meetings, and evangelical women began to assert themselves as leaders of various benevolent and social-reform movements.[15] Some women, such as Phoebe Palmer and Margaret (Maggie) Van Cott, became important evangelists.

Despite the temporary loosening of restraints during times of revival, nineteenth-century women rarely ascended to positions of religious authority. Whenever evangelical women aspired to leadership they were met with stern warnings. Presbyterian minister Ashbel Green, sometime president of the College of New Jersey, reminded his auditors in 1825 that Christ framed women "with that shrinking delicacy of temperament and feeling, which is one of their best distinctions, which renders them amiable." Green acknowledged that this female characteristic, "while it unfits them for command" and "subjects them, in a degree, to the rougher sex, gives them, at the same time, an appropriate and very powerful influence." Green concluded that women could not, however, expect that Christ, "who formed them with this natural and retiring modesty, and under a qualified subjection to men, would ever require, or even permit them, to do anything in violation of his own order."[16]

Did this mean that women had no spiritual role to play whatsoever? On the contrary, women must assume responsibility for the home and, in particular, for the spiritual nurture of the children. "The female breast is the natural soil of Christianity," Benjamin Rush, a fervent evangelical, opined.[17] "It is one of the peculiar and most important duties of Christian women," Ashbel Green wrote, "to instruct and pray with children, and to endeavor to form their tender minds to piety, intelligence and virtue."[18] Here was the proper sphere of female spirituality—as moral guardians of the home, in charge of the religious instruction and nurture of the children. "The family state," Catharine Beecher and Harriet Beecher Stowe wrote in 1869, "is the aptest earthly illustration of the heavenly kingdom, and in it woman is its chief minister."[19] Nineteenth-century evangelical literature fairly brims with examples of maternal piety and persistent prayers that eventually, sometimes even after her death, effect the conversion of a mother's children.[20]

This idea of women as spiritual titans was new in the nineteenth century and peculiar to America. "Although the women of the United States are confined within the narrow circle of domestic life, and their situation is in some respects one of complete dependence," Alexis de Tocqueville, the peripatetic French observer, wrote in 1835, "I have nowhere seen woman occupying a loftier position." After outlining Americans' distinctive and careful division of "the duties of man from those of woman," Tocqueville attributed America's "singular prosperity and growing strength" to "the superiority of their women."[21] Ann Douglas calls this development the "feminization" of American culture, the product of a collusion between nineteenth-century clergy, whose power and status were waning, and housewives eager for some emotional outlet.[22] Males came to be characterized as aggressive and indifferent to godliness, whereas women became the lifeblood of the churches. They were the repositories of virtue, meek and submissive—like Jesus himself.

Thus, female spirituality was upheld as an ideal, a notion taken to its extremes in Shaker theology and even in Christian Science, both of which asserted explicitly the superiority of the feminine and linked the perfection of humanity to womanhood. Women were implicitly more spiritual in nineteenth-century America. They were morally superior to men; they had a greater capacity for religiosity. Women, therefore, became responsible for the inculcation of virtue into their daughters, sons, and husbands. The evangelical women of Utica, New York, for instance, organized themselves in 1824 into a Maternal Association that met biweekly and required that each member pledge to pray for her children daily, to read literature on Christian child-rearing, to set a pious example, and to spend the anniversary of each child's birth in fasting and prayer.[23]

Other forces besides revivalism lay behind this transition from the spiritual patriarchy of the Puritan family to the evangelical household of the nineteenth century. The early republic witnessed the gradual emergence of a market economy and the stirrings of nascent industrialization. Men began to work outside the home and the farm. They eventually organized into guilds as their labor became increasingly specialized. Traditional family and kinship networks thus gave way to associations among fellow workers. Families were no longer self-sufficient; they depended on the fathers' wages. Gender roles became more distinct. "From the numerous avocations to which a professional life exposes gentlemen in America from their families," Benjamin Rush wrote, "a principal share of the instruction of children naturally devolves upon the women."[24] Men increasingly distanced themselves from domestic chores and activities, and women succumbed to the "cult of domesticity" or the "cult of true womanhood," marked by purity, piety, and domesticity.

Thus sentimentalized, women assumed responsibility for domestic life, especially the religious instruction of the children. For many, in fact, the two were inseparable. In his *Treatise on Bread, and Bread-Making*, Sylvester Graham, temperance lecturer and health reformer, explicitly assigned to mothers the responsibility for both the physical and the moral well-being of their children. It is the mother, wrote Graham, "who rightly perceives the relations between the dietetic habits and physical and moral condition of her loved ones, and justly appreciates the importance of good bread to their physical and moral welfare."[25] Indeed, the sphere of domesticity—including the home, the education and nurture of children, and religious matters generally—was the one area where the nineteenth-century woman reigned supreme, her judgments largely unchallenged. "In matters pertaining to the education of their children, in the selection and support of a clergyman, and in all benevolent enterprises, and in all questions relating to morals or manners, they have a superior influence," Catharine Beecher wrote in *A Treatise on Domestic Economy* in 1841. "In all such concerns, it would be impossible to carry a point, contrary to their judgement and feelings; while an enterprise, sustained by them, will seldom fail of success."[26]

An important theological development—a new focus on religious instruction and socialization—reinforced the importance of female nurture. The tides of revival early in the nineteenth century swept away strict Calvinist doctrines of depravity and original sin, thereby emphasizing the ability of the individual to control his or her spiritual destiny; eventually this downplaying of depravity and the elevation of human volition undermined the traditional emphasis on dramatic conversions. Indeed, Horace Bushnell's *Christian Nurture*, published in 1847, urged that children should be reared from birth as though they were Christian, and insisted that parents should not expect a dramatic conversion experience in their children. Hence, children should be educated and socialized in such a way that they would always consider themselves Christian or, in Puritan terms, among the elect. Who should perform this duty, especially in a society with increasingly differentiated gender roles? With men away at the mill or the factory all day, the task of "Christian nurture" fell to women.

The home thus became the sphere that both defined and delimited female influence. As the Victorian era unfolded, moreover, mechanized production and a commercial economy increasingly eased domestic burdens, especially for the middle-class mother, who often had a hired girl (usually a recent immigrant) to help with household chores. No longer must a woman spend her hours sewing, weaving, making soap, or butchering meat for her home. Instead, her husband's wages and the commercial economy gave her time to fuss over it. A passel of magazines, such as *Godey's Lady's Book*, instructed the Victorian woman on how to decorate her home with ornate woodworking and carvings and a vast array of furnishings—bookcases, clocks, overstuffed chairs—that lay within her budget. The invention of the power loom in 1848 made carpets plentiful and affordable. The parlor organ became a kind of domestic shrine, with its high verticality, its carved, pointed arches, and its nooks, crannies, and shelves for family photographs and mementos. The organ itself, used for family hymn-singing, both symbolized and reinforced religious notions and the ideal of feminine domesticity. *Mother* played the organ and thereby cemented her role as the religious keystone of the family.[27]

These notions about feminine spirituality have persisted among fundamentalists in the twentieth century. Many of the taboos devised by fundamentalists in their time of beleaguerment in the 1920s and 1930s centered on women. In reaction to the perceived moral laxity of the larger culture, which was careening stubbornly toward judgment, fundamentalists insisted that women forswear worldly adornments, especially jewelry and cosmetics. They devised elaborate parietal rules intended to protect the sexual innocence of their children, especially the girls, who were perceived as vulnerable to the animal cravings of less-spiritual males.

The Victorian myth of feminine spiritual superiority is so entrenched in twentieth-century fundamentalism that many preachers have felt obliged to shake men out of their spiritual complacency.[28] Consider, for instance, the machismo posturings of evangelist Billy Sunday, who insisted that in Jesus we find "the definition of manhood."[29] "God is a masculine God," the fundamentalist firebrand John R. Rice insisted to a male audience in 1947. "God bless women, but He never intended any preacher to be run by a bunch of women."[30] But the intensity of Rice's protestations merely verifies the pervasiveness of the myth. Presbyterian preacher Donald Grey Barnhouse confirmed this in his characterization of a typical Christian household. "The husband is not interested in the things of God, so the family drifts along without any spiritual cohesion," he wrote. "Perhaps they all go to church together on Sunday morning, and the wife goes to all the activities of the week, but the husband seems uninterested." Barnhouse then offered a familiar, albeit paradoxical, prescription for this malaise: feminine submission. "With delight she learns the joy of knowing it is her husband's house, his home; the children are his; she is his wife," he wrote. "When a woman realizes and acknowledges this, the life of the home can be transformed, and the life of her husband also."[31]

This notion reached its apotheosis in the 1970s with the enormous popularity of Marabel Morgan's book *The Total Woman*. The answer to a troubled marriage, Morgan preached, lay in becoming a "Total Woman," a wife who submitted abjectly to her husband and who burrowed herself ever deeper into the putative bliss of domesticity. "A Total Woman caters to her man's special quirks, whether it be salads, sex, or sports," Morgan wrote. "She makes his home a haven, a place to which he can run."[32]

Against the background of this ideal of feminine domesticity, fundamentalists have found the rapidly changing views of women in recent decades utterly disconcerting. Perhaps nothing—not even Darwinism and higher criticism, the issues of the 1920s—has contributed so greatly to their sense of cultural dislocation. American fundamentalists were caught off guard by *The Feminine Mystique*, and the ensuing feminist movement has left them confused and full of resentment because the domestic ideal that fundamentalism has reified since the nineteenth century is now derided as anachronistic by the broader culture. More confusing still is the fact that many fundamentalist women, like American women everywhere, have joined the workforce in the past two decades. On the one hand they are beset by calls from feminists for liberation and self-assertion, and on the other they are peppered from the pulpit by insistent rehearsals of the nineteenth-century ideal of femininity. Those who resist the workplace inevitably feel anger and even shame about being labeled "just a housewife," and they protest loudly about the nobility of tending the home. Often, however, general economic stringency, an unemployed husband, or divorce tips the balance in the general direction of the feminists. But those fundamentalist women are then left with what Leon Festinger calls cognitive dissonance: on the one hand, the necessity of employment; and on the other, the need they feel to perpetuate fundamentalist standards. More often than not, they feel guilt and confusion for "abandoning" their homes and families, thereby violating the fundamentalist feminine ideal.

A question-and-answer exchange in the May 1989 issue of James Dobson's *Focus on the Family* magazine illustrates poignantly this confusion and anger, as well as this pining for a halcyon past. "As a homemaker," the question from an anonymous reader begins, "I resent the fact that my role as wife and mother is no longer respected as it was in my mother's time. What forces have brought about this change in attitudes in the Western world?" Dobson's response is equally illuminating:

> Female sex-role identity has become a major target for change by those who wish to revolutionize the relationship between men and women. The women's movement and the media have been remarkably successful in altering the way females "see" themselves at home and in society. In the process, every element of the traditional concept of femininity has been discredited and scorned, especially those responsibilities associated with homemaking and motherhood.
>
> Thus, in a short period of time, the term *housewife* has become a pathetic symbol of exploitation, oppression, and—pardon the insult—stupidity, at least as viewed from the perspective of radical feminists. We can make no greater mistake as a nation than to continue this pervasive disrespect shown to women who have devoted their lives to the welfare of their families.[33]

Dobson, of course, failed to acknowledge that his "traditional concept of femininity" (and presumably the one shared by his distraught reader) was a nineteenth-century construct.

More significantly, Dobson's response identified the enemy: "radical feminists," the women's movement, and the media. In the face of such a conspiracy, fundamentalists have had to muster their troops, something they have done with remarkable success over the past decade. What is especially striking about the exertion of fundamentalist influence in the American political arena is the extent to which issues of gender—the Equal Rights Amendment, private sexual morality—have shaped their political agenda. Fundamentalists regularly attach the sobriquet "antifamily" to policies and to politicians they regard as inimical; and they have, curiously, attached singular attention to the issue of abortion.

In recent years, fundamentalists have tried, with considerable success, to propel abortion to the center of political debate. A group of activists calling itself Operation Rescue, many of whose members are fundamentalists, has picketed and blocked abortion clinics in

New York, Atlanta, Wichita, and other cities around the country. Anti-abortion hecklers regularly disrupted Democratic rallies during the 1988 presidential campaign.

The Supreme Court's *Roe* v. *Wade* decision on January 22, 1973, which effectively struck down existing state laws banning an abortion, was initially greeted with silence or indifference by fundamentalists; but by the end of the decade, as they began to mobilize politically, the abortion issue helped to galvanize them into a potent political force. Jerry Falwell, for instance, credited that decision with awakening him from his apolitical stupor, even though he had declared some years earlier that he "would find it impossible to stop preaching the pure saving gospel of Jesus Christ, and begin doing anything else—including fighting Communism, or participating in civil-rights reforms." Falwell thereby articulated a fairly common fundamentalist attitude in the mid-sixties. "Nowhere are we commissioned to reform the externals," he said. "We are not told to wage war against bootleggers, liquor stores, gamblers, murderers, prostitutes, racketeers, prejudiced persons or institutions, or any other existing evil as such."[34]

Roe v. *Wade*, however, together with what Falwell regarded as sundry assaults on the family, triggered an about-face. By the end of the decade Falwell had shed his political naïveté and had organized his "Moral Majority" to counter the evil influences in American culture that threatened to subvert the fundamentalist ideal of femininity. Other fundamentalist leaders have professed similar reactions and indignation to *Roe* v. *Wade*, and I have spoken with many fundamentalists who become visibly angry, almost apoplectic, when discussing abortion.

On the face of it, abortion is an odd issue to use as a rallying point. Fundamentalists pride themselves on taking the Bible literally, but, all of their tortured exegeses notwithstanding, nothing in the scriptures *explicitly* dictates a "pro-life" position. Nor does the fundamentalist fervor over abortion arise from any abstract commitment to the sanctity of all real and potential human life (in that respect, the "pro-life" moniker, which the activists prefer to "anti-abortion," is something of a misnomer). Many fundamentalists who decry abortion will, in the next breath, declare their unequivocal support for capital punishment. And fundamentalists have never been squeamish about the exercise of military force by the United States or its proxies, even when directed against civilians: witness their overwhelming support for the Contras of Central America, the U.S. bombing of Libya, and the wars in Vietnam, Grenada, Panama, and the Persian Gulf.

Why, then, have so many fundamentalists invested such extraordinary passion into this crusade? Why would hundreds of otherwise law-abiding citizens be willing to go to jail to underscore their opposition to abortion? I do not wish to trivialize fundamentalist convictions on this issue. I find some of their arguments compelling and most of them sincere; but it is difficult, at first glance, to understand the centrality of abortion to the fundamentalist political agenda.

I think the answer to this conundrum lies more in the realm of symbols than in ideology, and it relates in particular to the historical circumstances of fundamentalism in the twentieth century. For much of the century, fundamentalists have felt beleaguered and besieged by forces beyond their control. Whereas in the nineteenth century evangelicals had shaped much of the nation's social and political agenda, by the late 1800s rapid urbanization, industrialization, and the massive arrival of immigrants (most of them non-Protestants) made America look a good deal less congenial to evangelicals than it had during the evangelical heyday earlier in the century. Teeming, squalid tenements no longer resembled the precincts of Zion.

By the late nineteenth and early twentieth centuries, moreover, evangelicals felt the sting of evolutionary theory, which, pressed to its logical conclusions, undermined literal understandings of the Bible. The Scopes trial of 1925 finally convinced many fundamentalists that American culture had become inhospitable, even hostile, so they retreated into their own subculture of denominations, publishing houses, mission societies, Bible camps, and Bible institutes.

Although other factors played a role in their reentry into public life in the mid-1970s—a resurgent patriotism after the national ignominies of Vietnam and Watergate and following the presidential candidacy of a Southern Baptist Sunday-school teacher (whom they later abandoned)—fundamentalists latched onto the abortion issue with a vengeance. Given their own history, however, their identification with the fetus is not surprising. For fundamentalists, the fetus serves as a marvelous symbol, not only because of its Freudian or psychoanalytic connotations of crawling back into the womb to escape the buffetings of the world, but because they see it in their own image. "Abortion is the symbol of our decline," Randall Terry, head of Operation Rescue, told a reporter for the *New York Times*, "the slaughter of the most innocent."[35] Nothing is so pure and untainted as an unborn child; fundamentalists, in turn, view themselves as the guardians of moral purity in an immoral world.

At the same time, nothing is so vulnerable as a fetus, and fundamentalists for decades have seen themselves as vulnerable. "We are providing a voice and a defense for the human and civil rights of millions of unborn babies," Falwell wrote in 1987, explaining the political agenda of Moral Majority.[36] "The most dangerous place to be these days is inside a mother's womb," an anti-abortion activist in Iowa told me just before the precinct caucuses in February 1988. Many fundamentalists, I believe, readily identify with that sentiment. Despite their political successes in the past decade, contemporary fundamentalists, like their predecessors in the 1920s, still see American culture as alien and their own existence as precarious. They must exercise extraordinary vigilance lest the forces of evil and darkness, usually identified as "secular humanism," overtake them. In a fund-raising letter issued after the Supreme Court's *Webster* v. *Reproductive Health Services* decision, which allowed the State of Missouri to impose new restrictions on the availability of abortions, James Dobson reminded his readers that "the pro-life movement is only part of a much larger conflict that rages today. What is really at stake is the future of the Judeo-Christian system of values in this country." Dobson concluded the letter by assuring his readers (and contributors) that "we will fight to the death for the moral values in which we believe."[37]

Abortion, moreover, violates the cherished fundamentalist ideal of feminine domesticity. If women guarded their purity and contented themselves with their divinely ordained roles as mothers and housewives, abortion would never be thought necessary at all. For fundamentalists, the very fact that abortion is a political issue in the first place provides an index of how dramatically American culture has deserted their ideal of femininity. The roots of the "disorder," then, can be found in female restiveness, a popular unwillingness to accept the role that God had designed for women. According to Susan Key, a homemaker from Dallas, Texas, who devised a course for women called Eve Reborn, God gave women "a unique capacity for submission and obedience and when this capacity is thwarted by rebellion and deceit, it becomes a capacity to destroy which begins to work within her heart and then sulks out to her intimate relationships, widens to her acquaintances, to society, and then into history."[38]

But if benighted and wayward women contributed to the massive cultural malaise that fundamentalists so decry, women also, because of their exalted spirituality, hold the key to redemption. "I firmly believe the role of a woman today is to nurture our next generation," Maxine Sieleman of Concerned Women for America said during the 1988 presidential primaries, thereby echoing nineteenth-century evangelical notions of virtue. "She has the power within her hands to either make or break a nation. A good woman can make a bad man good, but a bad woman can make a good man bad. . . . Women are the real key for turning this country around. . . . I firmly believe that God has always worked through women."[39] Phyllis Schlafly, who almost singlehandedly defeated the proposed Equal Rights Amendment to the Constitution, said it more succinctly in *The Power of the Positive Woman*. The ideal woman, according to Schlafly, was not merely a housewife but a "patriot and defender of our Judeo-Christian civilization." Moreover, "It is the task of the Positive Woman to keep America good."[40] Compare the sentiments of Catharine Beecher in *A Treatise on Domestic Economy*, published in 1841:

> The mother writes the character of the future man; the sister bends the fibres that hereafter are the forest tree; the wife sways the heart, whose energies may turn for good or for evil the destinies of a nation. Let the women of a country be made virtuous and intelligent, and the men will certainly be the same.

Beecher added that "the formation of the moral and intellectual character of the young is committed mainly to the female hand."[41]

The political agenda of contemporary fundamentalists, then, represents a desperate attempt to reclaim the nineteenth-century ideal of femininity both for themselves and for a culture that has abandoned that ideal. For American fundamentalists, women serve as a kind of bellwether for the culture at large. If women allow themselves to be seduced by "radical feminists" into abandoning their "God-given" responsibilities in the home, America is in trouble. If, however, women cling to Victorian notions of submission, nurture, and domesticity, the future of the republic is secure. Far from the temptress of earlier Christian orthodoxy, the contemporary woman, in the rhetoric of American fundamentalism, can be a redeemer. What better demonstration of her superior spirituality?

Such notions, however, face tough opposition in the latter decades of the twentieth century. Despite their recent political success, American fundamentalists remain on the defensive, trying to shore up what the broader culture now considers a quaint, anachronistic view of women. Whatever the merits of their arguments, the fundamentalist political agenda and particularly their struggle against abortion may represent, at some (albeit subconscious) level, a battle for their own survival as well as a struggle for the preservation of a nineteenth-century ideal.

Notes

1. Bailey Smith, on *Larry King Live*, March 21, 1989.

2. Edward M. Brandt, "Mother," *The Way of Truth* 47 (May 1989): 2.

3. Tammy Deville, "Praying Mothers," *The Way of Truth* 47 (May 1989): 2.

4. Barbara A. Peil, "A Seasoned Approach," *Kindred Spirit* 11 (Spring 1987): 13.

5. "Motherhood in the '90s," *Focus on Family* 14 (January 1990): 2.

6. "Mother," *The Way of Truth* 47 (May 1989): [ii], 1.

7. Peil, "Seasoned Approach," p. 12.

8. Ibid., p. 13.

9. Ibid.

10. I shall use the term *evangelical* to refer to conservative Protestants of the nineteenth century. Because fundamentalists derive their name from the series of pamphlets published between 1910 and 1915, it would be anachronistic to refer to their nineteenth-century evangelicals forebears as *fundamentalists*, even though the two share many beliefs in common.

11. Cited in Rosemary Radford Ruether and Rosemary Skinner Keller, eds., *Women and Religion in America*, 3 vols. (San Francisco: Harper & Row, 1981–1986), vol. 2, p. 161.

12. Gerald F. Moran, "'Sisters in Christ': Women and the Church in Seventeenth-Century New England," in Janet Wilson James, ed., *Women in American Religion* (Philadelphia, 1976), pp. 47–65; Laurel Thatcher Ulrich, "Vertuous Women Found: New England Ministerial Literature, 1668–1735," in *Women in American Religion*, pp. 67–88.

13. Ruth H. Bloch, "The Gendered Meanings of *Virtue* in Revolutionary America," *Signs* 13 (1987): 37–58.

14. See Jan Lewis, "The Republican Wife: Virtue and Seduction in the Early Republic," *William & Mary Quarterly*, 3d ser., 44 (October 1987): 689–721.

15. Susan Juster writes: "The restoration of agency is the key to understanding women's experience of grace. . . . these women were empowered by recovering their sense of self through the assertion of independence from others." "'In a Different Voice': Male and Female Narratives of Religious Conversion in Post-Revolutionary America," *American Quarterly* 41 (March 1989): 53.

16. *Women and Religion in America*, vol. 1, p. 34.

17. *Women and Religion in America*, vol. 2, p. 402.

18. *Women and Religion in America*, vol. 1, p. 36.

19. Catharine E. Beecher and Harriet Beecher Stowe, *The American Woman's Home; or, Principles of Domestic Science; being a Guide to the*

Formation and Maintenance of Economical Healthful Beautiful and Christian Homes (New York: J. B. Ford, 1869), p. 19.

20. For one particularly well known example, see *The American Woman's Home*, pp. 28–29. See also Sandra S. Sizer, *Gospel Hymns and Social Religion: The Rhetoric of Nineteenth-Century Revivalism* (Philadelphia: Temple University Press, 1978), chapter 4.

21. Alexis de Tocqueville, *Democracy in America*, trans. Henry Reeve, ed. Henry Steele Commager (New York: Oxford University Press, 1947), pp. 401, 403.

22. Ann Douglas, *The Feminization of American Culture* (New York: Alfred A. Knopf, 1977).

23. Mary P. Ryan, "A Women's Awakening: Evangelical Religion and the Families of Utica, New York, 1800–1840," in James, ed., *Women in American Religion*, p. 107.

24. *Women and Religion in America*, vol. 2, p. 401.

25. Sylvester Graham, *A Treatise on Bread, and Bread-Making* (Boston: Light & Stearns, 1837), pp. 105–6.

26. Catharine E. Beecher, *A Treatise on Domestic Economy, for the Use of Young Ladies at Home, and at School* (Boston: March, Capen, Lyon, and Webb, 1841), p. 9.

27. These ideas of Victorian domestic culture are developed nicely by Colleen McDannell, *The Christian Home in Victorian America, 1840–1900* (Bloomington, Ind.: Indiana University Press, 1986).

28. The "feminization" of American Protestantism in the nineteenth century extended well beyond the evangelical ambit, and so did the various reclamation efforts undertaken early in the twentieth century. See Gail Bederman, "'The Women Have Had Charge of the Church Work Long Enough': The Men and Religion Forward Movement of 1911–1912 and the Masculinization of Middle-Class Protestantism," *American Quarterly* 61 (1989): 432–65.

29. Quoted in Douglas Frank, *Less than Conquerors: How Evangelicals Entered the Twentieth Century* (Grand Rapids: Wm. B. Eerdmans, 1986), p. 192.

30. *Women and Religion in America*, vol. 3, pp. 260, 261.

31. *Women and Religion in America*, vol. 3, pp. 261, 262.

32. Marabel Morgan, *The Total Woman* (Old Tappan, N.J.: Fleming H. Revell, 1973), p. 55.

33. "Dr. Dobson Answers Your Questions," *Focus on the Family* (May 1989): 8.

34. Quoted in Frances FitzGerald, "A Disciplined, Charging Army," *New Yorker*, May 18, 1981, p. 63.

35. Tamar Lewin, "With Thin Staff and Thick Debt, Anti-Abortion Group Faces Struggle," *New York Times*, June 11, 1990, p. A11.

36. Jerry Falwell, "An Agenda for the 1980s," in Richard John Neuhaus and Michael Cromartie, eds., *Piety and Politics: Evangelicals and Funda-*

mentalists Confront the World (Washington, D.C.: Ethics and Public Policy Center, 1987), p. 114.

37. Letter, dated August 1989, from James Dobson, *Focus on the Family,* pp. 2, 7.

38. Quoted in Carol Flake, *Redemptorama: Culture, Politics, and the New Evangelicalism* (Garden City, N.Y.: Anchor Press, 1984), p. 70.

39. Quoted in Randall Balmer, *Mine Eyes Have Seen the Glory: A Journey into the Evangelical Subculture in America* (New York: Oxford University Press, 1989), pp. 120–21.

40. Quoted in Flake, *Redemptorama,* p. 87.

41. Beecher, *Treatise on Domestic Economy,* p. 13.

Fundamentalism
& Gender
ed J. S. Hawley.
N.Y. : Oxford,
1994

3

Indian Islam:
The Shah Bano Affair

PETER J. AWN

Numerous scholars, when discussing issues of gender, single out the Islamic world for particularly sharp criticism, for what they perceive as its systematic oppression of women. Traditional patriarchies still wield enormous control in many Islamic societies, limiting women's access to the broader society and controlling their ability to make independent choices. But whether Islam as a religious system is the main support of this enduring patriarchal structure is not explored in the current study. Suffice it to say that Islamic religious law, while affirming the equality of men and women before God, nevertheless distinguishes clearly between the rights of men and women. And men, time after time, are afforded greater rights than women.

The history of the women's movement in the culturally diverse Muslim world is complex and cannot easily be summarized in a paragraph. In some Muslim societies, European and American models of women's liberation have had a significant impact. In others, women have expressed a desire for a model of liberation that integrates more fully the structures of the traditional extended family and the assignment of roles that this implies. At the same time, however, one can detect in many parts of the Islamic world a growing backlash against women and the women's movement.

The primary catalyst for this backlash has not been the women's movement itself, but the claim by a vociferous minority of religious zealots that the Muslim world faces a profound crisis that threatens its very existence. The rhetoric of many Islamic revivalist movements integrates a condemnation of women's desires for greater freedom into a broader critique of the pernicious effects that European and American social, economic, and political institutions have had on the Muslim world.

The manipulation of conservative religious ideals and institutions to confront sociopolitical crises has become a trademark of Muslim revival movements. The controversy sparked by the Shah Bano affair, which became a cause célèbre in India during 1986, is a particularly compelling example, since it pitted the Indian Muslim community against both the Hindu majority and the government of Rajiv Gandhi. The issue at stake was no less than the preservation of Muslim communal identity, symbolized by Islamic religious law (sharī'ah), which, many Muslims fervently believed, was under attack by secularizing, assimilationist forces.[1]

A brief review of the details of the case will illustrate clearly the inherent conflict between Islamic religious law and Indian public policy. The drama unfolded in the state of Indore, where Shah Bano Begum was married in 1932. During the many years of her marriage, she bore her husband several children, both male and female. In 1975 Shah Bano was thrown out of the family home because her husband took another wife. Although the husband initially provided her maintenance payments amounting to 200 rupees per month, support ceased in 1978. Eventually, Shah Bano was persuaded by family and friends to sue her husband under Article 125 of the Indian Code of Criminal Procedure, which requires that a husband provide 500 rupees a month maintenance to an indigent wife. Included in the category "wife" are divorced women who have not remarried.

In response to the suit, Shah Bano's husband divorced her, using the least approved (but frequently employed) method of Muslim divorce called talāqu 'l-bid'ah, according to which the husband pronounces three times "I divorce you, I divorce you, I divorce you." Upon divorce, Islamic law requires that the husband return to his wife her dowry (mahr), if she has not already claimed it, and Shah Bano's husband did so. Therefore, he argued, he had fulfilled all obligations stipulated in both Islamic religious law and the civil code. His assertion was based not on Article 125 of the Code of Criminal Procedure, but on Article 127 of the same code, which states that the provision for maintenance included in Article 125 is voided if a sum legislated by any personal law (that is, the religious law of a particular community—in this case, Islamic religious law or *shari'ah*) has been paid by the man to the woman on divorce.

The husband claimed that his return of the dowry (3,000 rupees) constituted the necessary payment on divorce referred to in Article 127 and absolved him of any further obligation to provide maintenance under the terms of Article 125. India's Supreme Court, however, rejected the husband's argument, ruling that the dowry was not a payment made on divorce, but a payment made on marriage.

Islamic religious law states unequivocally that the wife may claim part or all of her dowry at any stage of the marriage. She may, for example, demand a portion at the beginning and the remainder on her husband's death. Or she may take no portion at the beginning but, in the event of divorce, may require that the total sum be returned. The central point of the court's ruling was that the dowry (*mahr*) is not a sum of money to be paid specifically on the occasion of divorce. The husband's petition was denied, and he was required to pay his divorced wife 25 rupees per month in maintenance. (At a later date, Shah Bano petitioned the court for increased maintenance; and the award was adjusted from the original 25 rupees to 180 rupees per month.)

In an attempt to legitimate its ruling further by demonstrating the decision's conformity to Islamic religious principles, the court quoted Qur'ān 2:241–42:

> Making a fair provision for women who are divorced
> is the duty of those who are God-fearing and pious.
> So does God pronounce His decrees
> that you may understand.

The court also reaffirmed Article 44 of the Indian Constitution, which states that the nation is committed to working toward the eventual promulgation of a unified civil code for all religious communities in India.

The stage was set for a fierce debate that was to be articulated primarily in religious terms. The original outcry arose from groups within the Muslim community who claimed that the court and, by association, the central government were interfering in the religious law of the Muslim community. Most Muslims consider the *shari'ah* to be divinely inspired legislation forever binding on all Muslim men and women. In their eyes Islamic law is not a human invention but is derived from revealed sources. Human input is restricted to the formulation of legal theory by scholars during the first three centuries of Islamic history, and to the subsequent application of this theory to different situations by lawyers and judges. The *sharī'ah* cannot be altered or abrogated by the state as part of any effort to adapt religious law to changing social patterns or political structures. The purview of *sharī'ah* is both the public and the private spheres of human relations, and its obligations are incumbent on all Muslims, wherever they may live.

The Islamic law of divorce does not provide for the continued maintenance of the divorced wife. Marriage is a contract; once the contract is terminated, no legal relationship persists between the parties. The exception is the three-month period of *'iddah* following the divorce, during which time the husband is obliged to pay maintenance to the wife. Maintenance during the period of *'iddah*, however, should not be confused with alimony; it is, on the contrary, support provided during a three-month waiting period to ensure that the woman is not pregnant by her recently divorced husband. If she is found to be carrying his child, additional legal obligations become incumbent on the parties.

The ruling of the Supreme Court was perceived by certain elements within the Indian Muslim community as a frontal attack on the legal right of the Muslim minority to live by its own religious law. Specifically, they saw in the appeal to Qur'ānic authority by the court a none-too-subtle attempt by the civil authorities to alter the regulations on divorce found in the *sharī'ah*. Finally, the court's decision was criticized as a blatant effort by the state to force the assimilation of Muslims into the broader Indian (and predominantly Hindu) culture. Thus, the court's reaffirmation of Article 44 of the Indian Constitution was not hailed as a call for compromise and cooperation; it was condemned as an effort to impose uniformity and thus destroy Muslim identity.

The battle provoked by the Shah Bano decision was waged initially in the Indian press, but it soon spilled over into Parliament. The catalyst for the countrywide discussion was a three-part article entitled "The Shariat" (*sharī'ah*), by the respected journalist Arun Shourie, published in the English-language feature magazine, *The Illustrated Weekly*, on January 5, 12, and 19 of 1986.

In these articles, Shourie formulated a devastating rationalist critique of religion in general, and of Islamic law in particular, demanding finally that religion conform to reason and logic, and not hide behind uncriticized truth claims. One cannot hope to shut off inquiry and debate, Shourie insisted, "by asserting divine origins."[12]

Despite Shourie's secularist intellectual stance, Indian readers of the series could not have failed to recognize the writer's own religious and cultural heritage. Shourie's intellectual leanings were initially Marxist, but he comes from a Hindu family and has increasingly espoused what many observers perceive as Hindu causes. For some in the Muslim community, therefore, Shourie's attack on the notion of divinely revealed truth was tantamount to a Hindu polemic against Islam.

At the heart of Shourie's analysis was an examination of the origins of Islamic law and of the foundations on which it is based, namely Qur'ān, *ḥadīth* (the traditions), *qiyās* (the principle of analogy), and *ijmā'* (consensus). Islamic law, as we encounter it today, is, in Shourie's opinion, "completely frozen. There is not the slightest possibility of reform from within the corpus."[3] Consequently, the choice Muslims face, Shourie suggested, is either to capitulate to the traditional view that *ijtihād* (the use of human reason to create new legal theory) is no longer possible or to struggle to reform Islamic law by reintroducing the classic notion of *ijtihād*. Muslim tradition affirms that "the gates of *ijtihād*" were closed around 900 C.E., when Muslim legal scholars concluded that the essential structures of the legal tradition had already been fully articulated. All that remained for future scholars to do was to apply the law to new situations.

Shourie identified a further dilemma for Muslims in what he saw as the contradiction between Islamic legal theory and its practice. In theory, Islamic religious law is immutable, unchanging, and divinely revealed, true for all men and women at all times, regardless of the historical period or cultural milieu. Yet, as Shourie pointed out, the various opinions (*fatwā*, pl. *fatāwā*) offered by legal scholars over the centuries, do, on close inspection, reveal the effects of historical and cultural conditioning.[4]

Shourie's detailed discussion of the two primary bases of Islamic law—namely, Qur'ān and *ḥadīth*—further inflamed Muslim resentment by presuming to examine them solely from an outsider's perspective, with little sensitivity to insiders' understanding of the nature of religious texts. For Muslims, the Qur'ān is a collection of God's actual words, transmitted through the mediacy of the Prophet Muhammad, who is in no sense the author of the text. By definition, therefore, the truth of the Qur'ān is divinely certified. Muslims do not deny the need to elaborate through commentary the meaning of the text. But when a conflict arises between the insights derived from reason and the truths articulated in the revelation, most Muslim scholars choose revelation over reason, since all human faculties are by nature fallible and imperfect.

Shourie, however, asserted that reason should be the final arbiter of truth and the primary tool of Qur'ānic interpretation. To illustrate his point, Shourie ridiculed certain verses that he viewed as illogical and contradictory—for example, those relating to inheritance. In addition to caricaturing the text, Shourie expressed doubts about the moral fiber of the classical legal theorists who interpreted the Qur'ān. Are jurists, he asked, not charlatans when they devise legal stratagems (*ḥīlah* pl. *ḥiyal*) to achieve ends that appear to subvert the legal provisions found in the sacred texts (for example, by providing legal means to circumvent the prohibition against charging and collecting interest)?

While from the perspective of the outsider these criticisms may appear legitimate, they are ultimately misguided. For Muslims, the Qur'ān cannot ultimately be contradictory, because it is God's divinely revealed Word. If it appears to be contradictory, the problem is with our feeble rational faculties, not with the text. Shourie's criticism of the methods of legal scholars and his defense of the spirit of the law thus reveal a lack of familiarity with Islamic legal theory. Law is meant to free, not solely to bind. If, for example, the law forbids one from taking interest per se, but allows one to achieve effectively the same end through other means, there is no religious or legal reason why one should not pursue this alternative avenue of action.

Perhaps the most inflammatory aspect of his articles involved Shourie's critique of a second important body of Islamic sacred literature, the *ḥadīth*—traditions codified primarily during the ninth century C.E. After hundreds of thousands of popular traditions were collected, classical Muslim scholars labored to distinguish the authentic ones from the fraudulent or less reliable ones, through careful examination of the chain of transmitters (*isnād*) of each. Most Muslims today believe, therefore, that the six most revered collections of *ḥadīth* contain authentic traditions going back to Muhammad himself. Shourie, however, echoed the opinions of many non-Muslim scholars who have concluded that, while some of the tradition literature is historical and goes back to Muhammad and his early companions, much in the "authenticated" *ḥadīth* emerged at a considerably later date. Some non-Muslim scholars go so far as to assert that *ḥadīth* were deliberately fabricated to deceive the population and to promote the particular views or short-term interests of the fabricators. Such an extreme polemical stance has little merit and cannot be substantiated.

Clearly this divergence of opinion between Muslim and non-Muslim scholars on the question of the authenticity of *ḥadīth* is an issue of enormous sensitivity. Shourie echoed many of the standard non-Muslim views about the questionable historicity of *ḥadīth* and concluded that they must, therefore, be discarded as corrupt. To discredit *ḥadīth* in this way is tantamount to declaring all Islamic legal theory spurious, as being based on fabricated texts.

According to Shourie, the key to reform is to dethrone religious texts and treat them as fallible human documents. The laws of the *sharī'ah* could then be scrutinized anew and evaluated without reference to any supposed divine origin: "We thus have no alternative but to examine each provision of personal law by itself. If it is excellent, we must urge that it be applied to all. If it is medieval, there is no ground on which we can justify the subjection of any one to it."[5] From this perspective, a divorce law that does not provide continued support for the wife discriminates unfairly against women and should be revised. Similarly, laws permitting polygamy should be repealed. What is "medieval"—that is, based on traditional notions of revealed truth—must go; what is "modern"—that is, based primarily on rational analysis—must be embraced.

Shourie, unfortunately, ignored a basic reality: outsiders and insiders frequently differ on questions of interpretation and of the historical authenticity of religious texts. An argument articulated in terms of either authenticity or reasonableness ignores the actual function of the documents within the Muslim community. Rather than condemn the traditions as outdated or forged—a position that can only elicit a negative and defensive response—one might understand them in less polemical terms.

Muslim traditions, whether or not they all represent authentic sayings of Muhammad and his early companions, are precious interpretive documents—some reflecting Muhammad's own words, others reflecting insights arrived at much later and yet put into the mouth of the Prophet-Founder. The creative value of *ḥadīth* lies in their having provided continuity for the nascent Muslim community during its formative period, integrating change within the framework of the original ideals expressed in the Qur'ān and elsewhere by Muhammad. The traditions thus provided the bases for formulating a social and legal theory that has withstood the test of centuries.

In the final installment of Shourie's article, he emphasized that change has occurred in a number of Muslim societies, and that this change has been based on a number of religious and legal principles. Yet even here, while recognizing the fact of positive change, Shourie belittled the methods used to bring it about:

Many have tried to dress the reforms up by asserting that they are derived from or based on the Shariat itself. Some have invoked "the principle of necessity" and instituted reforms on this basis. Some have based these on "*takhsis-al-qada,*" the right of a ruler to specify what will and what will not be within the jurisdiction of the courts.

Another, even more openly eclectic, method has been *talfiq*—i.e., "patching up" by combining the opinions of different schools and jurists.

Others have been even more inventive and have enlarged the latitude of choosing one school of Islamic law or another out of recognition. They have decided to choose not just this school or that, but to choose school "X" on point "A," school "Y" on point "B" and so on. . . .

Now, one can raise anything to the point of principle and sanctify it by giving it an Arabic or a Persian name. And, I suppose, if a fig-leaf helps, it is good. But these are transparent subterfuges. The main points to remember are: because of the press of reality almost all Muslim countries have reformed personal law, as also every other aspect of Islamic law; and that in doing so they have derived the new formulations from widely disparate sources—the Napoleonic code, the codes of Britain, Italy, even Japan.[6]

Here, Shourie accurately summarized the principles employed by Muslim legists and politicians to promote change within modern societies. As an outsider, however, he concluded, unfortunately, that these methods are mere subterfuges invented to circumvent the law. On the contrary, they allow for social and political development, without requiring the actual revision of the *shari'ah*. This is possible because religious law is not and never has been the sole legal arbiter within the community. Since the death of Muhammad, Islamic polities have supported two intertwined yet distinct legal power bases: the Muslim religious and the Muslim political establishments. As a result, parallel court systems developed, each with its own jurisdiction.

The dynamic tension between the changing legal structures imposed by Muslim political authorities and the changeless truths embodied in the religious legal tradition has been a source of genuine creativity within Muslim communities throughout history. For Shourie, the outsider, however, this tension can only appear as an illogical and contradictory conflict between opposing powers.

In the same way, Shourie's caricature of Muslim scholars' appeals to different legal schools in order to obtain the most favorable ruling reveals a lack of familiarity with Islamic legal procedure. For the insider versed in religious law, such appeals to different legal schools afford individuals the greatest latitude the law will allow. To the outsider, however, they appear merely to be cynical attempts to circumvent legal obligations.

Shourie found little hope for the system of religious law in Islam as it now exists. In his concluding remarks, he outlined once again the classic secularist position: the Muslim *shari'ah*, with its reliance on texts inaccessible to serious rational scrutiny because of their sacred status, cannot but impede the Muslim community's efforts to integrate itself fully into the modern world. The blueprint for true reform must be found elsewhere:

- Each provision of each of our codes—and not just the Muslim one—must be re-examined in the light of modern secular principles;
- A new draftcode based on what is best in them as well as in codes in force elsewhere in the world should be drawn up;
- The task of preparing this code must be entrusted not to the clerics and priests and theologians of any religion but to modern, secular jurists;
- Once prepared the code should first be enacted as *an option* so that all Indians can choose whether they want to be governed by this code or by the one specific to their religion;
- As a final step of course, this modern, secular, common code, should replace the existing parochial codes.[7]

The responses to Shourie's articles were voluminous and diverse, both from within and from without the Muslim community. A formal two-part rejoinder, "In Defence of the Shariat," was published in *The Illustrated Weekly* by Dr. Rafiq Zakaria on March 2 and 9, 1986. Professor Zakaria's arguments, interestingly, mirrored the flaws present in Shourie's work. Whereas Shourie exhibited little understanding of the insider's views and the internal processes of evolution within the Muslim religious community, Zakaria for the most part ignored the perspective of outsiders.

In fact, Zakaria refused to address the crux of Shourie's argument—namely, that reason, not revelation, must be the final judge of the viability of religious laws in a modern nation-state. Zakaria's approach was to begin with an ad hominem attack, accusing Shourie of prejudicial attitudes inherited from European orientalists, who, with great regularity, belittle Islam. Zakaria's rebuttal consisted of quoting other Europeans, including H. G. Wells, who proclaimed Islam the ideal religion—"'the broadest, freshest and cleanest political idea that has come into actual activity'"[8] — and Edmund Burke, who characterized Islamic religious law as "the most enlightened jurisprudence that ever existed in the world."[9]

Thus, while Shourie challenged Muslims to address the actual state of Islamic communities in the twentieth century, Zakaria chose to focus on an ahistorical, idealized vision of Islamic society. For the outsider, such a model of "true" or "perfect" Islam has little relevance. The Islam of real interest and concern is the Islam of current history, with all its strengths and weaknesses.

To Zakaria's credit, however, he did take time to explain more cogently the insider's understanding of the function of the four bases of Islamic law — namely, Qur'ān, ḥadīth, qiyās (the principle of analogy), and ijmā' (consensus). Moreover, he described in detail the function of independent reasoning (ijtihād) within the context of Islamic legal theory.

Zakaria argued that Islamic history demonstrates a plurality of approaches to problems, legal and otherwise. Thus, in the modern period, many Muslim thinkers from various cultural areas have proposed ways to promote the continued adaptation of Islam to life in the twentieth century. But although this fact is significant to an insider, it cannot fully satisfy an outsider like Shourie who refuses to grant sacred texts more inherent relevance than the findings of human reason. No matter how firmly and sincerely Zakaria might laud and affirm ijtihād as a critical tool for developing legal practice, he must ultimately concede that its validity rests on its conformity to the fundamental texts of the revelation — namely, the Qur'ān and ḥadīth.

The impasse is clear. The outsider wishes to desacralize religious texts and the laws derived from them, treating this body of literature like any other human construct. The insider, on the other hand, precariously balances universal truth claims embodied in the sacred texts with human efforts to elucidate these documents in ways that will permit the community to respond creatively to new situations.

Throughout the history of Islam, development and adaptation have not been the problem; only innovation is condemned. Innovation (bid'ah) implies that the change being introduced is alien to and not in conformity with the overarching religious and social ideals articulated in the sacred texts. Shourie's proposed model falls into this proscribed category, while Zakaria's model struggles to link change to tradition.

Zakaria's concluding remarks are perhaps the most telling. The reason for the fierce Muslim reaction against the Shah Bano ruling by the Supreme Court, he suggested, is not the legal question of maintenance after divorce. Rather, the response was provoked by the way in which the case was handled and by the resulting criticism of Islam by non-Muslims:

> Unfortunately, the Supreme Court used this case as a hammer against the Shariat; many of its *obiter dicta*, particularly the reference to the degradation of women in Islam, were not only uncalled for but also unjustified. They smacked of prejudice against Islam, which naturally hurt the sentiments of the Muslims, coming as these observations did from the highest judiciary of the land. . . . The judicial forum was used to politicise the issue. On their part the Muslims feared that the basis of their religion, which is the Qur'ān, was being tampered with and their religious identity threatened. Kuldip Nayar, the noted columnist, writes: "Sectarian riots and discrimination against them in jobs and vocations have made them develop a siege mentality. At every step they see dangers threatening their identity. And since they have often come to grief, they have gone to the other extreme of seeking protection from maulvis and mullahs or those who speak like them. The Supreme Court would have done better if it had not made the remarks it did on a common civil code."[10]

Zakaria's analysis is cogent. A religious minority that perceives its identity, even survival, threatened may respond by falling back on the most conservative (and therefore unyielding) religious structures to shore up its defenses. As the Shah Bano debate progressed, moderate Indian Muslims who had long worked for the evolution of Islamic practice in the face of twentieth-century social challenges found themselves unable to counter the voices of archconservatives who branded them as traitors and lukewarm Muslims for refusing to defend the immutability of revealed truth. The leaders of the conservative minority thus became the most influential spokespersons for the entire Indian Muslim community. Muslim politicians labored to persuade the government to provide legal exemption for Muslims from Article 125 of the Penal Code, which, they claimed, threatened the integrity of Muslim religious law.

The political struggle waged in Parliament eventually resulted in what appeared to be a victory for the Muslim conservatives: the adoption of the Muslim Women (Protection of Rights on Divorce) Bill of 1986. Its provisions stipulate that the only maintenance to be paid to the divorced wife by the husband is the *sharī'ah* requirement for support during *'iddah*. In addition, two years of child support are required, as well as return of the dowry (*mahr*). Finally, all properties owned by the wife, from whatever sources, are to be returned to her.

Rather than imposing on Muslim men the obligation for maintenance prescribed for other Indians by Article 125, the Muslim Women Bill of 1986 provided that a divorced Muslim woman, if she remains unmarried and without independent means, must be financially maintained by those relatives who stand to inherit from her upon her death. If she has no relatives, or if the relatives cannot provide maintenance, support is to be provided by local boards entrusted with distributing assets derived from pious bequests called *waqf* (pl. *awqāf*). These Waqf Boards, therefore, were to become the legally responsible benefactors of last resort.

Thus, in the minds of the legislators, appropriate provisions had been made for the support of divorced women, without infringing on the requirements of Islamic religious law. But did this solution ultimately constitute a victory for the Muslim community?

The Muslim Women (Protection of Rights on Divorce) Bill itself was fraught with problems for Muslim women. How was a woman to be assured of maintenance from her financially able relatives if they refused to comply? How many women would feel at liberty to take their relatives to court? Would not such actions cause women to be ostracized from their extended family, the basic unit of Indian society?

When relatives are unable to provide support, the *waqf* system is expected to fill the void. Here, too, the proposed solution ignores the realities of the situation. The *waqf* system is not always efficiently administered. Consequently, it cannot be counted on to act successfully as a social service agency for indigent, divorced women. If the local *waqf* board is in disarray, what options remain available to the abandoned wife?

Finally, the 1986 legislation absolves the husband of all legal responsibility toward the wife after the three-month period of *'iddah* expires. With no further legal recourse available to the divorced wife against her husband, because of the provisions of the new law, her situation is potentially more vulnerable now than it was before enactment of the new legislation.

From a political perspective, however, many within the Muslim community hailed the Muslim Women Bill of 1986 as a resounding success. The *sharī'ah* had been defended successfully, and the integrity of the community had been preserved intact. The latest onslaught by the forces of assimilation had been stemmed.

Although many Muslim politicians were elated at the parliamentary victory, the long-range consequences of this success were ambiguous at best. First and foremost, the Shah Bano affair demonstrated that a vociferous minority that espouses ultraconservative religious principles can monopolize the public forum and silence a more moderate majority by creating an atmosphere in which moderation is equated with religious insincerity and communal indifference or treachery.

Second, the Gandhi government's capitulation, while it may have appeared at the time to signal a political victory for Muslims, may prove to be a setback in the long term. When a minority community is permitted, through political pressure, to retain practices that many outside the community brand as regressive, such a "victory" may give the impression that the community in question is incapable of joining forces with the majority in its struggle to mold a modern society. If the Muslim community insists on retaining an immobilized legal system that does not respond to modern needs, is it capable of participating fully in the national agenda of growth, development, and modernization?

Third, the decision of the Gandhi government sends the wrong signal to fundamentalist Hindu groups in India by demonstrating that radical religious forces have the power to extract favorable concessions from the state. If Muslims can achieve their ends through political coercion, Hindus can do the same. Moreover, Hindu nationalists interpret the capitulation of the government to Muslim demands as an attack on the essential Hindu character of Indian culture.

Radical Hindu forces have learned well the lessons of the Shah Bano affair, a fact dramatically illustrated by their destruction of the 16th-century Babari Mosque at Ayodhya in December of 1992. The claim of the Hindu nationalists was that this mosque had been built on the site of the birthplace of the god Rama and must be returned to Hindu control. For a considerable period, the government forbade entrance to the site by either Muslims or Hindus, but when Hindu nationalists began to take to the streets, it relented. Even that proved insufficient. What began on the surface as a religious dispute was transformed into a strident political and cultural confrontation, culminating with the demolition of the mosque by a Hindu mob.

The specifics of the historical debate over the Babari Mosque are not of central relevance. The heart of the conflict is the claim by Hindu fundamentalists that Indian culture is Hindu culture and that, for India to survive and progress, Hindus must regain control of their country and exorcise the foreign, corrupting elements.

Finally, it is impossible not to see the Shah Bano affair as a symbol of the systematic erosion of women's rights by conservative religio-political forces. More than once, communities in the Muslim world have attempted to combat a perceived threat by shoring up traditional patriarchal institutions at the expense of women's hard-won rights. Efforts to control women's sexuality, dress, career, and movements provide ultraconservatives with potent weapons against the incursions of more egalitarian social ideals and freer sexual mores, as espoused in America and Europe. And the success or failure of these efforts to control women becomes an important barometer of the success or failure of the community's broader efforts to reassert its traditional identity in the face of outside threats.

Muslim traditionalists are not fantasizing when they identify divorce, abortion, more open sexual experimentation, sexually transmitted diseases, and women's demands for equality in the workplace and in decision-making as threats to traditional values. American and European society attest to the strain under which the traditional family labors, even as new and varied models for partnering and parenting emerge. Should these practices be allowed to infiltrate traditional Muslim society? If so, which ones can be assimilated without destroying the community's identity?

It would be naive to believe that fundamentalist movements can completely prevent the infiltration of Western ideas of gender equality into traditional societies. Certain fundamentalist movements, however, have demonstrated that they can slow the process considerably either through coercion or by linking traditional values to political goals.

Coercion is best exemplified by the morality police who wander the streets and bazaars in Iran and Saudi Arabia. They preserve through terror public conformity to traditional values. What goes on privately, however, is more difficult to evaluate.

The more successful way to control the infiltration of new social values is to identify them as weapons used by Americans and Europeans to corrupt traditional societies. If the traditional society is sapped of its strength, the foreign power is able to maintain economic and political control. To reject foreign values is to reject foreign hegemony. To embrace traditional sexual roles proudly is to embrace the ideal of independence, to stand up in militant opposition to the aggressor.

As these considerations suggest, any rethinking of the role of women in Muslim societies cannot be based solely on models imported from America or Europe; it must emerge from the Muslim communities themselves. In the meantime, national governments should not allow religious conservatives to coerce women into conforming to a monolithic vision of Islam.

Traditionalist Indian Muslims won the battle over Article 125 and the question of maintenance after divorce. Whether the Shah Bano victory provides the Indian Muslim community with increased political strength to promote internal social development and cooperation with the Hindu majority is far from certain. On the contrary, the victory could be seen as the coming to power of extremist elements whose agenda is isolationist, and antagonistic toward cooperation within a pluralistic environment.

One rarely discovers in the revivalist rhetoric of ultraconservative religious movements a detailed social blueprint for adaptation to a changing world. More often than not, religious revivalists couch their aspirations in general terms of a return to a mythic past in which the seamless fabric of society reflects at every level the universal and unchanging principles of the traditional faith.

Unfortunately this mythic past never existed; nor is there great reason for hope that such a theocratic utopia could ever be created, in India or elsewhere. The increasing reliance of minority communities on restrictive, exclusionary notions of ethnicity and nationalism and on conservative religious agendas to promote the reassertion of identity does not bode well for creative interaction among communities. Such a view of the world, supported by religious principles that find pluralism antithetical, cannot help but brand the "other" as a threat, thus contributing to increased alienation and fragmentation in the world community. The Shah Bano case, while only one political skirmish fought using religious rhetoric as the weapon, reflects a disheartening trend that can be charted within a number of Muslim societies as well as in other newly emerging nations.

Notes

1. The Shah Bano affair generated sufficient controversy that it is now the subject of a considerable bibliography. Among the most significant works in English are the following: Asghar Ali Engineer, *The Shah Bano Controversy* (Bombay: Orient Longman, 1987); Asghar Ali Engineer, *Status of Women in Islam* (New Delhi: Ajanta Publications, 1987); Janak Raj Jai, *Shah Bano* (New Delhi: Rajiv Publications, 1986); Susheela Kaushik, ed., *Women's Oppression: Patterns and Perspectives* (New Delhi: Shakti Books, 1985); V. R. Krishna Iyer, *Justice V. R. Krishna Iyer on the Muslim Women (Protection of Rights on Divorce) Act, 1986* (Lucknow: Eastern Book, 1987); Shahida Lateef, *Muslim Women in India: Political and Private Realities 1890s–1980s* (London and Atlantic Highlands, N.J.: Zed Books 1990); Sunil Maitra, *Muslim*

Women's Act: Deathknell of Secularism (New Delhi: Natural Book Centre, 1986); Mohammad Farogh Naseem, *The Shah Bano Case: X-Rayed* (Karachi: Karachi Legal Research Center, 1988); H. Y. Siddiqui, *Muslim Women in Transition: A Social Profile* (New Delhi: Harnam Publications, 1987); and Indu Prakash Singh, *Indian Women: The Captured Beings* (New Delhi: Intellectual Publishing House, 1990).

2. Arun Shourie, "The Shariat," *Illustrated Weekly*, January 5, 1986, p. 8.

3. Ibid., p. 14.

4. Ibid.

5. Arun Shourie, "The Shariat," *Illustrated Weekly*, January 19, 1986, p. 20.

6. Ibid., p. 22.

7. Ibid., p. 23.

8. Quoted by Rafiq Zakaria, "In Defence of the Shariat," *Illustrated Weekly*, March 2, 1986, p. 42.

9. Quoted by Zakaria, ibid.

10. Rafiq Zakaria, "In Defence of the Shariat," *Illustrated Weekly*, March 9, 1986, p. 47.

4

Hinduism:
Satī *and Its Defenders*

JOHN S. HAWLEY

Only half a decade ago, the phrase "Hindu fundamentalism" would have had an odd ring. Americans thought of fundamentalists as Christian, Muslim, or even Sikh, but not as Hindu or Buddhist: these religions did not seem to lend themselves to militancy. Recent events in India and Sri Lanka have greatly altered this perception. Hinduism no longer seems so tolerant and quiescent, and it has become commonplace for the press to designate as "fundamentalists" the Hindus who confronted Muslims and their one-time protectors, the secular state, over the issue of whether a temple to the god Rama should be constructed on the site in Ayodhya where he is supposed to have been born.

From 1528 until December 6, 1992, a mosque built by one of the lieutenants of the Mughal emperor Babar stood there. Now it is gone—torn apart by clubs, pipes, ropes, and pickaxes in the hands of young men and ascetics dedicated to restoring "Rama's rule" to India. Hundreds of thousands watched and cheered as the mosque was being pulled down. The police guard, almost all of whom were Hindu, looked the other way or found ways to lend their support. Members of the crowd took home pieces of the erstwhile structure as souvenirs. And thousands of people, mostly Muslims, have died in riots associated with the controversy, both before and after the demolition of the Barbari Mosque itself.

Many who write in the Western press have expressed the fear that events at Ayodhya may signal an ominous reorientation of Indian political life in the direction of "Hindu fundamentalism." They are not alone in using the term: India's English-speaking elites have for some time followed suit. In Indian newspapers and periodicals, the word *fundamentalism* has gradually phased out such terms as *revivalism* and *obscurantism*, which reflected more closely the British ambience that has dominated English-language education in India. One sees the near hegemony of this term in English-language coverage of the Ayodhya affair, as if it represented a closing of linguistic ranks by secular writers opposed to the reality they were forced to describe. But the trend began earlier, in reports of a *sati* that occurred in Deorala, in the state of Rajasthan, in 1987; reactions to it filled the newspapers for many months thereafter. In hindsight the Deorala *sati* seems almost a dress-rehearsal for the confrontation at Ayodhya, and its effects have contributed in major ways to the remarkable momentum of Hindu religious revival that seems to be sweeping through India. For example, an influential pamphleteer in the Deorala affair went on to devote his efforts to expounding the Hindu case at Ayodhya, and a politician who made a name for himself as an advocate of *sati* was subsequently recruited—over much protest—to the national cabinet, presumably to attract his following among traditionalist Hindus.[1] Obviously, the Ayodhya confrontation has not been as specifically focused on women as were its two predecessors in India's struggles with religion and politics—the Shah Bano episode (1985–1986) and the *sati* of Roop Kanwar in Deorala (1987–1988). At Ayodhya the issue of Hindu manhood was far more to the fore than Hindu womanhood. Yet these two are closely intertwined.

My purpose in the essay that follows is to return to the controversy that surrounded the *sati* of Roop Kanwar, in an effort to discover the strength of the connection between it and the gathering cause of Hindu fundamentalism. I will suggest that the bond is strong and that issues of gender are by no means incidental to forging it.

The Sati *of Roop Kanwar*[2]

The word *sati* (or as nineteenth-century authors tended to spell it, "suttee") is used in European languages primarily to designate the custom whereby a Hindu widow is burned on the pyre of her dead husband. In Hindi and other Indian languages the usage is different.

There, *sati* refers primarily to the woman herself, who becomes *sati* when her inner truth (*sat*) manifests itself as she joins her husband in death. By those who participate in what has been called the "cult" of *sati*,[3] she is believed to keep her protective power at her husband's disposal as he continues on his journey, and she also radiates it outward to those who venerate her action.

The practice of allowing a woman to become *sati* has never been widespread in India, but it was observed with sufficient frequency in the early nineteenth century to arouse the indignation of British authorities and a number of elite Hindus. It was outlawed in 1829.[4] *Sati* is extremely rare today—owing at least in part to the fact that the British legislation prohibiting it generated a body of precedent that was taken over by independent India—but it does occur. According to official records, there have been twenty-eight instances of *sati* in Rajasthan (which was not a part of the Raj) since independence in 1947,[5] and a number of additional cases have been reported from the neighboring states of Madhya Pradesh and Uttar Pradesh. These are rural areas lying at some distance from the great centers of power; and most of the *satis* that occurred there caused no great furor, although the Indian press usually gave them brief notices and the phenomenon stimulated a few scholarly articles. All that changed in 1987.

On September 4 of that year, in the village of Deorala, some 50 miles north of Jaipur, in the Shekhavati region of Rajasthan, a young woman by the name of Roop Kanwar became a *sati*. Roop, a pretty Rajput girl of eighteen, had eight months earlier married a twenty-four-year-old Rajput man by the name of Mal Singh. The day after Mal Singh's untimely death from acute gastroenteritis or a burst appendix—or perhaps poison[6]—she mounted his funeral pyre with him; there her body was consumed in the flames along with his.

Although this event was witnessed by thousands, reports from the scene disagree about what actually happened. According to early accounts, Roop Kanwar willed her own death and carried it out with dignity and resolve. In commenting on this fact, sympathetic observers often say that Roop had prepared herself for such an event before she had any inkling that it might become a part of her own life. She is said to have visited the great *sati* temple at Jhunjhunu, and more than once to have journeyed to a *sati* temple in far-off Ranchi, Madhya Pradesh, where she spent much of her childhood because her father Bal Singh Rathore (or Bal Singh Shekhavati), a businessman, was employed there.

On the day of her own *sati*, all this preparation came to fruition. In the traditional fashion, it is said, she took her husband's head in

her hands as she seated herself on the pyre and submitted calmly
to the flames.[7] Icons issued to commemorate the event—primarily
tableaus composed from photographs taken independently of Roop
Kanwar and Mal Singh while both were alive and healthy—recall it
in just this way. For those who buy them, these serve not only as
mementos but as potentially forceful amulets that carry forward the
inner significance of the event.

In the minds of believers, a *sati* involves much more than what
happens on one particular day. It has an eternal resonance because it
is a hierophany—an occasion on which the boundary between the
human and divine planes is breached. In a true *sati*, according to
Rajput belief, a woman carries out a vow to make available to her
husband the power (*śakti*) that is hers as a woman beyond the confines of this particular mortal life. Her continuing presence at his
side is believed to shelter him from the potentially malevolent effects
of death, to cancel the karmic effects of his shortcomings in this life
(as well as any of her own), and to offer benefits as well to those who
surround her in the last moments of this life. These include both
members of her family and any others who come to seek her blessing
or merely to witness her action; for Hindus, the act of sight itself
(*darśan*) is regarded as empowering. If the woman pursues her desire
to become *sati* from motives of genuine devotion to her husband, the
truth of her stance is believed to become plain at the moment she
dies. As she enters the world beyond this life, her divinity becomes
manifest in this one: with no physical assistance from the outside,
the fire of her inner truth (*sat*) ignites her pyre.[8] People seek out such
a *sati* in the hours prior to this happening, for although her divinity
is concealed from public view, it is present nonetheless. She has the
power to protect by means of blessings and curses (*ok* and *srāp*), and
to speak the truth in a way that ordinary mortals cannot.

At such a time she is no longer an individual but a manifestation
of divinity. Once her *sat* bursts forth in flames, she becomes a "sati
mother" (*satimātā*) fully capable of nurturing and sheltering her "children" well into future generations. She joins other "sati mothers" in a
class so tightly knit that her worshippers are apt to refer to any member of it as if she were the whole. She is thus in some sense the
goddess Sati—a member of a sacred class to which the wife of Shiva
called Sati also belongs. There is no exact fit between the practice of
sati (*satipratha*) and the myth of Sati, Shiva's wife, but the connections are powerful. Sati killed herself in front of her father before he
could complete a huge sacrifice from which he had excluded Shiva as
a guest. Thus she diverted its power from the public, male realm to

the one in which women have power: the domestic arena that surrounds the life of a wife and a husband.[9] Hindus who revere *satis* feel that the same power of self-sacrifice continues to be manifest every time a new *sati* emerges; and each time, it is not just a human event but a divine one. In Rajasthan this has happened with sufficient frequency that many "sati mothers" stand between the "original" *sati*, Shiva's wife, and the present. As the effective focus of *sati* worship in Rajasthan, they are honored through the veneration of icons that show them cradling the heads of their husbands, recumbent on the pyre, as they serenely submit to the flames themselves.[10]

In opposing *sati*, the great Hindu reformer of early nineteenth-century Bengal, Rammohan Roy, attempted to drive a wedge between *sati* as a mythical ideal and *sati* as the practice of immolating real women. He saw the myth of the divine Sati as a celebration of female heroism, but he thought the practice of widow-burning (as he and the British called it) depended on a cruel devaluation of women in relation to men. Modern Indians, especially feminists, who continue Rammohan Roy's legacy often go much farther than he did in questioning the efficacy of the myth itself, for they are eager to strip the practice of *sati* of any divine aura. The faithful who came to celebrate Roop Kanwar's death bought photomontages in which wedding pictures of the handsome faces of Roop and Mal Singh were superimposed on a stylized rendering of their gorgeously draped bodies ready for a common funeral. But feminist critics, in writing about Roop's death, tended to project an actual photograph of her charred remains. Sometimes they went further, as Paul Courtright has explained, composing icons of their own. In one example we see Rajput men and women joining hands in homage to Roop Kanwar, but this traditionalist phalanx is undercut by a row of women who raise a barrage of clenched fists, the symbol of international protest on behalf of women.[11]

Similarly, these opponents' accounts of Roop Kanwar's death tell quite a different story from the one we have just heard. According to them, Roop Kanwar unquestionably did not act voluntarily. Most say she was drugged into submission by her in-laws. Even so, she had the strength to try once to escape from the pyre—some say as many as three times[12]—but was pushed back on. (The account offered by devotees says she fell from the pyre and was assisted in the task of mounting it again.) One version, published in a major newspaper, said that Roop had fled to a barn and was dragged back;[13] others assert that the funeral procession was attended by armed guards, lest she tried to get away.[14] And it has been widely reported that in her last moments Roop Kanwar called out to her father for help or uttered cries that could not be understood because they were drowned by the exuberant roar of the crowd.[15]

People who see the event from this point of view generally assert that Roop Kanwar's in-laws acted primarily from economic motives. How else to explain the fact that they arranged for her to be immolated on a plot near their own home, rather than on the town cremation grounds, as would have been customary? This bit of evidence leads critics to believe that Mal Singh's family expected large numbers of worshipful spectators to make offerings on the occasion of the *sati* itself, and to continue their generosity once a shrine (*sati sthal*) was established on the site of Roop Kanwar's death and transfiguration.[16] Their area of Rajasthan has a vivid (though not necessarily ancient) practice of honoring *satis*. The most magnificent temple in the region is dedicated to the Great Queen Sati (*rāṇī mahāsatī*) of Jhunjhunu, some 60 miles away, and an earlier series of *satis*, as many as one a year, in Deorala's own Sikar district had brought a measure of wealth to the families and villages involved.[17]

Of course, critics ridicule the idea that the pyre burst into spontaneous fire. It had to be lit, and the person responsible for touching a torch to the pyre was Pushpender Singh—a lad of fifteen and the younger brother of Mal Singh. This role would have fallen to Pushpender in the regular course of traditional Hindu mortuary practice, whether his brother's corpse had been joined on its pyre by his wife or not. For the role he played in the death of Roop Kanwar, this youth was arrested by the local police the day after the event and charged with murder. And when the local constabulary came under criticism for not having themselves taken steps to prevent the *sati* (and thereby uphold the law of the land), further arrests were made: Mal Singh's father and three other male members of his family were imprisoned.[18] Advocates of a woman's right to *sati* say that the number of people jailed by the authorities on suspicion of having conspired in the event soon rose to a hundred, but apparently all have since been set free, and no one has been prosecuted.

One critical figure, the family doctor who may have administered a sedative to keep Roop Kanwar as calm as possible during an ordeal she did not herself choose, has been untracked since the day of the *sati* itself. Another doctor also figures in the picture: a neuropsychiatrist in Jaipur to whom Mal Singh's family had earlier turned for help in treating a mysterious depressive disorder that may be related to whatever it was that ultimately claimed his life. In a recent analysis of medical evidence and police reports, Veena Talwar Oldenburg reads Mal Singh's death as a probable suicide, caused by his repeated failure in examinations for medical school—and, perhaps, failure in his marital life as well. Whatever the truth, the circumstances invite dark suspicions.[19]

Given the current legal context and the values expressed in India's secular constitution, it is perhaps to be expected that much of the discussion about Roop Kanwar should focus on the issue of whether this was a voluntary *sati* and on the question of what punishment should be meted out to those who share responsibility for allowing it to occur, whether voluntarily on her part or through coercion. Our concern, however, is somewhat different and has less to do with the *sati* itself than with the stir it subsequently caused. Why did this *sati* become such a celebrated case, when earlier examples of *sati*—even those that occurred in nearby villages—attracted little notice and little protest? Why did such huge crowds gather to observe the event and to participate in the *chunari*[20] ceremony solemnizing it after the fact? Still more to the point, when feminists and others gathered in Jaipur to protest the continued presence of *sati* in the fabric of Rajasthani life, why did tens of thousands of people march in counterdemonstrations, urging that the government had no right to intrude into the realm of religion by attempting to suppress the practice of *sati*? The virulence of this response by traditionalists— and its contemporaneity with seemingly comparable events in world affairs—has seemed to justify the use of the term *fundamentalism* in characterizing the point of view that it represented. Here we hope to see to what extent that label makes sense.

The "Fundamentalist" Response

Several important events followed the *sati* of Roop Kanwar. The first was a *chunari* celebration, held twelve days after the *sati* on the spot in Deorala where it occurred. This ceremony is named for the auspicious cloth—primarily red but flecked with yellow—that figures at its core. The *chunari* rite holds a place in the Rajput culture of Rajasthan that makes it roughly parallel to the *srāddh* ceremony (in Rajasthan, the *pagaḍi rasm*) performed an equal number of days after the death of a Rajput male. In the central ritual act, the ceremonial *chunari* dedicated to the woman who has died is held over a flame at the cremation site and is then released into the fire as a final act to honor her physical remains. At the *chunari* ceremony for Roop

Kanwar, her natal family provided the cloth, her married family participated in the ritual, and visitors showered numerous additional *chunaris* onto the place where the pyre had been.

Believers who were present say that the fire, which had miraculously stayed burning the entire twelve days, first rose to kiss the original *chunari* in a gesture of respect, and then receded before rising again, this time to consume the cloth. Other remarkable occurrences have also been claimed for the holy spot, including numerous cures that are attested by bits of colorful garments left at the *sati sthal* by grateful devotees.[21] More miraculous — and more threatening — to those who disapprove of the event is the sheer numbers of people who attended it. Despite the fact that the Rajasthan High Court, responding especially to efforts by women's organizations, forbade the assembly of great numbers of people at Deorala on that day, hundreds of thousands of people flocked to the site.[22] These were almost entirely Rajasthanis, who came by every conceivable conveyance, from jeep and truck to camel-cart; and there seem to have been noticeably more women among their number than men. Brahmin priests officiated, and the crowd reverberated with shouts of "Victory to Great Mother *Sati*" (*mahāsati mātā kī jai*).[23]

It can hardly be doubted that this convocation represented a considerable cross-section of the regional population, and one might well feel that a sufficiently substantial tradition of *sati* worship exists in this part of Rajasthan to make such a gathering intelligible on its own terms. Large numbers of people come together at annual pilgrimages to *sati* temples in not-far-distant Kotri, Jharli, Dhandeni, and of course Jhunjhunu, at roughly this time of year. Other observers are skeptical, however, that such an enormous crowd could have been assembled if Deorala had been the typical rural village it is sometimes made out to be. Visitors are often struck by the fact that Deorala is quite well-to-do, displaying an overwhelming proportion of solidly built brick dwellings, rather than mud ones. Much of this prosperity is attributable to the fact that the Brahmin and Rajput families who form Deorala's leadership almost invariably have one or two male members working in cities that lie in the general vicinity, especially Jaipur and Delhi. Delhi is only five hours away, and Jaipur less than half that. Hence Deorala is well connected to an information network that extends throughout the region, and is sufficiently wealthy and enterprising to be able to sponsor an effective poster campaign on its own behalf in neighboring areas, as did occur. The early involvement of women's groups in Jaipur and Delhi in the effort to suppress any subsequent celebrations of Roop Kanwar's *sati* may also have played a role in stimulating the remarkable gathering at Deorala on September 16, as a sort of backlash.

Who organized this backlash? The group most immediately concerned was formed shortly after Roop Kanwar's *satī*. At first it called itself the Sati Dharma Raksha Samiti ("Committee for Defending the Religion of *Satī*"), but after the Rajasthan High Court seemed to forbid precisely this activity—"the glorification of *satī*" was the court's language—in ordering against participation in the *chunarī* ceremony, the organization in question shortened its name to Dharma Raksha Samiti, the "Committee for the Defense of Religion."[24] The DRS is based in Jaipur, not in Deorala, and is run by educated Rajput men in their twenties and thirties. In 1987 the president was a man named Rajendra Singh Rajawat, the proprietor of a lucrative leather export business. When a group of women in Jaipur organized a public protest against the lionizing of Roop Kanwar, they were able to mount a solemn, silent demonstration involving some 3,000 people, almost entirely women. The DRS vastly outdid them, however. It responded with a demonstration two days later (October 8, 1987) that brought 70,000 people—mainly Rajput and often quite young, at least in the case of the men—into the streets.[25]

Further demonstrations ensued on both sides of the issue, from Delhi to Bombay; and especially in the metropolises the numbers on the two sides were more nearly equal than these figures might at first suggest. But the ability of *satī* fundamentalists to mobilize large numbers of people was beyond doubt in all cases, and it was especially impressive in Rajasthan itself. This became plain on September 22, 1988, the first anniversary of the death of Roop Kanwar, according to the lunar calendar used by Hindus. The government specifically forbade any gathering in Deorala for the purpose of glorifying *satī* on that day and deployed a force of 3,000 police, many of them plainclothesmen, to make sure that it did not happen. Even so, busloads of visitors arrived.

It is a measure of pro-*satī* sentiment in Rajasthan that the state government felt it advisable to compromise with organizers of the celebration, entering into an agreement that held to the letter of the law (with its anti-*satī* stance) while at the same time vitiating its spirit. The government continued to resist the holding of any rally specifically on behalf of Roop Kanwar's *satī*. No slogans to that effect were to be emblazoned on banners, and no ceremony of worship was to be permitted at the *satī sthal*, where local residents had been prevented by court order from erecting a permanent shrine. (The *satī sthal* has a flat stone foundation but remains an open space, one whose sacred boundaries are marked by police—who forbid entry to visitors—rather than by temple walls.) Yet the government did make a significant concession to the pro-*sati* forces represented by the DRS. A week-long recitation of the *Bhagavad Gītā* that was said on local posters to have been organized by Roop Kanwar's father and her father-in-law—the latter in jail—was allowed to reach its completion on the year anniversary of the *sati* itself, and 3,000 people were to be permitted to attend this ceremony, provided that they adhered to the other stipulations of the agreement.

Events transpired more or less according to that arrangement, except that by the end of the day the participants numbered about 8,000, again with a strong representation of young Rajput men. Furthermore, although the ban on written slogans was observed, the spirit of the agreement was substantially violated by the celebrants' oral glorification of *sati*. As the impressive procession moved in the direction of the *sati sthal* the now familiar chants arose of "Victory to Great Mother *Sati*," "Victory to Roop Kanwar," and "Victory to the holy spot Deorala."[26]

So far we have highlighted the role of a single group—the Dharma Raksha Samiti—in orchestrating the pro-*sati* response to the death of Roop Kanwar, but many other groups and figures have been involved. Some of these are religious, some political, some a mixture of both. The most obvious allies of the DRS have been other Hindu revivalist organizations around the country. One must not overstate the extent of this support: not every conservative Hindu group has rallied to the cause. But considering that *sati* is not as important a tradition in other parts of India as in Rajasthan and that to support it was to risk committing a criminal act ("the glorification of *sati*"), the extent of participation by organizations from around the country is significant.

The Vishva Hindu Parishad, which has played a prominent role in the temple/mosque affair at Ayodhya, remained officially silent, perhaps out of a desire to preserve its image as a group representing all Hindus, including the many who might be expected to question any adulation of *sati*. Other large Hindu organizations exhibited no such diffidence. The Hindu Mahasabha ("The Great Hindu Assembly") was one national religious organization that weighed in early on the side of pro-*sati* Rajputs,[27] and the Dharma Vishvavidyalay ("University of Religion")—a significant regional organization headquartered in Churu, Rajasthan—also joined the fundamentalist forces. Its leader, Svami Shivanand Maharaj, appeared on the dais during the first great Jaipur rally, praising the essential role of *satī* in true Hindu religion.[28] Finally, the Shankaracharya of Puri, a Rajasthani ascetic whose authoritative position in eastern India has made him one of the leading figures in traditional Hinduism, lent his support to the cause. On the other hand, the Shankaracharya of Kancipuram—his counterpart in the south of India, and a man who has traditionally exerted more influence across the subcontinent as a whole—did not adopt the cause of *satī*.

Among conservative political groups, similarly, there is no entirely unified position. Nonetheless, a strong contingent allied itself with the defenders of *satī*. Most important in this regard, undoubtedly, were the Janata Party and the Bharatiya Janata Party (BJP), both enemies of the then-ruling Congress Party. The Janata Party had in 1977 absorbed the influential Jan Sangh, a Hindu party, and thereafter had managed to build a coalition that unseated the Congress Party for a time, beginning in 1977. In 1980, however, the Jan Sangh element seceded, reshaping itself into the BJP. Leaders of both the Janata Party and the BJP in the state of Rajasthan (of which Jaipur is the capital) were intimately involved with the Rajput pro-*satī* cause from the beginning. Not surprisingly, the most important figures among them are Rajputs themselves.

Of the two parties, the BJP would seem the more likely to espouse the rhetoric of Hindu conservatism, so it is significant that early statements made to the press by several Janata leaders seemed to align them in the same cause. Evidently, they wished to portray the Janata as the ally of the local Hindu majority and to cast the Congress Party in the role of an outsider. This scenario was convenient, especially since the central government in Delhi did indeed attempt to suppress any celebration of Roop Kanwar's *satī*, albeit belatedly: Rajiv Gandhi, the Prime Minister, responded to pressure from anti-*satī* groups only on September 22—more than two weeks after Roop Kanwar's death in Deorala, and long after it had become a great public affair. Despite Rajiv Gandhi's hesitant entry into the fray, certain prominent Janata members sought to personalize the enemy by placing much of the responsibility for "government repression" on him. They took every opportunity to point out that his father was a Parsi, not a Hindu, and that his wife was Italian by birth. Thus, Bhakti Lal, a former Janata member of Parliament from Rajasthan, called the Prime Minister "a Parsi married to a foreign woman, who is insulting the Hindu religion."[29]

The head of the Janata Party in Rajasthan, Kalyan Singh Kalvi, had no reservations about connecting the language of religion with that of politics. Responding to an interviewer's suggestion that the practice of *sati* demeans women, he said, "In our culture, we worship the motherland, *dharma*, and *nari*," that is, the motherland, religion, and woman.[30] In this trio, an unspoken affinity exists between the two feminine entities, and religion is apparently the glue that keeps them together.[31] By religion, Kalvi meant specifically the Hindu religion—the majority religion—which he depicted as having been singly victimized by government policies. "Jains are known to die by fasting. Buddhists are known to immolate themselves. So why apply this law only to us?"[32] This feeling that only the religion of the majority suffers from discrimination at the hands of the supposedly secular government is a sentiment shared by many who support the cause of Hindu revivalism.

The Janata Party's ranks interweave naturally with those of such groups as the Dharma Raksha Samiti. A former leader of its youth division (the Yuva Janata) in Rajasthan, who was interviewed at DRS headquarters in Jaipur, tried to keep his political and religious devotions separate by saying "Here I am just a member of the Dharma Raksha Samiti; I am not a political person." Yet as the interviewers noted, this man immediately went on to combine the two in observing that a competing leader of the opposition had "lost Rajput hearts and votes by issuing a statement against the Deorala *sati*."[33] Furthermore, Janata Rajputs, the core constituent of an organization proclaiming itself the Rajput Commando Force, are conscious of the possible parallel between their case and that of Sikh activists in the Punjab. Indeed, on occasion they have threatened to pursue religiopolitical actions as extreme as those to which Sikhs have resorted, unless their protests against government intervention in the affairs of Rajasthani sovereignty and Rajput religion are heeded.[34]

Other parties than the Janata and BJP were to some degree also drawn in on the side of *sati*, including the Congress, which was the ruling party in Rajasthan during 1987 and 1988. When the Chief Minister of Rajasthan entered into an accord with the Dharma Raksha Samiti regarding the celebration of the first anniversary of Roop Kanwar's *sati*, he may well have been trying to head off Janata efforts to use this religious issue to unite formerly disparate segments of Rajput political opinion under its leadership. The Chief Minister's anniversary concordat was at the very least an attempt to employ government authority to maneuver the Congress Party into a position that would sever the strong bond between the BJP, the Janata, and the pro-*sati* organizations of Rajasthan, even if it meant opening the

Congress Party to charges of having deserted the anti-*sati* cause. The government's direct tie to the constabulary force charged with policing the situation locally provided Congress with further leverage on the religious vote. The party's eagerness to avoid offending pro-*sati* voters expressed itself in a local peacekeeping policy that, to interested outsiders, often seemed designed as a simple effort to keep the salient facts about Deorala from reaching the news, rather than as an earnest endeavor to prevent the worship of *sati* there.[35]

Finally one must mention the role of other organizations and communities. In the Roop Kanwar case, the national press has been almost entirely hostile to the forces they describe as Hindu fundamentalism, revivalism, or obscurantism; but this opposition has not been maintained at the regional level. The *Rājasthān Patrikā*, a newspaper published in Jaipur that is among the most widely read newspapers in Rajasthan, has been praised by pro-*sati* forces for presenting their cause in sympathetic terms, and the same assessment could be made of *Jansattā*, a competitor. *Jansattā* published a whole series of articles on the *sati* theme, the last of which compared the conflict between defenders and opponents of *sati* to the great battle described in India's epic, the *Mahābhārata*. In this latter-day epic battle, the humane tradition indigenous to India was pitted against wicked ideas brought in from the West, with the secular state as their broker.[36] It is noteworthy that *Jansattā* is exclusively a Hindi-language publication, and the *Rājasthān Patrikā* also publishes a Hindi edition.[37]

Finally, the partisans of Roop Kanwar's *sati* found a powerful ally in the Marwari community, the nation's most important group of merchants and industrialists. In the course of the past century, the Marwaris have fanned out from their caste home in the Shekhavati region surrounding Jhunjhunu and made their presence felt throughout the country.[38] Marwaris wield explicit and implicit political force in all major political arenas throughout North India.

The actions of the Dharma Raksha Samiti were entirely congenial to Marwari religious convictions, since the nation's largest and wealthiest *sati* temple—the one dedicated to Great Queen Sati at Jhunjhunu—is the focus of the Marwaris' own communal bond. Every year in August the clan retreats to Jhunjhunu, its ancestral home, to celebrate the anniversary of her *sati*, which is variously dated to A.D. 1295 and A.D. 1595.[39] The religious convictions of the Marwari clan are usually presented to the general Indian public in the form of temples and institutions that celebrate elements of Hinduism that are common to the whole country, or at least to its Hindi-speaking heartland. Marwari temples laud the *Bhagavad Gītā*, the *Rāmcarit-*

mānas of Tulsidas, and Mother India herself. But alongside these efforts to encourage the emergence of a common Hinduism that will tighten the cultural fabric of independent India—*sanātan dharma* ("old-time religion"),[40] as it is normally called—and alongside their generous donations to existing groups whom they perceive as promoting the core traditions of Hindu teaching and practice,[41] Marwaris attempt to advance the distinctive religious practices of their own clan. These focus on a devotion to the Great Queen Sati of Jhunjhunu, a maternal form of God who, on earth, was the bride in an unconsummated marriage, and yet was so dedicated to her husband that when he died she chose *satī*, at age fifteen. Recently enacted national legislation prohibiting "the glorification of *satī*" would clearly have an adverse impact on the Jhunjhunu temple and others like it, so Marwaris have been at the forefront of efforts to contest the new law. They have successfully petitioned to have their case heard by the Supreme Court, where it awaits judicial review.[42] Moreover they have established ties to the Rajput groups defending *satī* in various ways.[43]

Madhu Kishwar and Ruth Vanita, critical observers of day-to-day ritual practice at the *satī sthal* in Deorala, have noted that the informal ceremonies conducted there—most of them, once again, by young Rajput men—bear a stamp only dimly reminiscent of the traditional religion of Rajasthan. The formulas uttered by these educated youths seemed to Kishwar and Vanita more suitable to the milieu of political slogans than to that of religious chants: typically, one person would sound the first line of a two-line formula, and the others would respond with the antiphon that completed it. Moreover, Kishwar and Vanita observed that the song used to accompany the evening *ārati* ceremony—an offering of lights—was one phrased in Hindi (*om jay jagadīsh hare*) that has been made popular by the Bombay cinema industry and has no strong traditional roots. Similarly, both the use of an *ārati* and the distribution of *prasād* ("grace"; that is, sanctified food) at the *chunarī* ceremony are importations from general Hindu practice; they are unknown to the vocabulary of traditional Rajasthani *chunarī* ceremonies. No wonder, commented Kishwar and Vanita, its supporters called this *chunarī* a *mahotsav* ("great festival"), in contradistinction to the solemnity of traditional usage:[44] what they were observing was "a new-fangled cult," an expression of "phoney religiosity"[45] after the pattern of recent developments in the religious practices of the Marwaris. "The phoney revival of this cult is more a creation of the Marwari than the Rajput community."[46]

The Fundamentalism of Satī:
Analysis and Comparisons

Kishwar and Vanita are feminists of the Delhi school. The magazine for which they are primarily responsible and in which they publish is called *Manushi*, which means simply, "Woman." In their view, the *satī* of Roop Kanwar is essentially nothing more than a ritualized instance of violence against women—something that forms part of the same fabric as female infanticide, the aborting of female fetuses after amniocentesis, and the murdering of young brides whose natal families have failed to pay a dowry that satisfies the groom's family. The illustration used on the first page of Kishwar and Vanita's essay, in fact, consists of a collage of newspaper articles reporting on these themes.[47] Much of their argument attempts to show that the Deorala *satī* is illegitimate on the very terms by which the pro-*satī* forces wish to validate it. Kishwar and Vanita seek to demonstrate that the underlying motivation of the fundamentalists is not religion but "phoney religion"—politics in a very thin disguise. In pursuing this line of analysis, they explicitly protest against the sort of religious "mystification" that serves the cause of oppressing women.[48] They are clearly concerned that, if *satī* is accepted as a valid religious practice, it will be entitled to protection from state interference under new judicial decisions designed to interpret and enforce the Indian constitution.

Kishwar and Vanita highlight several aspects of the Roop Kanwar *satī* that are of great interest to anyone attempting an inquiry into "comparative fundamentalism." First and most obvious is the close connection between religion and politics, which Kishwar and Vanita demonstrate and deplore. As a concept for the 1980s and 1990s, the term *fundamentalism* almost always refers to a form of religion that has a political dimension, and this case is no exception. What is not always so clearly seen is that the connection between religion and politics works both ways. On the one hand, as is so often said, politicians "exploit" the cause of religion, and religionists enter politics. On the other hand, religion absorbs aspects of political usage. This was vividly illustrated when crowds at and on their way to the *chunarī* of Roop Kanwar adopted styles of diction that would seem more appropriate at political rallies and other secular gatherings. Consider, for example, the following chant (in translation):

> One, two, three, four
> Victory to Roop Kanwar.[49]

A second (and not unrelated) point is that, in a fundamentalist context, practices that may masquerade as religion the way it always was—"old-time religion," as the *sanātan dharma* phrase has it—often prove to be quite recent creations. These typically draw on old roots and even old forms, to be sure. Otherwise one would find it hard to explain why large numbers of genuinely traditional people are so obviously and effectively attracted to the cause—an attraction that Kishwar and Vanita generally ignore in their analysis of the Deorala movement, and at most treat simply as a social danger that ought to cause alarm. But as Kishwar and Vanita clearly see, the vessels into which the old wine is being poured are quite modern ones—the newly vulgate Hinduism of cinemas, videos, and pamphlet literature. This late-twentieth-century form of Hinduism is the "Marwari" religion embraced by threatened Rajput elites.

Similarly, Sudesh Vaid and Kumkum Sangari have argued that the central notion of the self-lighting fire is a very recent invention; and Veena Oldenburg has pointed out that the idea of building a temple to *satī* (rather than honoring a *satī* stone) is not much older.[50] Against the background of traditional Rajput village culture, some of these motifs seem importations. But one can turn the tables and note that they also enable a local or special conviction—the Rajput tradition of *satī*—to symbolize and galvanize the commitment of Hindus in general.

The aping of Marwari practice by Rajputs at Deorala is especially significant in this regard. It relates Rajput religion to a network of new-like-old Hinduism that has already transformed traditional Hindu piety, creating new patterns of uniformity where expressions of Hinduism were once disparate from region to region, community to community, and caste to caste. And if the veneration of *satī* could bolster the attempts of *nouveaux riches* Marwaris to legitimate themselves regionally, why should the selfsame homogenized, up-to-date Hindu practice not be expounded by Rajputs trying to display themselves favorably to a national (and perhaps even specifically Marwari) audience?

Like many of their Christian counterparts in the United States, these Rajput fundamentalists represent segments of the population who understand themselves as having been mainstream in an earlier era, but who are now faced with the task of prospering in a world they no longer define. Of course, as in the American Christian case, this erstwhile mainstream status is not an obvious historical truth; it is an artifact that took some time to construct—after the fact. With the Rajputs, the British attraction to the concept of a "martial race"

and the Indian nationalists' need for paradigms of struggle from earlier decades of Indian history played significant creative roles in this
development. Fundamentals in the social sense—groups whose position is critical to defining the broader society—have to be kneaded
out of a larger amorphous mass, much as a body of doctrine has to be
worked over to yield the material that adherents subsequently view
as "the fundamentals."

A third aspect of the Deorala case to which Kishwar and Vanita
have drawn attention, and one that must be considered alongside
what has just been said, is the fact that Deorala is not a total backwa-
ter. The principals involved in Roop Kanwar's *satī*, including Roop
herself, were educated people. For instance, Roop's father-in-law,
Sumer Singh, was a teacher in the local school before his arrest.
These people, like Roop's businessman father, have access to a world
considerably larger than that of a traditional Indian village, and they
travel back and forth readily between urban and rural settings. Deorala's location part way between Jaipur and Delhi facilitates this pattern
of interaction in a way that would be difficult for many Indian villages to replicate. It is well enough connected to the cities by railway
lines and highways that men from Deorala's Rajput and Brahmin
families can work there and still visit their family homes with relative ease; yet it is far enough away that the village itself still symbol-
izes the force of tradition.

Such people can be expected to feel the conflict between modern
and traditional values more acutely than most, and some of them
must deal with the painful fact of commanding a comparatively good
level of education in an economy that cannot put all its educated
young people to work. But what happened at Deorala cannot be explained merely as a function of this sort of economic squeeze. Kishwar, Vanita, and others have emphasized that the village of Deorala
is fairly well-to-do. More to the point, this is a village that no longer
controls its own economy. Its leaders are no longer leaders primarily
because of their traditional status or their contribution to the task of
regulating village life. Instead, they often owe their economic power
to connections with the outside world, which is far less predictable
than a traditional agricultural village and is ultimately beyond their
control. Visitors to Deorala invariably report the villagers' deep-
seated suspicion of foreigners. Much of this has to do with Deorala's
specific notoriety, of course: this is a culture that sees itself as having
been under siege. But some of it is undoubtedly a more general response to the values and incursions of outsiders.

Both at Deorala and far beyond in Hindu society, a special wrinkle in this fabric of reaction and invention ("stress and response," as Karen Brown has called it more generally[51]) is the question of who constitutes the majority. Is it the insiders—defenders of the fundamentals, of religion as it is believed to have been—or is it the outsiders, who seek to tear all this apart? In many parts of the world, groups that take militant religion-inspired action against the perceived proponents of secular antireligion consist of people who think they have the weight of an idealized past on their side. They see themselves as a clan whose members used to exercise authority and control over this past, but who have somehow come to doubt that this is any longer natural or (in some cases) even possible. Such people consider themselves the voice of a "moral majority" that once existed and, they hope, still does; and when they encounter challenges to that morality, they are offended not only by the moral dimension of the attack, but by their opponents' defiance of what they conceive to be the will of the majority.

Many Rajputs of Rajasthan—Rajput males in any case, and probably a fair number of the women, too—are "moral majority" people in this way. They understand their primary identity in history as having been earned in heroic battles against outsiders—most of them successful; but the most legendary of all, sacrificial. There is no more famous Rajput man than Maharana Pratap Singh, king of Mewar (r. 1572–1597), who at great cost fended off attacks by the forces of the central Mughal government, both from his fortress at Chittor and afield. Queen Padmini holds a similar position among Rajput women. It was she who, some centuries earlier, led the women of Mewar to a massive suicide inside the fort at Chittor when it seemed clear that they would otherwise be taken captive and defiled by the invading Afghan armies of Ala-ud-din.[52] The stories of both the hero and the heroine have centrally to do with resistance, but it is resistance of a particular type: the resistance of a class of people who felt themselves to be responsible for protecting a majority culture in a larger political context within which they had become peripheral, a minority. And in both cases the struggle is remembered as having had an important religious dimension. The invaders were always aliens in a religious sense, despite their having been established for some time at the power center of the Indian subcontinent: both Mughals and Afghans were Muslims.

Some modern-day "Muslims," according to the perception of Hindu activists, are indeed Muslims. The heat that has been generated all over North India and into the South by the Ayodhya mosque affair is evidence of this. Old scores are still being settled. But some

"Muslims" are not adherents of Islam. They are instead elements of the invading force that succeeded the Mughals as possessors of the traditional centers of power in the subcontinent: Europeans; and specifically, the British. Both the Mughals and the British attempted to outlaw *sati*, which bears rather close associations in Rajput understanding with the communal *jauhar* ("suicide") of Padmini and her court. Both administrations tried to alter a practice that lay near the heart of Rajput identity, so it is not hard to understand why the Rajputs of Jaipur, the modern-day capital of the Rajput state within India, would want to resist any further evidence of the aliens' desire to extinguish the embers of Rajput identity altogether.

Especially interesting is the degree to which pro-*sati* Rajputs were evidently able to gain the sympathy of Hindus more broadly. Here again one must reckon with the strains that modernity has introduced into Indian society as a whole; and one must understand that many Hindus, like Rajputs, perceive themselves as a majority that is treated by the laws of the land as if it were a justly persecuted minority. Certainly this became evident in the rhetoric of the Shankaracharya of Puri as he took up the pro-*sati* cause. Many Hindu religious leaders, the Shankaracharya among them, have felt the pinch of secular authority in recent years as tax laws have been revised to apply to revenues that accrue to temples and monastic institutions. Typically such institutions have had to become public institutions overseen by a board of trustees, and they have had to forfeit a portion of their lands and/or revenues to the government unless they can satisfactorily document their status as nonprofit organizations. Rightly or wrongly, Hindus have often accused the Congress Party, which for almost forty years controlled the central government and that of most states, of being unwilling to tighten the screws in a similar way on the religious institutions of minority groups, since it relies upon their votes to compensate for the incomplete hold it has over Hindus at the core of Indian society. In modern, secular India, votes matter.[53]

For many Hindus—and important religious authorities are apt to be among them—the manner in which the Congress government reversed itself in the Shah Bano case illustrates the point.[54] Federal law accords Muslims, like Christians and other minority religious groups, the privilege of regulating their own actions in the realm of family law, whereas Hindus are expected to live up to the general civil code. Hindu leaders feel that the conduct of Hindu religion and of affairs in the Hindu family ought to be exempted from government interference in a similar way. By rights, the fact that Hindus comprise the majority in Indian society would make it all the more imperative that their sensitivities be listened to in matters religious. Currently the situation is just the reverse.

Nor does the Hindu sense of beleaguerment stop there. Ever since the drafting of the Indian constitution in 1947, and in some ways for a decade and a half before that, upper-caste Hindus have seen special consideration given to the "scheduled" or "backward" castes in matters affecting political representation, admittance to educational institutions, and hiring for government jobs. Such "affirmative action" programs mandated by the central government have led to deadly riots in recent years as upper-caste Hindus have found it increasingly difficult to gain entrance to the best universities and professional schools. Prime Minister V. P. Singh's attempt in 1990 to implement the Mandal Commission Report, which concluded that the oppressed classes were still oppressed, only made matters worse. His proposal to raise the number of specially reserved positions in government and education to about 50 percent brought on a storm of devastating confrontations.

Interestingly—and tragically—suicide by immolation has been a major method of protest for students and other young people directly affected by this reallocation of quotas. At the end of October 1990, it was reported that more than 159 such suicides had been attempted, 63 with success.[55] It was as if the legacy of *sati* for mainline Hindu groups had found a new avenue of expression. The language of *sati* itself was not prominent, but the idea of such a death may have played a part in enabling young women to take as active a part in the protest movement as their male counterparts—an unusual phenomenon even in urban India. One Hindu girl of sixteen wrote in her suicide note, "V. P. Singh, you can see that it is not just the boys but also the girls who are making sacrifices."[56]

From the point of view of the Hindu upper castes, members of several of the groups who stand to benefit from special-consideration legislation have sometimes added insult to injury by disavowing Hinduism itself. They have insisted that Hinduism is a religious system invented by the upper castes in large part to oppress those over whom they wish to assert power; so they have declared, "We are not Hindus."[57] With such groups disavowing their religious loyalty to the whole while at the same time reaping special benefits from the government, many high-caste Hindus feel that they have become second-class citizens under their own country's laws. They see themselves as victims of policies put into effect by Westernized elites that until very recently maintained total dominance in the urban centers of education and political power. No longer, they vow. The increasing spread of a certain level of education through male Hindu society and the access of distant areas of the country to modern communications media have challenged the power of these elites. V. P. Singh's own Janata Party government was largely brought down by the disaffection of Hindus such as these, who resented his vigorously pursued (and carefully calculated) "affirmative action" policies and saw him ultimately as an opponent in the Ayodhya controversy. His alliance with the newly powerful BJP had enabled him to dislodge Rajiv Gandhi and the Congress Party in the first place. When the BJP broke ranks with him, his government fell.

The analogy that was perceived to exist between the Shah Bano case and the controversy involving Roop Kanwar had more than one component. Those who saw the parallel considered them both to be issues of religious liberty, and concluded that the government's modernist, neocolonial, politically motivated anti-Hindu prejudice had denied Hindus the same freedom from government interference that Muslims had received. But there was also a gender dimension to the analogy. In the Shah Bano case, the government, under pressure, had refrained from trying to overrule through legislation the understanding of women's social position held by a particular segment of society—the Muslims. Should it not do the same in relation to *sati*? Part of what made both affairs so powerful was that they both raised the issue of who and where a woman should be in relation to matters of religion. Indeed, with *sati* the relationship is especially intimate, for to believers a *sati* is at once a woman and a goddess.

The Shah Bano and Roop Kanwar affairs, like the Christian fundamentalist protest in the United States over the issue of abortion, involve resistance to the idea that women are autonomous beings—people whose identity need not be articulated primarily in relation to men. The men involved in both of these Indian controversies seem to feel a general threat to the integrity of their social and cultural worlds from outside, secular, modernist forces—the forces of at least one important "other." Over these forces, which seem to be aggressively expanding, they have only limited influence; but in relation to another "other," they have usually been able to exercise more control. That other is woman. As Simone de Beauvoir said so many years ago, women are the implicit other for all men;[58] yet to use a phrase with which Ashis Nandy has described relations between Indians and the colonial British, they are "the intimate enemy."[59] As the force of the other within, women are potentially the most dangerous enemy of all, but they are typically perceived in this light only at a subconscious level. Conscious rhetoric by men—and to a degree, by women—tends to exalt them: the American housewife is put on her pedestal; Hindu women are in some way understood as goddesses.[60] But efforts by men to control these very same women, often expressed through the language of religion, seem to tell quite a different story. As Arjuna warned Krishna in the first chapter of the *Bhagavad Gītā*:

> In overwhelming chaos, Krishna,
> women of the family are corrupted;
> and when women are corrupted,
> disorder is born in society.[61]

Every report of the Deorala affair indicates that, although Roop herself was the principal actor, the action was orchestrated—at least after the fact, if not before—almost entirely by men. It is true that women appeared at the *sati sthal* in great numbers and that the local women of Deorala have shown open hostility to people whom they perceive to be investigators from the outside (perhaps particularly the women among them). It is also true that these women do not want the *sati* of Roop Kanwar to be understood as a variant on the same pattern that produces the deaths of so many urban brides who are judged by their in-laws to have brought an insufficient dowry into their marriages. Village women are quick to distinguish these irreligious horrors from their own tradition-honored practices.[62] But for all this, the fact remains that the main actors in the drama are men. Men serve in religious roles at the *sati sthal* itself; men run the Dharma Raksha Samiti; and but for a few symbolic exceptions—the sister and mother of Roop Kanwar—men sit on the dais in Jaipur when a rally is organized in defense of *sati*. Men collect the money, men give the speeches, and men search the texts to justify the practice.

I do not wish to say, with Kamla Bhasin and Ritu Menon, that we are presented here with a simple case of oppression of women in a patriarchal society.[63] It is equally hard to accept Modhumita Mojumdar's short-circuiting assertion that voluntary *sati* is impossible—a contradiction in terms.[64] But the religion of *sati* advances a vision of the cosmos in which women are restricted to a clearly delineated place, a place that defines them in relation to men. In this respect it shares a hallmark of many independent expressions of that peculiar form of reactive modern/traditional religion we call "fundamentalist."

In the case of *sati* this could scarcely be more obvious, since a *sati* dramatically enacts the principle that a woman's religion is the service of her family, as personified in her husband. Hers is the religion of *pativrata*, "devotion to her lord"; and when her lord passes on, the highest path open to her is to pass on with him, so that she can protect him in the there and then as she would have done in the here and now.[65] A *sati's* devotion thus becomes the epitome of a general pattern in Hindu women's religion, which focuses far more than men's on the performance of vows (*vrats*).[66] Here self-abnegation generates a power that can be concentrated and passed on to others—paradigmatically by a woman to her husband and family. Such a vision of *sati* (and this understanding of women's religion in general) acknowledges forthrightly that women do have power—a power that must be channeled if it is to be devoted to the betterment of men and, through men, society. A great fear among members of fundamentalist groups seems to be that the modern world will free this force from the traditional restraints that have directed it to the service of religion, virtue, and social cohesion. If these floodgates be breached, who knows what will happen?

Obviously, many factors distinguish the pro-*sati* forces in India from the anti-abortion forces in the United States. In a certain superficial way, in fact, they seem virtual opposites. One group argues for "right to death," the other for "right to life." One group argues that under certain circumstances a woman has a right to take her own life; the other insists that under no circumstances has she the right to take a developing life inside her.

Yet not far beneath the surface lie important parallels. Both groups are loath to see a woman claim an identity that places her outside the matrix of husband and family. A Shekhavati Rajput woman whose husband predeceases her, particularly one who has yet had no children, is a danger to her in-laws—the family with which she lives—because she has a moral right to her husband's share of the property and because she may adopt a child from outside the family to care for her and enable her to exercise that right.[67] But this is so in a more general way, too. A *sati* is exalted—as are the many "*sati* mothers" who compose the goddess Sati, including Sati the wife of Shiva—for having an identity so totally absorbed by her relation to her husband that even the force of death is insufficient to break the bond. Such exaltation is especially strong in the case of a young, newly married woman like Roop Kanwar. It is even more powerfully appropriate for a woman whose marriage has never been consummated, like Narayani Devi, the great *sati* of Jhunjhunu. But here, too, Roop Kanwar was not far from the ideal. She had spent only a few weeks of her short married life in the presence of her husband, since he had often been ill and away from home; she was almost a virgin bride. Thus she was highly suited to the role of a woman whose whole life (at least from a male point of view) was summed up in sacrifice.

That an American woman could sacrifice the life of another person—a fetus, the outgrowth of a man's presence in her body—to salvage some aspect of her own life and autonomy seems the ultimate perversion of such a vision of woman as sacrificer. Just as traditional Hindus judge a husband's untimely death to be evidence that his wife has failed to protect him, failed to sacrifice herself sufficiently on his behalf, so do fundamentalist Christians judge the death of an unborn child by abortion to be evidence of a woman's unwillingness to live as a woman and to protect the gift entrusted to her by her human impregnator and the masculine God. Symbolically, both specters strike at the adult version—especially the adult male version—of a child's need to believe that Mother will sacrifice everything for Me.[68] Certainly in the Hindu case one has ample evidence that Mother possesses another aspect, this one to be feared. In the way in which Kali and Shitala are conceived—mother goddesses with horrific attributes and the power at once to protect and to destroy—one senses the extremity to which human fear can go in imagining the destructive potential of a woman's energy. Goddesses who function within the ambit established by the gods whom they serve as consorts typically display a sunny, placid demeanor, but let a goddess slip beyond the control of a male counterpart, and she is apt to seem the most threatening of creatures.[69]

What does the control of women, as exemplified by the issues of *sati* and abortion, have to do with religion? These are matters of symbol and psyche that reach far back into every person's past— so far back that "adult" institutions governing political, social, and economic relations cannot quite touch their root. Religion, with its overarching symbolic capabilities, can. Hence, in both Indian and American societies, a special resonance is felt between the powers and sentiments of women and the realm of religion. In both societies women tend to be seen, at least by men, as the natural vessels of religion. Men may be needed to define and defend that special relation, but women are at its core as participants. To defend a woman's right to incarnate religion—to express the sense that the driving force (or forces) in the universe is ultimately "on our side" and willing to sacrifice for us—is precisely what the defense of *sati* is all about. Perhaps every society contains elements that tend to efface its sense that the universe coheres in such a way, but the institutions of modern society are downright virulent. By seeming to commodify or individualize women, removing them from their archetypal roles, modern society strikes a dangerous blow. Hindu and Christian fundamentalists respond by insisting that women somehow embody a nobler, truer sense than modernity can imagine of the way the universe really is. Not everyone in the social world of which these fundamentalists are a part will take this insight as far as they do, but somewhere in their bones many people—including many modern people, and in particular many men—feel the force of the argument.

Notes

1. On the pamphleteer Dharmendra ji Maharaj, see Sudesh Vaid and Kumkum Sangari, "Institutions, Beliefs, Ideologies: Widow Immolation in Contemporary Rajasthan," *Economic and Political Weekly* 26(17), April 27, 1991, p. WS-12. On the politician Kalyan Singh Kalvi, see page WS-7 n. 17 and note 32 below, and *New York Times*, December 28, 1990.

2. Several pages in this section of the essay are substantially the same as the description offered in my introduction to *Sati: The Blessing and the Curse*. A number of readable accounts of the death of Roop Kanwar and subsequent events have appeared since this chapter was drafted. They include especially Elisabeth Bumiller, *May You Be the Mother of a Hundred Sons: A Journey Among the Women of India* (New York: Random House, 1990), pp. 62–74; Mark Tully, *The Defeat of a Congressman and Other Parables of Modern India* (New York: Alfred A. Knopf, 1992), pp. 191–215; and Sakuntala Narasimhan, *Sati: Widow Burning in India* (New York: Doubleday, 1992), pp. 1–10 (cf. pp. 91–97, 133–35, 143–46).

3. Vaid and Sangari, "Institutions, Beliefs, Ideologies," p. WS-12. The phrase *sati dharma*, of which "the religion of *sati*" might serve as a translation, has been used by advocates of *sati*. An example is Guru Shivanand Maharaj of the Dharma Vishvavidyalay of Churu, Rajasthan, in a speech delivered on October 8, 1987 (*Indian Today*, October 31, 1987, p. 19).

4. It has been argued that in the early nineteenth century, when it was banned, *sati* occurred in a more concentrated fashion in the domains of Bengal (where the British presence was most vividly felt) than in more traditional Hindu areas, and that this is in large part to be explained as a response to the cultural dislocation that the British themselves caused. (Ashis Nandy, "Sati: A Nineteenth Century Tale of Women, Violence and Protest," in Nandy, *At the Edge of Psychology: Essays in Politics and Culture* [New Delhi: Oxford University Press, 1980], pp. 1–31.) According to this argument, the central British administrators would have perceived it as a much more prevalent phenomenon in Hindu society than it actually was. For further relevant evidence, some of which calls into question the picture painted by Nandy, see Anand A. Yang, "Whose Sati: Widow Burning in Early 19th Cen-

tury India," *Journal of Women's History* 1(2) (1989): 8–33; and Sanjukta Gupta and Richard Gombrich, "Another View of Widow-Burning and Womanliness in India," *Journal of Commonwealth and Comparative Politics* 22(3) (1984): 252–58.

5. This is the figure cited by Ranjani Majumdar et al. in their videotape "Burning Embers" (New Delhi: Mediastorm, 1987). The *New York Times* gives even sparser figures, saying that *satī* occurs "only once or twice in a decade" throughout the whole of India. ("India Seizes Four After Immolation," September 19, 1987, p. 2. This estimate was repeated in the following day's *Times*.)

6. Some have alleged that Mal Singh took his own life after failing the exams for admission to medical school a second or even third time. See *Link* (New Delhi), September 29, 1987, p. 5; and a fuller discussion by Veena Oldenburg, "The Roop Kanwar Case: Feminist Responses," in Hawley, ed., *Blessing and Curse* (in press).

7. Just how far into the past this "traditional" pose can be traced is a matter of some dispute. Many iconographical representations of *satī*—including many rather old ones—do not depict this pose but another, in which the husband and wife are recumbant on the pyre together (cf. Paul B. Courtright, "The Iconographies of Sati," in Hawley, ed., *Blessing and Curse* [in press]). Several scholars have emphasized that *satī* is not a monolithic tradition, but a composite one, and that it has evolved in major ways in recent years. See, for instance, Vaid and Sangari, "Institutions, Beliefs, Ideologies," pp. WS-3, WS-7–10; and Veena Oldenburg, "The Continuing Invention of the Sati Tradition" (in press).

8. Vaid and Sangari have questioned the historical depth of this perception ("Institutions, Beliefs, Ideologies," pp. WS-10–12), but they do not dispute that it was prevalent in Shekhavati Rajasthan at the time Roop Kanwar died.

9. The myth is told in several versions, only some of which actually state that Sati's death was through self-immolation. The effects, however, are the same.

10. Lindsey Harlan, who has done fieldwork on this subject in western Rajasthan, reports that she has never heard the myth of Sati proper cited in descriptions of *satī*. She also cautions that, in speaking of *satīs* from earlier generations, the Rajput women of Udaipur and surrounding areas never relinquished the sense that they were ancestors, and therefore did not group them with gods and goddesses such as Shiva and Parvati. (Lindsey Harlan, personal communication, June 6, 1989.) Quite a different impression is provided, however, by icons of Narayani Satimata from Rajasthan such as are presented in figure 1 of Paul Courtright's "The Iconographies of Sati," in which Shiva and Parvati provide the background for the action performed by the *satī*, raining celebratory flowers on her. Compare also the somewhat indeterminate but definitely heaven-dwelling goddess who serves as background to Roop Kanwar as a *satī* in Rajeswari Sunder Rajan, "The Subject of Sati: Pain and

Death in the Contemporary Discourse on Sati," *Yale Journal of Criticism* 3(2) (1990), figure 2.

11. Courtright, "The Iconographies of *Sati*" (in press). Figure 5 in Courtright also appears as the cover illustration of Meena Menon, Geeta Seshu, and Sujata Anandan, *Trial by Fire: A Report on Roop Kanwar's Death* (Bombay: Women & Media Committee, Bombay Union of Journalists, 1987).

12. *Link*, September 27, 1987, p. 6.

13. *The Statesman*, October 21, 1988. So also Menon et al., *Trial by Fire*, unpaginated [p. 5], in which this information is attributed to a Congress Party worker in Deorala, who received it from relatives present there at the time [p. 4].

14. Menon et al., *Trial by Fire*, unpaginated [p. 5]. Sakuntala Narasimhan speaks of "sword wielding Rajput youths" in *Sati: Widow Burning in India*, p. 83.

15. *Hindustan Times*, September 17, 1987, back page. See also Menon et al., *Trial by Fire*.

16. E.g., Modhumita Mojumdar, "A Visit to Deorala 'Peeth'," *Mainstream*, December 26, 1987, p. 22. According to Mojumdar, the sum that had been gathered by Roop Kanwar's in-laws by December 12, 1987, was said to be in the neighborhood of Rs. 950,000.

17. Kumkum Sangari and Sudesh Vaid, "Sati in Modern India: A Report," *Economic and Political Weekly* 16(31) (August 1981): 1287. Sangari and Vaid report seven *satis* in the seven years preceding 1980.

18. *New York Times* September 20, 1987. On Pushpender, see *Hindustan Times*, September 17, 1987.

19. Oldenburg, "The Roop Kanwar Case" (in press).

20. The *chunari* rite, practiced among Rajputs, occurs twelve days after a *sati*'s death and is analogous to the *śrāddh* ceremony performed at that interval after the death of a Rajput man. The feminist magazine *Manushi* criticizes its practice in the case of Roop Kanwar as being a *chunari mahotsav*, "a great *chunari* festival," not the solemn occasion that tradition would dictate. Madhu Kishwar and Ruth Vanita make this point in "The Burning of Roop Kanwar" (*Manushi* 42–43 (1987): 18) and also discuss the institution of *pagaḍi rasm*, on which see below.

21. Mojumdar, "A Visit," p. 20; cf. Narasimhan, *Sati*, pp. 92–93.

22. Crowds of this size at *chunari* celebrations in Sikar district are not without precedent. A similar gathering in the village of Jhardli, in 1980, is estimated to have attracted 200,000 people (Sangari and Vaid, "Sati in Modern India," p. 1285).

23. *Hindustan Times*, September 17, 1987, p. 1.

24. Problems having to do with the translation of *dharma* as "religion" will enter into our discussion shortly. Suffice it to say at this point that "duty," "tradition," and even "propriety" are conceivable alternatives in this context; but on the whole, because of the magnitude of the area being desig-

nated and the existence of a secular authority whom the DRS sees as its implicit enemy, "religion" seems the most plausible translation.

As to the legal history associated immediately with the Roop Kanwar case, the succession is briefly this: After the Rajasthan High Court issued an injunction against participation in the *chunarī mahotsav*, the Governor of Rajasthan signed a formal ordinance forbidding *satī*, on October 1, 1987. That ordinance was converted into a bill by the upper house of the Rajasthan state legislature on November 10, 1987. A similar bill prohibiting the glorification and practice of *satī* was passed by the national Parliament on December 15–16, 1987. Each of these acts has been criticized as being superfluous, considering the Republic of India's retention of legal precedent associated with the 1829 law criminalizing *satī*, and as being damaging in other ways. See Vasudha Dhagamvar, "Saint, Victim or Criminal," *Seminar* 342 (February 1988): 34–39.

25. The overwhelmingly male composition of the second demonstration may be judged by both the reporting and the picture printed in *India Today*, October 31, 1987, p. 38. The ratio of its size to that of the earlier demonstration interestingly echoes the figures given by William Darrow for the rallies against and, subsequently, in support of Ayatollah Khomeini's proclamation of the *chador* as mandatory public dress in Iran in 1979: 5,000 demonstrators protested against the action; 100,000 in its favor. See William R. Darrow, "Women's Place and the Place of Women in the Iranian Revolution," in Y. Y. Haddad and E. B. Findly, eds., *Women, Religion, and Social Change* (Albany: SUNY Press, 1985), p. 315.

26. I translate *satī mātā kī jay, rūp kanvār kī jay,* and *deorālā dhām kī jay,* as reported in *India Today*, October 15, 1988, p. 38. Anther frequently used translation for the word *jay*, which occurs in all three formulas, is "long live." *India Today* prefers this alternative.

27. Founded in 1913, the Mahasabha is among the most venerable of the groups dedicated to pursuing Hindu causes in the public arena. Since 1951 many of its members have expressed their political will through different parties than the Sabha itself: first in the Bharatiya Jana Sangh, and then in the BJP.

28. Some of his speechmaking has been preserved on videotape and made accessible by Ranjani Majumdar and her colleagues in "Burning Embers."

29. *India Today*, October 31, 1987, p. 19.

30. Ibid., p. 20. On the translation of *dharma* as "religion," see note 24.

31. A similar bond is discovered by Lata Mani in her analysis of what was at issue on both sides of the debate about *satī* in colonial Bengal. The debate was ostensibly about women, but her conclusion is that "What was at stake was not women but tradition." (Mani, "Contentious Traditions," *Cultural Critique* 7 [Fall 1987]: 153.)

32. *India Today*, October 31, 1987, p. 20. On other aspects of Kalvi's sentiments and involvements, see Menon et al., *Trial by Fire*, unpaginated [pp. 3–4, 13], and Narasimhan, *Sati*, especially p. 103.

33. Kishwar and Vanita, "Burning," p. 20. I have taken the liberty of respelling certain words in this oral quotation and slightly altering punctuation to accord with the conventions adopted in this essay.

34. *India Today,* October 31, 1987, p. 19.

35. Eloquent testimony on this point is provided by both Mojumdar, "A Visit," pp. 21–22, and Kishwar and Vanita, "Burning," pp. 22–23.

36. *Mainstream,* December 26, 1988, p. 22. A summary and rebuttal of an important three-to-four-page appeal entitled "The Connection Between Man and Woman" (*Nar-nārī Sambandh*) by Banwari in *Jansattā* (September 29 to October 1, 1987) appears in Kumkum Sangari, "Perpetuating the Myth," *Seminar* 342 (February 1988): 28–29. See also Sujata Patel and Krishna Kumar, "Defenders of Sati," *Economic and Political Weekly,* January 23, 1988, p. 130.

37. The Women and Media Committee of the Bombay Union of Journalists devotes a special section of its report to the treatment of the Deorala *sati* in the Rajasthan regional press and in the Hindi-language national press (Menon et al., *Trial by Fire,* unpaginated [pp. 30–33]). The Committee emphasizes the editorial favor with which Roop Kanwar's *sati* was regarded there and the high profile given to the incident, in comparison to what one read in the English-language press. Reportage on demonstrations and legal actions against "the glorification of *sati*" was often minimal.

38. Confusingly, the term *Marwari* ought by rights to imply a person or group from Marwar, the region centered at Jodhpur, in western Rajasthan. Usually, however, it does not; instead, it refers to groups whose ancestral home is in the Shekhavati region many miles to the east. In the eighteenth and nineteenth centuries, the term *Marwari* apparently came to be used in other parts of India than Rajasthan to provide a general designation for merchant-caste groups from Rajasthan. The most influential segment of this Marwari population is composed of Shekhavatis, as is shown overwhelmingly by the statistics provided in Vaid and Sangari, "Institutions, Beliefs, Ideologies," p. WS-9.

39. Sangari, "Perpetuating the Myth," p. 29. Both dates are typically incorporated into the history of the temple that is explained to visitors.

40. I owe the translation to Philip Lutgendorf, *The Life of a Text: Performing the Rāmcaritmānas of Tulsidas* (Berkeley: University of California Press, 1991), p. 363.

41. For instance, Marwaris are major supporters of various religious institutions in Brindavan, which celebrate the god Krishna, who is worshipped at least as widely throughout the Hindu fold as Rama is.

42. The beginnings of this judicial battle, at the Calcutta High Court, are reported in *India Today,* October 15, 1988, p. 38. On other aspects, see Narasimhan, *Sati,* pp. 102, 147.

43. See Vaid and Sangari, "Institutions, Beliefs, Ideologies," p. WS-12.

44. Kishwar and Vanita, "Burning," pp. 17–18.

45. Ibid., p. 18.

46. Ibid., "Burning," p. 19. This note is also sounded in Sangari, "Perpetuating the Myth," p. 25. Sangari views the great expansion of the Marwari *sati* temple at Jhunjhunu and its related educational institutions as an attempt by merchant-caste Marwaris to equate themselves with warrior-caste Rajputs, who had traditionally been the most honored group in Rajasthan.

47. Kishwar and Vanita, "Burning," p. 15.

48. The same point is made — and in just this language — by Sudesh Vaid, "Politics of Widow Immolation," *Seminar* 342 (February 1988): 23.

49. *Ek do tin chār, rūp kanwār kī jayjaykār* (*Link*, September 27, 1987, p. 7). Modhumita Mojumdar reports that she found the same chant used by those surrounding the *sati* site when she visited ("A Visit," p. 21); cf. also *India Today*, October 15, 1988, p. 38. Examples of other "slogans" are provided by Kishwar and Vanita, "Burning," p. 17.

50. Vaid and Sangari, "Institutions, Beliefs, Ideologies," pp. WS-4–5, WS-10–12; and Oldenburg, "Continuing Invention" (in press).

51. Brown, "Fundamentalism and the Control of Women," her essay in this volume, esp. pp. 178–82, 197–98.

52. See Lindsey Harlan, *Religion and Rajput Women: The Ethic of Protection in Contemporary Narratives* (Berkeley: University of California Press, 1992), especially Chapter 6 on Padmini. In personal correspondence (June 26, 1989), however, Harlan cautions against assuming that erstwhile female aristocrats from Mewari Rajput families generally celebrate Roop Kanwar as a successor to Queen Padmini — or indeed, as an authentic *sati* at all. As more or less direct descendents of Padmini, they are in a position to adopt a purist perspective on the matter. This would be less natural for most Rajputs — not to mention other groups — especially those residing in eastern Rajasthan. These have been substantially influenced by a campaign undertaken in the 1950s to broaden the legacy of Rajput heroism so that it could serve as a general ideology for Rajasthan (cf. Vaid and Sangari, "Institutions, Beliefs, Ideologies," pp. WS-7–8).

53. A brief exposition of the Puri Shankaracharya's version of this accusation is given in *India Today*, May 31, 1986, p. 79. He is said to have explicitly referred to "a feeling of helplessness among Hindus" in the face of such a situation.

54. On the Shah Bano controversy, see Peter Awn's essay in this volume. The affair occupied national attention from April 1985 to May 1986, when the Muslim Women (Protection of Rights on Divorce) Bill was passed by the lower house of India's Parliament, overturning an earlier ruling on the matter by the Supreme Court. One comment on the tie between the Shah Bano and Roop Kanwar cases is provided by Imrana Qadeer, "Roop Kanwar and Shah Bano," *Seminar* 342 (February 1988): 31–33.

55. *India Today*, October 31, 1990, p. 10.

56. *India Today*, October 31, 1990, p. 11.

57. *Ham hindū nahī*. In regard to the use made of this phrase by Ad Dharmi Untouchables, see Mark Juergensmeyer, *Religion as Social Vision*

(Berkeley: University of California Press, 1982), pp. 74, 301. In its initial context, the phrase was Sikh: see Joginder Singh, "Bhai Kahan Singh's Ham Hindu Nahin: Polemic or a Social Document?" *Journal of Sikh Studies* 14(1) (1987): 65–74; and Kenneth W. Jones, "*Ham Hindū Nahīn*: Arya–Sikh Relations, 1877–1905," *Journal of Asian Studies* 32(3) (1973): 457–75.

58. Simone de Beauvoir, *The Second Sex*, translated and edited by H. M. Parshley (New York: Alfred A. Knopf, 1957), pp. xv–xvii. I am indebted to Karen Brown for directing me to this classic passage.

59. Ashis Nandy, *The Intimate Enemy: Loss and Recovery of Self Under Colonialism* (Delhi: Oxford University Press, 1983).

60. For example, the designation *devī*, "goddess," is a commonly appropriate term of address for a married woman. However, a growing literature examines the apparent disparity between the exaltation of female figures in the form of Hindu goddesses and female saints and the treatment often accorded to real women in India. See, for example, Madhu Kishwar, "Introduction," *Manushi* [Tenth Anniversary Issue: Women Bhakta Poets] 50–52 (1989): 6; Renuka Viswanathan, "S. S. Vasan's Avvaiyar," *Manushi* 50–52 (1989): 33; and Sonal Shukla, "Traditions of Teaching—Women Sant Poets of Gujerat," *Manushi* 50–52 (1989): 64.

61. *Bhagavad Gītā* 1.41, as translated by Barbara Stoler Miller, *The Bhagavad-gita* (New York: Columbia University Press, 1986), p. 26.

62. This perceived difference is often ignored. In an otherwise capable article on dowry deaths, for example, Barbara Crossette glosses bride-burning as *satī* (*New York Times*, January 15, 1989, p. 10). A more cautious pairing of *satī* with the phenomenon of dowry burning is achieved by Elisabeth Bumiller, *Mother of a Hundred Sons*, pp. 44–74, and new dimensions to the dowry aspect of Roop Kanwar's own situation are brought out by Veena Oldenburg, "The Roop Kanwar Case" (in press).

63. Bhasin and Menon, "The Problem," *Seminar* 342 (February 1988): 12.

64. Mojumdar, "A Visit," p. 22. Her argument is essentially that every "voluntary" *satī* is an instance of false consciousness; and this interpretation is not to be quickly dismissed. For a fuller statement, see Kumkum Sangari, "There Is No Such Thing as Voluntary Sati," *Times of India Sunday Review*, October 25, 1987, or Sakuntala Narasimhan, *Sati*, passim.

65. A handy review of the literature on this topic can be found in I. Julia Leslie, "Suttee or *Satī*: Victim or Victor?" *Bulletin of the Center for the Study of World Religions, Harvard University* 14(2) (1988): 13–20. See also P. V. Kane, *History of Dharmaśāstra*, vol. 2, fasc. 1 (Pune: Bhandarkar Oriental Research Institute, 1974), pp. 624–36; and Lindsey Harlan, "Perfection and Devotion: Sati Tradition in Rajasthan," in Hawley, ed., *Blessing and Curse* (in press).

66. See Mary McGee, "Feasting and Fasting: The Vrata Tradition and Its Significance for Hindu Women," Th.D. dissertation, Harvard Divinity School, 1987. See also McGee, "Desired Fruits: Motives and Intention in the Votive Rites of Hindu Women," in I. Julia Leslie, ed., *Roles and Rituals for*

Hindu Women (Rutherford, N.J.: Fairleigh Dickinson University Press, 1991), pp. 71–88.

67. For information on an instance of *sati* in which this pattern formed part of the background, see Vaid and Sangari, "Institutions, Beliefs, Ideologies," p. WS-4. See also Sangari and Vaid, "Sati in Modern India," p. 1285. In relation to Roop Kanwar, see Oldenburg, "The Roop Kanwar Case" (in press).

68. For a taste of the literature on the coddling of children by their mothers in Hindu families—and in Rajasthani families in particular—see Morris Carstairs, *The Twice-Born* (Bloomington, Ind.: Indiana University Press, 1967), pp. 65–68; on the presumed strength of the child's (especially the male child's) reaction when that coddling ceases, and its relation to various aspects of Hindu religion, see pp. 156–69. On similar themes, see Sudhir Kakar, *The Inner World* (Delhi: Oxford University Press, 1981), pp. 79–112; and Stanley N. Kurtz, *All the Mothers Are One: Hindu India and the Cultural Reshaping of Psychoanalysis* (New York: Columbia University Press, 1992), pp. 29–53. In relation to *sati*, see Karen McCarthy Brown, "Good Mothers and Bad Mothers in the Rituals of Sati," in Hawley, ed., *Blessing and Curse* (in press).

69. See J. S. Hawley, "Introduction," in J. S. Hawley and D. M. Wulff, eds., *The Divine Consort* (Boston: Beacon Press, 1986), p. xi; and the article in the same volume by Frédérique Apffel Marglin, "Types of Sexual Union and Their Implicit Meanings," pp. 298–315. For a review of the literature on this subject and a somewhat more complicated perspective, see Kurtz, *All the Mothers Are One*, pp. 20–28.

5

Japanese New Religions: Profiles in Gender

HELEN HARDACRE

In a Yokohama branch church of a Japanese Buddhist New Religion, a small, elderly man stands in his stocking feet at the head of a large meeting room. Tensely resting his right hand upon the doilied lectern before him, he taps with his thumb on the larger beads of his tasseled wooden rosary. He is not pleased; he is not sure his message is getting through. He pauses to survey his audience. About 150 in all, every one is a member of his church, and virtually all are women. They are sitting formally on their knees upon the straw-matted floor, listening to this monthly sermon by the head of their church, the *kyōkaichō*. The leaders among them are dressed in black, as befits a Buddhist gathering in Japan. Some are taking notes. The *kyōkaichō* tries again:

> You women know that in the animal world, it is the males who are the most powerful. Take the gorilla for example—did you ever hear of a female gorilla leading the pack? No, of course not! And it is the males who are the prettiest. Who ever paid any attention to a drab female duck? Or a female peacock? Ridiculous! Being the stronger and most powerful, naturally the males are the most attractive as well. What I'm trying to tell you today is that it's the same way with human beings. It's the men who are superior, and the women who are behind all the trouble in the world.

This vignette comes from my fieldwork on the Buddhist religion Risshōkōseikai, founded in 1938 and currently the second largest New Religion organization in Japan, with some 5 million members. The message from the Yokohama *kyōkaichō* was unambiguous: male superiority and authority, a sociobiological argument for female submission and deference. He later connected the assertion of female inferiority with a need to reinstate the *ie* — a patriarchal family form discussed in detail later — in which the authority of elders and the dominance of males were rigidly institutionalized and given legal force under prewar law.

Direct as this man's message was, however, it was not at all clear how to draw a correct interpretation of the whole situation. The women in the audience, it later emerged, had come to pay tribute to the female founder of the religion, Naganuma Myōkō (1889–1957), whose death anniversary was the occasion for the monthly sermon, and to socialize with each other. Naganuma was a visionary charismatic who kept her younger male cofounder Niwano Nikkyō (1906–   ) firmly in check during her lifetime, which may account for the present male leadership's desire to write her out of Risshōkōseikai's history. The *kyōkaichō* himself seemed to recognize that the women sitting so deferentially before him might in fact be ignoring what he had to say, patiently waiting for the end of his tiresome harangue so that they could get on with the business that had really brought them to the church that day: interacting with other women.

Men such as the Yokohama *kyōkaichō* have no impact on Japan's social policy, because the government steers clear of any association with religion in that context, no matter how many politicians might personally agree with what was said in the church that day. On the other hand, in terms of the members' thought and religiosity, years of exposure to so vigorous a denigration of women have certainly had a cumulative effect. How many of the women present that day ignored this proclamation of male superiority? To how many does its presentation in religious guise lend a sacrality to its content? For those women, what is the character of religious experience based on the doctrine of their own inferiority? How many will raise their daughters to believe in their own inferiority and to defer to men who proclaim it from the pulpit? When will even one woman have the courage to denounce such a leader in public? Assessing the significance of radical patriarchalism in the New Religions is by no means an easy task.

Most scholars who have studied the New Religions of Japan would probably agree that there is a certain kinship between these religious associations and fundamentalism. Yet this is at best a similarity of ambience: a hewing to social and political conservatism; a perception that an enemy ideology exists in left-of-center thought and communism in particular; and a pervasive sense that "traditional values," closely associated with the patriarchal family, are both sacred and under attack. These tendencies are more pronounced in newer groups, however. In the older ones, with histories of more than a century, they are absent or negligible. Creationism, opposition to abortion, and insistence on textual inerrancy are weak or entirely lacking among the Japanese New Religions. Since the perception of similarity is so amorphous, and since some of the hallmarks of fundamentalism are so conspicuously absent, the appropriate starting point for a comparative investigation is by no means obvious.

Overall it may seem inappropriate to think of the Japanese New Religions as fundamentalist, because they lack the characteristic antimodernism of the fundamentalist phenomenon as a whole. Their affirmation of rationalism, bureaucratism, scientism, and nationalism initially strikes one as being contrary to a normal fundamentalist agenda. Yet as other chapters of this book remind us, fundamentalist antimodernism is selective. The vaunting of nation, science, bureaucratic order, and rationality—alongside a critique of the deleterious effects of "secular modernism"—is a prominent feature among many Christian, Islamic, and even Hindu fundamentalist groups. In this regard, then, the Japanese New Religions deserve to be considered alongside the rest—especially since, on the whole, they share with fundamentalist groups in other religious traditions the characteristically conservative stance in regard to family, gender, and interpersonal relations that commands our attention in this book.

The New Religions: Background Information

The New Religions of Japan currently number over 3,000 organizations, large and small, and include between one-fourth and one-third of the Japanese people, that is, between 30 million and 40 million people. A single organization, Sōka Gakkai, accounts for some 12 million persons. While perhaps fifteen of these organizations are truly massive and powerful, with memberships of 3 million or more, most are much smaller in size.[1]

The term "New Religions" refers to religious associations founded since roughly the beginning of the nineteenth century down to the present that exist outside the ecclesiastical structures of temple Buddhism and shrine Shintō. In terms of their doctrine, the New Religions included Buddhist, Shintō, Christian, and completely novel organizations. The New Religions typically feature a number of elements found in more traditional forms of religious association, such as ancestor worship, healing, and shamanic practices. The novelty of the New Religions thus lies not in the list of their various practices and beliefs, but in the way these are assembled into a shared perspective on human problems—a common orientation that can be described as a shared world view. In their incorporation of more traditional practices, we can see a continuity with past religious history; at the same time, however, the New Religions, whatever their doctrine, have developed a distinctive approach to religious life and have adapted traditional beliefs and practices to modern circumstances.

The New Religions were founded in three distinct waves, each in the context of particular social and historical conditions. The first wave occurred during the period from 1800 to the Meiji Restoration (1868). Of the organizations founded during that time, three are most significant: Kurozumikyō (f. 1814), Tenrikyō (f. 1838), and Konkōkyō (f. 1858). All were founded in the relatively prosperous area of western Japan: Tenrikyō in what is now Nara Prefecture; and both Kurozumikyō and Konkōkyō in Okayama Prefecture. Contrary to the notion of New Religions' being founded by the poor and oppressed, the founders of these three organizations came from stable, even prosperous economic circumstances. Each experienced revelations or religious insight after a severe illness or a series of disastrous yet inexplicable misfortunes.

While none of the founders of these organizations intended to establish a Shintō sect, by the early twentieth century all of them had assumed Shintōized doctrines and practices. During this period, the state sponsored Shintō and pressured other religions to conform to Shintō's mythology and emphasis on such state-centered values as loyalty and national service.

The second wave of New Religions came in the early twentieth century, with the establishment of Sōka Gakkai (1930), Seichō no Ie (1929), and Reiyūkai Kyōdan (1919–1925). Both Sōka Gakkai and Reiyūkai were Buddhist, while Seichō no Ie expounded the unity of all religious creeds. Sōka Gakkai remained relatively small until 1945, but its growth thereafter was stimulated by the martyrdom of its founder, Makiguchi Tsunesaburō (1871–1944), who was arrested and died in prison. Seichō no Ie's founder, Taniguchi Masaharu, was an eclectic thinker and prolific writer who incorporated such diverse elements as psychoanalysis, spiritualism, and meditation in the thought and practice of his religion. Reiyūkai Kyōdan collected its earliest following from among a very poor stratum, recent migrants to Tokyo from rural areas, largely through the evangelism of its female cofounder, Kotani Kimi (1900–1971), while its male cofounder, Kubo Kakutarō (1892–1944), concentrated on developing doctrine. Until 1945 it preached a doctrine of laypersons' ancestor worship combined with frank anticlericalism; it also was a strong supporter of the prewar regime, as was Seichō no Ie. Reiyūkai Kyōdan spawned a number of schisms, which nevertheless have retained many of the parent organization's doctrines and practices — especially the emphasis on ancestor worship — suggesting that it captured a religious impulse that numerous adherents of the New Religions regard as central to religious life.

The third wave of New Religions arose in the postwar era, when hundreds of organizations were founded. Many of the founders who emerged during this wave would doubtless have established religions earlier had they not been prevented from doing so by the repressive prewar state, and many of the organizations formed at this time in fact represented the reconstitution of religions suppressed before 1945. Thus, the appearance of so many New Religions immediately after the war, "like bamboo shoots after the rain," as the Japanese media have often said, is somewhat misleading. These organizations did not simply emerge in response to the crisis precipitated by defeat in war, although no one would deny that the defeat was a "crisis" by any definition; but with the lifting of restrictions on the establishment of religious groups, many persons became able to do so for the first time and sought earnestly to adapt their vision of the truth to the urgent circumstances Japan faced after 1945.

Of the many New Religions founded since 1945, several stand out. Perfect Liberty Kyōdan (f. 1946) represented the reconstitution of an organization severely persecuted before the war, as did Sekai Kyūsei Kyō. P. L. Kyōdan took as its slogan the expression "Religion is art" and fostered the practice of the arts in daily life. Sekai Kyūsei Kyō practiced faith healing and natural farming without fertilizer. Tenshōkōtai Jingūkyō, informally known as the "dancing religion" because of its "dance of no ego," was founded in 1945 by the highly charismatic Kitamura Sayo (1900–1967), who had begun even before the war's end to castigate the emperor as a puppet, and civil servants as his "maggot beggars."

Women in the Japanese New Religions

The New Religions of Japan present impressive examples of religious change.[2] Of these, none is more significant than the appearance of large numbers of women in active and powerful positions in virtually all lay societies founded since 1800. This represents a major change from the way women participate in more traditional religious associations such as the parishes of temples and shrines. Women's participation in the New Religions has been facilitated by such attitudes as anticlericalism after the Meiji Restoration of 1868 and by such social changes as compulsory education for all and urbanization, which have loosened the hold of older religious associations. These changes alone do not, however, account for women's phenomenal participation in new religious movements. That phenomenon rests not only on parallel religious and social change, but on innovation in religious thought about women.[3] The New Religions offer women a relation to soteriology different from that of other religious groups.

Women's roles in the Buddhist or Shintō parish have largely been restricted to serving male clerics or assisting male lay leaders by performing domestic services (cooking, laundering, cleaning), and these services have not been linked to the salvation of the women concerned. Furthermore, an ideology of pollution has been used to bar women from clerical roles and to insist that it is more difficult (if not impossible) for them to achieve salvation than for men. For women or men in temple Buddhism or shrine Shintō, salvation is likely to be viewed as a distant goal over which laypersons have limited control, and for which clerical mediation is crucial.

By contrast, in the New Religions, salvation is typically believed near at hand and within the believer's power to effect. Pollution notions, while present, are used in a different way and do not typically constitute a barrier either to women's full ritual participation or to their enjoyment of the rewards of dedicated practice. Women expect to experience such this-worldly miracles as physical healing and repair of fragmented human relations, and they anticipate that improved health and relationships will result in greater economic stability and good fortune. They exert themselves vigorously to bring about these results, and they understand their achievement to constitute proof of salvation's imminence.

Women's sustained participation in this mode of religious activity in such large numbers for nearly two centuries would be inconceivable without basic changes in religious consciousness, leading them to believe that such achievements are indeed possible. One of the most basic changes relevant to women's participation in the New Religions is the shared world view of these associations.

The Common World View of the New Religions

As the foregoing discussion indicates, there is great variety in the doctrines of the New Religions.[4] While some, such as Reiyūkai Kyō-dan, derive from Buddhism and contribute significant innovations to traditional Buddhist doctrine and rites, others are purely eclectic. Still others have at one time or another in their histories assumed a Shintō identity to escape persecution, but without necessarily originating in Shintō doctrine or having institutional connections to Shintō establishments. That being the case, where lies the unity of the New Religions, and in what sense can we speak of them as having something in common?

The New Religions adopt a common perspective on human problems. Typically they present themselves to potential converts as specializing in solving problems of sickness, economic instability, and interpersonal relations. The New Religions, whatever their doctrine, regard human beings as able to gain control over their circumstances through sincerity, harmony, loyalty, filial piety, modesty, and diligence. In contrast to such Western religions as Christianity, they reject the idea that human affairs are determined by the unknowable will of a single creator deity. When a problem arises, they believe, it is because the self has not been sufficiently cultivated in the values they espouse; and the problem's solution lies in renewed effort in the practice of these virtues. The self exists in a matrix of relations with the body, other persons, society, nature, and the supernatural world. When it is perfected in virtue, the self will naturally be in harmony with each level of the matrix.

This formulation is inverted in a specific way to diagnose and solve a problem; let us take sickness as an example. An adherent who consults a leader of one of the New Religions regarding illness will typically be questioned about the quality of personal relations in the household and be advised to look there for the origin of the sickness. In addition, repentance for a lapse of personal self-cultivation may be recommended. It is assumed that illness arose because the self is not in harmony with the body or with other persons; and hence, if harmony is restored, a return to health will follow as a matter of course. Sometimes the diagnosis indicates that the sickness arose because the patient has not been sufficiently attentive to ancestral spirits. This idea represents an adaption of the ancient practice of ancestor worship to the contemporary world; the New Religions typically advise members about how to worship their ancestors in such a way that they will maintain harmony with these most proximate representatives of the supernatural world.

It goes without saying that the world view of the New Religions has limited applicability in treating such diseases of modern life as cancer, but it is undeniable that thousands of adherents of these groups believe that they personally have experienced a healing of a major or minor ailment through the ministrations of their religion. Whatever the status of their therapies in purely medical terms (and it is by no means self-evident that medical institutions in all cases preserve a more "objective" viewpoint about illness than the religions do), the psychological reality of healing through a restoration of harmony, however, it may be conceived in the doctrine of a particular group, is widespread and remarkably persistent, quite independent of the progress of medical science. Investigations of cases of faith healing often reveal a profound dissatisfaction with Japanese medical practice and the social conventions observed in dealing with doctors.

Ideologies of Gender and the Family

Gender encompasses more than the roles assigned differentially to the sexes; it includes ideas and images of masculinity and femininity that demarcate the limits of acceptable behavior and possible attainments. These ideas and images are mutually constructed; that is, the categories of women and men as types of human beings are portrayed not as freestanding entities but in relation to each other. Religion as a cultural force in human history has been remarkably powerful in establishing long-lasting, influential motifs of gender.

The Japanese New Religions' ideologies of gender present a difficult paradox. Their female founders typically defy social convention and achieve a public voice only by throwing off restrictions of marriage and motherhood—the very restrictions they spend their careers depicting to other women as the one true path to salvation. In the postwar period, many New Religions have adopted an agenda of social issues on which reestablishing a patriarchal ideology of the family (which received state sponsorship during the prewar era) heads the list. The prewar family system that they seek to reinstate institutionalizes male dominance and the authority of elders and keeps women's status low by restricting their sphere of choice in matters of marriage, reproduction, and divorce. This older family form is imbued with religious significance in such a way that to be a good wife and mother is not only proper, it is essential to women's salvation.

Female gender characterizations among the New Religions idealize the qualities of gentleness, modesty, deference, humility, and self-sacrifice in relation to men, in whom the qualities of forthrightness, assertion, and pride are prized. These idealizations of femininity and masculinity are shared with the rest of Japanese society in broad outline; one distinguishing characteristic of their formulation among the New Religions is the premium placed on exaggerated expressions of humility and deference by women to men, apparently as a demonstration of complete acceptance of the principle of male dominance. Women's rightful arena is the domestic sphere, while men represent the domestic sphere to the outside world. Women should not attempt to take a place alongside men in the public world, or the domestic sphere will be thrown into chaos.

In order to understand the situation in Japan, we must review major trends in postwar social change and the ideals held in Japan of a "traditional family"—an entity as mythicized as its American cousin. The composition of that coresident group organized to share the tasks of socializing children and providing economic sustenance has changed greatly over the course of Japanese history; and at any given time there have been significant regional and class variations and differences of linguistic usage, as well as wide variations in patterns of descent, inheritance, and succession.[5] The range of variation that is presently known is probably an index of recent scholarly interest in the history of families and households in Japan, just as contemporary Western scholarship has shown great interest in the topic during the postwar period.[6] As our knowledge of the historical variation in family forms increases, we can assert with confidence that there never existed a single and invariant organization of the domestic group.

Much former regional and class variation in custom was papered over by the Meiji Civil Code, enacted in 1898, by which the new nation adopted the mores of the former samurai class as a standard.[7] The ideal of the family embodied in this code, which remained in effect until 1947, lives on as an ideal in the minds of many older Japanese, who hold what we may identify as a semifundamentalist mentality. The Meiji Civil Code upheld the *ie*, or household, as the single form of the family to be given legal status.

The *ie* has been characterized as a "joint-stem family," composed primarily of a core of consanguines but sometimes also including unrelated persons who were employees or retainers, existing over generations and including currently living members, deceased ancestors, and as-yet-unborn generations. The *ie* is a corporate group that serves as an economic unit, as the agent of primary childhood socialization, and as a ritual group focused on the worship of ancestral spirits. It rests on the twin principles of the authority of elders and male dominance. The *ie* is inseparable from a code of social ethics founded on its role structure, which upholds the values of filial piety, obedience to elders, repayment of benefice, and loyalty to the group. Ancestor worship is carried out by *ie* units and constitutes a ritual practice sacralizing the *ie*, its roles, and its values.

In most cases an elder male served as its head, a position given legal status under the Meiji Civil Code; and he would, except in unusual cases, be succeeded by his eldest son. Daughters and all sons but the eldest normally moved out at maturity, to marry into other *ie* and take the new *ie*'s name or to set up branch households. Both the main branch of the *ie*, called the *honke*, and the branch or collateral households, *bunke*, of which there might be several, were ideally perpetuated by the succession of first sons and their wives.

At any given time in the evolution of a particular *ie*, it might assume one of several different forms. Starting with a three-generation form, there would be an elder couple residing with their first son, his wife, and the children of this second generation. If the elder generation died before the second generation produced children or before the children of the successor married, the household would have only one or two generations until the first son (the first grandson of the original couple) had married and produced a child, at which time there would again be three coresident generations as the core members of the *ie*. At any point in the cycle, employees and retainers employed in the business of the *ie* might or might not reside with core members.

The position of the househead *(koshu, kachō)* carried considerable authority in the Meiji Civil Code. In particular, the househead held authority over all *ie* property, which made it nearly impossible for women to hold property in their own right. He legally held the ancestral tablets and any related ritual equipment that marked the *ie*'s existence as a ritual unit, and he normatively presided over corporate rites of ancestor worship. He also had considerable authority over the marriages of his children: none of them could marry or establish a separate residence without his consent. If a son's bride did not please him, the househead could divorce her without his son's (her husband's) consent and send her back to her natal family. If she bore no children or no *male* children, that was sufficient reason to divorce her, even if her husband was infertile.[8]

In the case of infertility or lack of sons, adoption was frequently used to procure a successor. In general, distant kin were preferred over unrelated persons. Adoption had many forms, including adoption of a man to marry a couple's daughter, after which he took the wife's surname; this type is known as *mukoiri kekkon*. Alternatively, a childless couple might adopt a boy or a girl and later a spouse for the child, or they might adopt an already married couple. The possibilities were and are wide-ranging.

Women's legal capacity was severely limited under the Meiji Civil Code. Women could own real property only in very exceptional circumstances; for the most part, any property a woman brought to a marriage belonged to the husband who could dispose of it thenceforth without the wife's consent. It was conventionally believed that women's main duty to the *ie* into which they married was to bear and raise children. Prewar government policy prohibited use of and education about contraceptive devices. Men could divorce women for adultery, but women could not do the same; women could only initiate divorce proceedings under very special circumstances. A woman who was divorced was not automatically entitled to financial support from her former husband; and children of their marriage typically were assigned to the man's custody, as members of his *ie*. Besides these legal strictures, a woman newly married into her husband's *ie* was normatively under the authority of the househead's wife as well as under the authority of her husband and his father. Tensions between these two women were extremely common.[9]

The reality of prewar society, of course, was far from embodying the Meiji Civil Code. It has been estimated that many household units did not conform to the *ie* ideal, not because of a temporary cyclic change in the evolution of that household, but because they were based on various other arrangements, from the nuclear family, to single-person households, to coresident groups of assorted, unrelated persons who lived together for any number of different purposes. Nevertheless, the *ie* remains an ideal family form for many today. Its role structure of househead, wife-of-househead, successor, successor's wife, and the unmarried children of the successor generation remains a powerful grid shaping thought about family life for many people who have never actually lived in the ideal form.

Meanwhile, however, postwar social changes have largely succeeded in relegating the *ie* to the status of a minority form in contemporary society. The Allied Occupation introduced sweeping reforms in the 1947 revision of the Civil Code. The *ie* was deprived of all legal significance, as was the position of househead. Marriage became an arrangement contracted between the principles, requiring the consent of no one else. Primogeniture was replaced by equal inheritance among all children. Women were empowered to own property in their own right and to initiate divorce on terms equal with men. The ritual status of the *ie* no longer has a determinate form, because the ownership of ancestral tablets, genealogies, graves, and ritual equipment can now be bequeathed and inherited like any other property. In place of the *ie*, the nuclear family became the legally recognized form of the family.[10]

Just as the Meiji Civil Code was not a blueprint of social reality, neither was the 1947 Civil Code. Occupation authorities recognized that equal inheritance of agricultural land would result in ruinous subdivision of already tiny plots, so no one objected when it became more or less customary for a single child (usually a son) to inherit agricultural land, with other children ceding their right to inherit. Similarly, inheritance of the equipment for ancestor worship continues to devolve disproportionately on first sons, as does the major responsibility for caring for aged parents, although the latter burden is so heavy that daughters are likely to be called on as well. Many people continue to think of main and branch households, even where the links are quite attenuated; and frequently the authority of the main house is undermined by branch houses whose wealth far exceeds that of the main house.

The percentage of households of the nuclear family type has increased during the postwar decades to around 65 percent of the total, while the percentage of households of the *ie* type—that is, a married couple, with or without children, plus one or both parents of one spouse—has decreased from about 23 percent in 1960 to about 15 percent in 1980.[11] As discussed earlier, some residential patterns conforming to the nuclear family represent a developmental stage in the *ie*, but this sustained decrease in the number of *ie*-type households is definitive evidence of the *ie*'s decline. As Robert J. Smith has said, "The household [*ie*] ideal has been abandoned in favor of the ideal of the conjugal family, which is no longer a stage along the way to the establishment of a stem family."[12] That the *ie* is abandoned by many is undoubtedly true, but today a distinguishing characteristic of the sector of Japanese religious life that resembles fundamentalism is its determination to reinstate the *ie* by limiting women's sphere of choice over marriage, reproduction, and divorce.

During the postwar decades, the population of Japan has become increasingly urban. As of 1955, the balance between rural and urban areas had shifted so that a majority of the population now lived in urban areas; since that time, agriculture areas have undergone further depopulation. In addition, the number of persons per household has decreased dramatically over the postwar decades, from 6.0 in 1955 to 4.5 in 1985. The birth rate has continued to decline as well, from 25.47 per thousand in 1950 to 12.26 in 1986; in other words it has been cut in half in the postwar era. And while well over 90 percent of the population marries, the rate of divorce, minuscule by the standards of Western societies, has climbed from around 1 percent in the early postwar period to about 1.39 percent in the late 1980s—a factor that alarms many traditionalists.[13]

Perhaps the most dramatic change in postwar society has been that affecting the female life cycle. Japanese women now have the longest life expectancy in the world, at 80.1 years; thus the changes in the life cycle relative to the prewar period, when the life expectancy of a woman born in 1920 (for example) was less than 60 years, have been radical. Women born in the prewar era could expect to live only about fifteen years beyond the birth of their last child, while now they live more than fifty years beyond that time—about eighteen years after the marriage of their last child. Whereas women in 1950 typically gave birth to 3.65 children, the average number of children per couple in 1986 was 1.72. In other words, the birth rate has declined by more than 50 percent in thirty-five years. Comparable changes have occurred in other developed nations only over a much longer span of time.[14]

Women have also become increasingly conspicuous in the labor force during the postwar era. There is now a well-established tradition of women working before marriage and until the birth of a first child. Furthermore, from 1965 to 1982, the number of employed married women rose from 38.7 percent to 50.2 percent; if one includes women who are actively seeking employment, the increase is from 54.4 percent to 73.0 percent.[15]

The reality that the majority of married women are employed coexists uneasily with the persisting ideal that married women should remain at home. Many married women are employed in a family business or at part-time jobs, so they do spend most of their time at home. The issue as religious traditionalists see it is connected to the *ie* ideal, since the wife's role in that system is a highly professionalized one. Being a wife and mother is recognized in Japan as a full-time occupation no less important than men's work, and it cannot be combined with employment outside the home without compromising performance of the wife-mother role, which is universally accorded greater priority than any other.[16] Hidden within this ideology of full-time motherhood is a fear of married women having independent access to a cash income. This prospect is fearsome because it would allow women to become economically less dependent on if not independent from their husbands.

The postwar years have seen a marked increase in women's social participation. They are entitled to equal education, and they may work and marry without anyone's consent. Nonetheless they remain subject to massive and systematic discrimination. The male–female wage differentials in Japan are among the largest of the developed world, with women earning on average only 57 percent of men's wages,[17] and in spite of new legislation promoting women's employment in managerial posts, most are barred from advancing in a career on equal terms with men. Many parents fear giving their daughters "too much" education, and thus the majority of college women are enrolled in two-year junior colleges. Furthermore, while women are free to marry whom they wish or not to marry at all, the pressure brought to bear on women of marriageable age is typically quite intense, both to marry someone—anyone—rather than to remain single, and to marry someone regarded by their parents as "suitable."[18]

The dramatic decline in Japan's birth rate during the postwar era was due to a reversal of the prewar government's pronatalist policy and its encouragement to couples to limit fertility through widespread use of condoms and induced abortion. The drop in the birth rate and the availability of condoms and abortions do not, however, indicate that women can now (as they could not under the Meiji Civil Code) exercise full control over their reproductive capacity. Indeed, Japanese family planners cite husbands' lack of cooperation as a major reason for contraceptive failures, leading to decisions to abort by some married women. Furthermore, the government's refusal to sanction the prescription of oral contraceptives and physicians' failure to prescribe and fit diaphragms and other female barrier methods of birth control, as well as their general indifference to the state of women's knowledge of their own bodies, perpetuate ignorance of basic reproductive functions. A major study, *Family Planning in Urban Japan*, attributes Japanese couples' low "family planning performance"—that is, "taking the initative to find an appropriate contraceptive method and then cooperating with one's partner for effective use"—in significant measure to women's low status in marriage.[19]

The changes in women's social position since the prewar period and the changes in their legal status under the revised Civil Code of 1947 relative to the Meiji Civil Code are highly complex and impossible to summarize briefly. The same can be said of changes experienced by women living in the United States during the same period, yet certain patterns are clear. The diversification of the American population undermined Caucasian pretensions to cultural hegemony, and Europe's decline further shook the confidence of Caucasians. Simultaneously, the economic rise of Japan and its evident superiority in exercising something remarkably like the Protestant work ethic frightened the Caucasian middle class. The so-called sexual revolution of the 1960s was associated with a rise in the rate of divorce, and economic change gradually moved the majority of married American women into the labor force. All these developments seemed to call into question the viability of "the traditional family," an idea that flourished in the 1950s (as Randall Balmer has shown in his chapter) on the basis of the cult of domesticity that grew up in nineteenth-century America. In addition, women raised to perpetuate the 1950s family had to confront the fact that many things they had previously placed in the category of the God-given suddenly, unexpectedly, and frighteningly had now shifted into the category of things about which women themselves could actually make informed choices.

For one thing, it became clear that women could support themselves economically; they did not have to accept a position of dependence and servitude to a male. That is not to deny that many could live at a higher level when solely supported by a male, because of discriminatory hiring practices and salary differentials. Yet evangelical women could see numerous examples of self-supporting women around them. Such women have increasingly been portrayed favorably and sympathetically in the all-powerful media. But if a woman's economic support does not depend entirely on securing the permanent financial allegiance of an employed male, then marriage changes from an essential to an optional institution. The woman's economic need to seek marriage was lessened, and this change precipitated basic questioning about the divine sanction matrimony was purported to enjoy.

Similarly, married or not, a woman involved in a heterosexual relationship could, for the first time in human history, control her own fertility and choose when and whether to have children. The contraceptive technologies that became available in the 1960s ended exclusive reliance on abstinence, late marriage, and potentially faulty condoms. Crude and insufficiently tested as many of these technologies were and are, they have been enthusiastically adopted by American women across the religious spectrum for their relative reliability and for the control over contraception that they place in women's hands. Thus, within a remarkably short time, marriage, self-support, and control over fertility became matters of choice, representing a complex of revolutionary changes for women, for the character of their relations with men, and for the course of the female life cycle. The branch of American religious life identified as fundamentalist has registered sustained horror at these changes and seeks to return to an idealized past when men were men and women knew their place. This reaction of horror is what most unites American fundamentalism with the New Religions of Japan.

In actual situations both choice and compulsion are seldom absolute, and real decisions incorporate varying degrees of initiative and constraint. The mixture is probably more complex and aspects of choice and compulsion more inextricable the weightier the decision. Choices regarding marriage, divorce, and reproduction are by any standard among the most significant in human life, and hence are among the most difficult to analyze. Especially for women, pressure to choose in these areas among a limited number of unpleasant alternatives frequently makes choice an illusory freedom. Nevertheless, we can say that in Japan, relative to the prewar period, the sphere in which women can exercise some choice without fear of violating the law has widened. At the very least, women may marry without their parents' consent, they may take steps to control their fertility, and they may initiate divorce. Since they could not do these things without violating civil law in prewar Japan, it appears that the principles of male dominance and the authority of elders have weakened since that time.

I do not mean to suggest either that choice was absent from prewar women's lives or that compulsion in marriage, reproduction, and divorce is absent in postwar Japan. The change is relative, and undoubtedly many postwar marriages have been contracted largely to satisfy convention, many pregnancies carried to term for the same reason, and many divorces heartily wished for by women who—while supposedly "free" to do so—refrain because to do so would expose them to severe economic hardship, given the discrimination they face in the labor market. Similarly, humane househeads, who neither abused their authority nor used it to railroad their children into unwanted marriages and divorces, may have existed before 1945.

Nevertheless, the idea of an increased sphere of choice for women in postwar society may facilitate this essay's effort to articulate a comparison between Japanese and American fundamentalists.

Identifying Fundamentalism
Within the New Religions

Recent changes in the leadership of such organizations as Reiyūkai Kyōdan and Risshōkōseikai have resulted in efforts to raise the level of women's political awareness and participation, and these may act to broaden women's sphere of choice. Nevertheless, the emphasis on ancestor worship—which is an index of partriarchalism, and which seems to be linked to a sacralization of the *ie*, a desire to reinstate it, and an intention to restrict women's sphere of choice as a means to reinstate the *ie*—may provide an important key for further research that could delimit the field of the New Religions and determine more clearly which may be usefully compared with fundamentalism.

The New Religions showed some slight activity in the 1980s aimed at increasing women's social awareness, and it may be that in the future these will be linked to changes in the general conservatism found there regarding the family, gender, and interpersonal relations. The activity was initiated by male leaders and completely directed by them, so it would be surprising if basic change in this area resulted from these activities. The situation in Reiyūkai Kyōdan and Risshōkōsaikai is informative.

Reiyūkai Kyōdan has been a longtime supporter of various conservative politicians, mostly from the Liberal Democratic Party, the party that has been in power nearly continuously since 1945. Among them, Ishihara Shintarō, whose dialogue with the founder Kotani Kimi is discussed later, has maintained a sustained relationship with the religion. In the 1980s, and especially after 1985, significant energy was devoted to considering how the religion could most appropriately contribute to Japan's social and political development; and a body within the organization, called in English the Inner Trip Ideologue Research Center, was formed to coordinate these efforts. One of its activities has been to provide educational programs for women to raise their level of political understanding.

In interviewing Reiyūkai women associated with the research center, I learned that the program consists of occasional lectures to interested women by the wives of politicians, such as Ishihara, who are financially supported by Reiyūkai. At these lectures, the wives describe to Reiyūkai women the role of the politician's wife: she is expected to await her husband's return each evening, ready to offer hospitality to distinguished guests no matter how late the hour, and in other ways to be prepared to offer a congenial atmosphere for political guests who require a place where they can discuss political machinations in confidence. Reiyūkai women in the audience reported that they were gratified by the chance to hear about the inner workings of the political world and that they were personally impressed with the women who spoke before them. They said also that these programs had raised their level of interest in politics in a general way, and that they now read the newspapers more and sought to be better informed on current events. They did not, however, anticipate initiating any political activities of their own.

A second manifestation of this new type of activity for women in the New Religions can be seen in Risshōkoseikai's "No Poi" campaign. *Poi to* is an onomatopoetic adverbial expression attached to verbs for "to throw away," as when one speaks of tossing away a bottle or other piece of trash. This expression provides the origin for the No Poi campaign, which aims to combat littering. I found out about this campaign in the course of interviewing at Risshōkoseikai's Kosei Institute of Peace and Justice, when I asked whether women were involved in any political activities sponsored by the religion. The No Poi campaign is centered at the Saitama prefectural headquarters of the religion, and its activities consist of having women clean parks and streets on a voluntary basis. The institute's theory on the matter holds that the questions of peace and justice must ultimately be addressed at an individual level, in terms of the problems that directly affect a community. Of these, trash and the need to assume an attitude of responsibility for the cleanliness and sanitation of one's immediate surroundings are apposite examples. In interviewing in Saitama, however, I did not find any clear reflection of this political theory among women participants.

The two examples just presented of activities among the New Religions in the 1980s aiming to increase women's level of political awareness do not seem to presage any dramatic change in the stance of the organizations concerned on the family, gender, and interpersonal relations. They remain male-initiated and male-controlled. It may be that they constitute rather lukewarm responses to more broad-based efforts in Japanese society during the 1980s to raise women's levels of social and political awareness and participation.

Abortion and Pronatalism

Opposition to abortion is conventionally expressed by Japanese Buddhism and Shintō; in addition it is a minor theme in some of the New Religions. Nevertheless, neither temple Buddhism nor shrine Shintō has played a significant role in public debate on abortion or other issues of medical ethics. When called on to express their views, they are remarkably self-contained and insular, apparently unaware of the history of the discussion.[20] Furthermore, like doctors, Buddhist priests have an economic stake in preserving induced abortion as a means of contraception, regardless of the physical and emotional costs to the women involved. Buddhist temples of virtually every sect reap huge profits from performing rites to pacify the souls of aborted, miscarried, and stillborn children (*mizuko kuyō*). Thus they do not wish to displace one of their most reliable sources of income by preaching against the practice of abortion.

Among the New Religions, Seichō no Ie has taken the most vehement stance against abortion. Seichō no Ie was founded in 1929 and currently has about 3 million members. While its influence outside its own adherents is limited, the voluminous writings of its founder, Taniguchi Masaharu, are widely available and have probably spread the religion's teachings somewhat beyond the group's membership. The group's opposition to abortion is based on the twin ideas that abortion prevents the birth of a spirit who should have received human life, and an "anatomy equals destiny" argument holding that women have a duty or "mission" to bear children: "When a woman obeys this 'command of heaven' [i.e., to give birth] she is satisfied and can attain a feeling of 'carrying out the mission.' . . . When it is abandoned through abortion, she is tortured by a sense of guilt which says 'I've killed our child.'"[21]

Implicit in Seichō no Ie's opposition to abortion is the idea that women have a duty to procreate, and that this duty is sacred because it originates in heaven. The sacralization of motherhood is thus invoked to support opposition to abortion; or it might be more correct to say that abortion is opposed because it gives women the option to shirk their duty to reproduce and is tantamount to homicide.

The idea that women have a duty or mission to bear children also appears in the *ie* ideal. There it derives its rationale from the goal of perpetuating the *ie* over time. Old-timers in the New Religions typically invoke the desirability of perpetuating the *ie* to support the notion that women are obligated to bear children. In the past, they opine, women endured more, were more self-sacrificing, and seldom considered their own interest. In that way, they conformed more closely to the shared gender ideology, which so strongly insists on male dominance.

Seichō no Ie is an eclectic religion that does not derive directly from either Buddhism or Shintō, but the fundamentalist agenda of restricting women's sphere of choice regarding marriage, reproduction, and divorce as a way of reviving the *ie* is very strong in Buddhist groups as well, particularly in Reiyūkai Kyōdan and the thirty-odd organizations that originated by schism from it.

Reiyūkai Kyōdan has not, for the most part, attempted to exert political influence to realize its social agenda, but it patronizes a number of sympathetic politicians in the right wing of the Liberal Democratic Party. One such politician, Ishihara Shintarō, a longtime protégé of Reiyūkai, conducted a series of conversations with the former president of Reiyūkai, Kotani Kimi. The following excerpt exemplifies the group's pronatalism in religious guise:

Kotani: Women these days seem to have stopped having many children. Usually they have about two. What do you think about that, Mr. Ishihara?

Ishihara: I think they ought to have five or six, myself.

Kotani: I think so, too [Kotani had no children of her own]. Why is it that women these days won't bear children?

Ishihara: Well, to make a long story short, they're thinking of nobody but themselves. They aren't thinking of mankind as a whole. They have no desire to produce descendants, and in a nutshell, they think only of their own comfort. They think children are a bother, so they put off having them for as long as possible. A concern for humanity is lacking in modern man.

Kotani: If we go on like this, the Japanese people will decrease drastically, as in ancient France.

Ishihara: Well, people talk about a population problem, but when the number of children decreases, I think it's a problem of selfishness on the part of people who ought to become parents. I'm afraid that our great possibilities as Japanese are slipping away. As for me, when my first child was born, for the first time, there were ancestors and descendants, like the links of a chain that had been connected. I felt that I'd become a link in the chain for the first time.

Kotani: That's so true. It's exactly as you say. That's because it is also through children that karma is transmitted. When people do good, good karma is created.[22]

In Reiyūkai Kyōdan, the declining birth rate is seen as a social evil attributable to women's selfishly shirking the duty to reproduce. That men might share responsibility for the decline is not considered. In the organization's view, the solution to the problem is to encourage women to marry early and to have numerous children. Although childless herself, Kotani saw no irony in her own position as essentially a female religious professional deriving a livelihood from preaching that "a woman's place is in the delivery room."

Reiyūkai Kyōdan also sees a great evil in divorce, and it charges the foreign (to them, unambiguously American) officials of the Allied Occupation with having confused centuries of stable Japanese social life by granting women the legal power to initiate divorce. Women are more vehement than men in expressing this idea, and during Kotani's presidency it was very strong indeed. The *ie* can only be protected when women lack this postwar legal right.

The foregoing examples show how the New Religions seek to limit women's choices and to increase compulsion over them in matters of marriage, reproduction, and divorce. Although the Japanese New Religions do not make an issue of textual inerrancy and do not bear some of the other hallmarks of American fundamentalism, they do seek to reimpose an older model of the family. The *ie* model of family life, which appeals to the New Religions, is distinguished in their thought as imposing restrictions on women and as limiting women's exercise of choice. Further explorations of "comparative fundamentalism" on the basis of family and gender ideology may prove fruitful in other cases as well.

One way in which the gender ideologies of American fundamentalism and Japanese fundamentalism differ relates to the presence or absence of fear of female sexuality. The religious right in the United States shows an overwhelming anxiety about sexuality in general, and about female sexuality in particular. While Marabel Morgan's *The Total Woman*, published in 1973, does not entirely represent American fundamentalists' attitudes toward female sexuality, its vast popularity says something about the enthusiasm with which large numbers of conservative Christians responded to a picture of woman's sexuality that was aggressively harmless—confined to pink baby-doll pajamas and bubble-bath episodes. The absence of female lust and passion in *The Total Woman* is conspicuous and suggests a self-conscious effort by Morgan to render it harmless and nonthreatening.

Neither does passionate sexuality occupy center stage in the hagiographies of female founders of the New Religions; but there is such passion in their single-minded pursuit of religious goals, and men are not expected to fear that passion. While pollution notions applied to women and associated with menstruation and childbirth are not absent in the New Religions, they are frequently used to claim new kinds of power for women—for example, the power to enter a trance and to discover the cause of illness or misfortune, as in Nakayama's biography. In that sense and to that extent, women's sexuality receives a much more positive valuation in Japanese fundamentalism than it does in American fundamentalism.

Notes

This chapter substantially reproduces the essay "The New Religions, Family, and Society in Japan" that appeared in *Fundamentalisms and Society: Reclaiming the Sciences, the Family, and Education*, edited by Martin E. Marty and R. Scott Appleby, copyright © 1992 by The University of Chicago. All rights to portions of the essay that are printed in *Fundamentalism and Society* are reserved. In that form, it was composed for the Fundamentalism Project of the American Academy of Arts and Sciences. Reprinted sections appear here courtesy of the University of Chicago Press.

1. Material in this and the following sections is largely based on Helen Hardacre, *Kurozumikyō and the New Religions of Japan* (Princeton: Princeton University Press, 1986), chapter 1.

2. Material in this section is drawn from Helen Hardacre, "Gender and the Millennium in Ōmoto Kyōdan: The Limits of Religious Innovation," in Michael A. Williams, Collett Cox, and Martin S. Jaffee, eds., *Innovation in Religious Traditions: Essays in the Interpretation of Religious Change*, Religion and Society Series, vol. 31 (Berlin and New York: Mouton de Gruyter, 1992), pp. 215–39.

3. This paper adopts the distinction between religious change and religious innovation delineated by Michael A. Williams in "Religious Innovation: Towards an Introductory Essay" (Working paper, University of Washington, January 1988), in which "religious change" refers to changes of an institutional nature or large-scale change in the climate of thought (such as a shift from pro- to anticlerical attitudes), while "religious innovation" indicates the creation of new myths, ideas, and symbols that may stimulate religious change.

4. Material in this section is based on Hardacre, *Kurozumikyō and the New Religions of Japan*, pp. 7–36.

5. Fukuo Takechiro, *Nihon kazoku seidoshi gaisetsu* (Tokyo: Yoshikawa Kōbunkan, 1959).

6. Robert Netting et al., *Households: Comparative and Historical Studies of the Domestic Group* (Berkeley: University of California Press, 1984).

7. Harumi Befu, *Japan: An Anthropological Introduction* (San Francisco: Chandler Publishing, 1971), pp. 50–52.

8. Igeta Ryoji, "Meiji minpō to josei no kenri," in Joseishi sōgō kenkyūkai, ed., *Nihon joseishi*, vol. 4: *Kindai* (Tokyo: Tokyo Daigaku Shuppankai, 1982), pp. 58–72.

9. Igeta, "Meiji minpō."

10. See Kurt Steiner, "Postwar Changes in the Japanese Civil Code," in John Huston, ed., *Legal Reforms in Japan During the Allied Occupation* (Special edition of *Washington Law Review*, 1977), pp. 97–123; see also Sakae Wagatsuma, "Democratization of the Family Relation in Japan," in Huston, *Legal Reforms in Japan During the Allied Occupation*, pp. 125–45.

11. Shigeru Yamate, "Seikatsu no hendo to kazoku no hendo," in Hamasumi Otohiko et al., eds., *Nihon no shakai*, vol. 1: *Katsudō suru nihon shakai* (Tokyo: Tokyo Daigaku Shuppankai, 1987), p. 91.

12. Robert J. Smith, *Kurusu: The Price of Progress in a Japanese Village, 1951–1975* (Stanford: Stanford University Press, 1978), p. 46.

13. Statistics Bureau, Management and Coordination Agency, *Japan Statistical Yearbook* (Tokyo: Japan Statistical Association, 1988), pp. 51, 53.

14. Ibid., pp. 53, 55; also, Yoriko Meguro, "Josei mondai to josei seisaku," in Hamasumi Otohiko et al., eds., *Nihon no shakai*, vol. 2: *Shakai mondai to kyōiku seisaku* (Tokyo: Tokyo Daigaku Shuppankai, 1987), p. 193.

15. Yamate, "Seikatsu no hendo," p. 95.

16. Suzanne H. Vogel, "Professional Housewife: The Career of Urban Middle Class Japanese Women," *Japan Interpreter* 12(1) (1978): 16–43.

17. Statistics Bureau, *Japan Statistical Yearbook*, pp. 100–101.

18. Takie Lebra, *Japanese Women: Constraint and Fulfillment* (Honolulu: University of Hawaii Press, 1984), pp. 50–100.

19. Samuel Coleman, *Family Planning in Japanese Society* (Princeton: Princeton University Press, 1983), pp. 126, 149–54.

20. See the selections by religious leaders in Nakayama Tarō, *Nōshi to zōki ishoku* (Tokyo: Simul Press, 1989).

21. Quoted in Coleman, *Family Planning*, p. 63.

22. Quoted in Helen Hardacre, *Lay Buddhism in Contemporary Japan: Reiyūkai Kyōdan* (Princeton: Princeton University Press, 1984), p. 50.

Conclusions
in Contradiction

6

"Fundamentalism": Objections from a Modern Jewish Historian

JAY M. HARRIS

In recent years it has become quite trendy to extend the term *fundamentalism* from its original Protestant context to include a wide variety of religious and political phenomena. Fashionability aside, we must ask ourselves what this extension accomplishes. Does the term illuminate diverse cultural phenomena and allow them to be understood better, by virtue of calling attention to other human manifestations of essentially the same thing? Or does the term obfuscate, leveling important distinctions that must be maintained if we are to understand the world about us?

In the discussions that led to this book, we identified a number of characteristics that seem to fall within the purview of the term. These characteristics included: opposition to modernity; a literalist or "inerrant" approach to the reading of sacred texts; an ideology of gender control; and a perception of being beset.[1] With the partial exception of the second one, it is easy to locate all of these characteristics within Jewish communities during the modern period; and with the exception of the first (obviously), it is possible to locate all of them in premodern forms of Judaism. One question we must address is whether these traits as expressed in the modern period differ in essential ways from premodern traditional patterns of religious life; and if they do not, we must ask what the term *fundamentalism* actually means. Perhaps of greater import is the question of whether these traits, understood specifically rather than generically, are sufficiently similar in American fundamentalism to their manifestation in other religious communities to justify our concluding that we have identified a phenomenon we can label *fundamentalism*? Is, say, the "opposition to modernity" of Jewish "fundamentalists" a reaction against challenges similar to those confronted by other religious communities, or is it sufficiently different to negate any generic identification? For that matter, are there no distinctions to be made with regard to various Jewish "fundamentalisms"?

The Politics of Nomenclature

Before attempting to respond to these concerns, it is important to understand the motives underlying the extension of the term *fundamentalism* from its American Christian point of origin—an extension for which both the mass media and the academy are responsible. The word *fundamentalism* has come to imply an orientation to the world that is anti-intellectual, bigoted, and intolerant. It is applied to those whose life-style and politics are unacceptable to modern, Western eyes and, most particularly, to those who would break down the barrier we have erected between church and state. The political side of this is important, since we do not attach the label to groups whose members are content to live in isolation from us, without impinging on our lives in any appreciable way. Thus, the Amish and some Hasidic groups (at least in the United States) are not generally identified as fundamentalist. Their opposition to abortion, say, is not generally translated into a concerted effort to make abortion inaccessible to the rest of us, and therefore we can respect—or ignore—their principled opposition. We may even consider it, with more than a tinge of contempt, quaint.[2] We do not, however, bother to apply the potent, discrediting weapon of calling them "fundamentalist."

No, the term *fundamentalism* is reserved for those who have the temerity to attempt to project their world view onto others—to formulate a kind of Christian man's burden. Against such people we lash out with a label that immediately delegitimates them, that immediately says these people are out of *the* mainstream and therefore deserve to be given an *ad hominem* dismissal. "We" immediately know that "they" are not like us, or even worthy of our time, since clearly "we" cannot deal with "them." Further, "we" would like very much to believe that we would never behave as they do—and that we have never done so.[3]

I submit that this is one of many strategies we employ to allow ourselves to ignore the ugly and imperialistic side of modern culture. It enables us to ignore the fact that the post-Enlightenment modern West has been and often remains as absolutist and intolerant as the "fundamentalists" with whom we do battle. It enables us to sustain the illusion that the term *modernity* is synonymous with pluralism, democracy, respect for difference—all the things the "fundamentalists" presumably are not. It enables us to pretend that the values to which American "high culture" pays homage represent what modernity is and always has been. This is, however, entirely an illusion.

From the very beginning of modernity, with the Enlightenment itself, difference and particularity have been inherently suspect, at best. We would do well to remember the plaintive words of Karl von Eckertshausen (1752–1803), an anti-Enlightenment leader in Bavaria:

> O tolerance, tolerance, what a wonderful word! frequently exclaimed but seldom practiced in our "enlightened" century! The false philosophers of the *Aufklärung* shout imperiously: Think as we think! or else we will brand you as obscurantists in our writings and whip and scourge you through half the world. . . .[4]

Plus ça change. . . .

The reality is that *modernity* itself is not synonymous with any kind of political or cultural orientation; it is a largely meaningless construct that we invest with meaning as we go along. In general, in the discussion of fundamentalism, *modernity* connotes all that is good and wholesome, while the "medieval" world, to which we contrast it, represents all that is worthy of supersession. Many things are wrong with this representation, but I cannot deal with them fully here. It is important to recognize, though, that our whole inquiry is governed by this contrast. The notion that opposition to modernity requires explanation is rooted in the sense that such opposition is inherently irrational. We thus feel compelled to invoke such explanations as "social stress" or "disempowerment," as if there ever were a time without social and economic stress or a time in which most people were not disempowered. What we intend to suggest through this effort to diagnose their underlying mentality is that these people do not deal with the anxieties of stress and disempowerment as well as we moderns do. They need to flee to irrationality, while we boldly advance to meet the challenges of the day rationally.

By treating the opponents of modernity as know-nothing bigots, we justify ourselves, *a priori*, in rejecting their fundamental critique of modern life. In particular, we ignore their criticism of the modern movement away from communitarian identities that is at the heart of many of the so-called Jewish fundamentalisms. We remember well the oppression that can result from such communitarian identities — the loss of individual freedom, the mindless violence — and yet we ignore the fact that we have replaced it with the tensions of individualist and statist identities, whose realization has hardly been free of oppression and violence.

What seems particularly disturbing to us about "fundamentalist" movements is their total rejection of pluralism, their absence of respect for cultural or religious difference, and their denial of an individual's right to flee from his or her cultural heritage. This is understandable for those of us who reside in the United States, where a significant portion of our legal protections — and a much smaller portion of our popular culture — is directed toward maintaining an atmosphere in which pluralism is possible. But the modern age did not emerge in Europe with the same respect for cultural distinctions, and most Jewish "fundamentalisms" have their roots in Europe. As noted by von Eckertshausen, and many others since, the *philosophes* were scarcely tolerant of differing points of view.

Even the two most often noted devotees of respect for cultural difference in the eighteenth century, Lessing and Herder, were in fact Eurocentric and "Protestanto-centric" in their approach to other cultures. Despite Lessing's stirring adaptation of Boccaccio's tale of the three rings in *Nathan the Wise*, the remainder of this play and his many other writings suggest that Lessing fully expected all premodern cultures to be absorbed by the newly emerging rational one. Much the same is true of Herder: despite his warnings against cultural haughtiness in *Yet Another Philosophy of History*, and despite the commitment to the uniqueness of all cultures that marked the early German historicism (of which he represented the avant garde),[5] when he came to write his magnum opus, *Ideas on the Philosophy of History of Mankind*, Herder presented all human history as moving toward the emergence of modern Europe. It was in Europe — Christian Europe — that his ideal of *Humanität* was most fully realized.[6] Similar views were expressed by many of the most "enlightened" voices in Europe. Thus, even the least imperialistic and intolerant figures of the Enlightenment and Romantic movements could not view the history of culture in genuinely pluralistic terms. This is critical to any discussion of Jewish "fundamentalism," since, with one exception, every trend in the Jewish community that has been identified as fundamentalist has its roots in late-eighteenth- and early-nineteenth-century cultural shifts in Europe.

At times, the politics of nomenclature leads to some interesting uses and extensions of the term *fundamentalism*. In his recent book, *For the Land and the Lord: Jewish Fundamentalism in Israel*, Ian Lustick explains that, for his purposes, the term signifies a belief system "insofar as its adherents regard its tenets as uncompromisable and direct transcendental imperatives to political action oriented toward the rapid and comprehensive reconstruction of society."[7] As he makes clear, the term need not denote a religious movement at all; and it could certainly be applied to many nonreligious revolutionary and reactionary movements—could be, but isn't. Why, then, use the term at all? The answer, I submit, lies in the disclaimer: "It is employed here not to refer to hyper-religiosity, not to evoke images of fanaticism or simplistic thinking, but to focus attention on a certain kind of politics." The beauty of the term for Lustick lies precisely in the fact that it does evoke images of fanaticism and simplistic thinking in his readers; but at the same time he can claim to be writing an unbiased account of a particular kind of politics. It is not difficult for the reader to discern that the author does not approve of the political movements he describes.

Yet another example comes from a recent article by Avishai Margalit on the "ultra-Orthodox" community in Israel.[8] Margalit identifies this community as "fundamentalist"; then he explains that they are not really biblical fundamentalists, since (as he well knows) such textual fundamentalism is thoroughly eschewed in Jewish thinking. Rather, they are "talmudic fundamentalists." But within a paragraph Margalit realizes that this phrase won't do, either, since the Talmud, like the Bible, is subject to many differing but legitimate interpretations. Thus, they are "halakhic fundamentalists." I do not know what this term means, other than that it refers to people who are strongly committed to observing Jewish law. Margalit's desperation to hold onto the term *fundamentalist*, even though he realizes that it does not fit the situation and communicates nothing informative, can only be explained by the word's political resonance. He knows that if he calls his subjects "fundamentalists," no matter how many somersaults he has to do to make the term fit, he will have told his readers, in modernist code, that these people are anti-intellectual, close-minded folks who threaten right-thinking people.

Further indicative of the confusion surrounding the term, and the political edge to the whole discussion, is the fact that today different scholars argue over which Jewish groups should be called "fundamentalist." Some identify the Neturei Karta group; others, Gush Emunim; still others, both. Yet other scholars use the term for yet other "ultra-Orthodox" groups. Almost all begin from the premise, prominently highlighted in this volume, that fundamentalists are reactive groups, fighting against something we call "modernity." To identify which Jewish groups are fundamentalists, we must first make a judgement regarding what aspects of Jewish life are—or more to the point, should be—normative in the modern world. Once we have done this, it is easy to identify the most threatening and vociferous opponents of these goals as fundamentalists. If modern Jews should be religiously pluralistic and should be engaged in modern philosophical and theological discourse, then all "ultra-Orthodox" groups are fundamentalists. If one is a Zionist (or for some other reason assumes that Zionism is a normative Jewish stance), then the anti-Zionist Neturei Karta are fundamentalists. If one is not sympathetic to Zionism, then the "ultra-nationalist" Gush Emunim are fundamentalists. If one has a taste for Zionism but prefers it "over easy," then both Neturei Karta and Gush Emunim may be fundamentalists.[9] If one thinks that modern Jews are too well-informed to believe in the Torah as the revealed word of God, than anyone who does still believe in this is a fundamentalist.[10] If one thinks that it is all right to believe in this, but that one shouldn't be too strident about it all, than Hasidic Jews and Orthodox Jews whose roots are Hungarian and in some cases Lithuanian are fundamentalists, but so-called "centrist" Orthodox Jews, whose roots are in the German and (other parts of) the Lithuanian Jewish communities of the nineteenth century, are not. If. . . . The point is that all such categorizations depend on the normative judgment of the scholar or journalist about how other well-informed people ought to live; that is, the fundamentalist is very much the demonized creation of the modernist, and of his or her normative judgments. For this reason, we display little interest in understanding each "fundamentalist" group in its own unique historical context. We prefer to level all distinctions, for all "fundamentalists" have one thing in common: they do not conform to our views of how life should be lived.

We in the academy must be aware of the political uses of the term *fundamentalism*, and we must resist the extension of the term beyond the communities that identify themselves as such—unless it can be shown that the term provides us with an accurate picture of a common feature of religious life. I would like, then, to turn to this issue, using modern Judaism as the test case. Two manifestations of Jewish religious life in modern times are most often called "fundamentalist": (1) the contemporary "ultra-Orthodox" groups who descend, primarily, from the Hasidic communities of Eastern Europe, as well as the non-Hasidic Hungarian and Lithuanian Jewish communities in the nineteenth century and their twentieth-century offshoots (I would include the Neturei Karta as a subgroup within this group);[11] and (2) Israelis (and their American sympathizers) who oppose the return of any occupied territory, ostensibly on biblical grounds. As we have seen, the latter group's alleged fundamentalism is not necessarily religious, although it does draw on religious symbols and history. Let us investigate the extent to which either of these groups genuinely manifests the four characteristics outlined earlier, and let us then examine whether they do so in a sufficiently similar way that they can be meaningfully labeled by a single category, "fundamentalism."

Opposition to Modernity

Virtually all discussions of fundamentalism insist that one of its defining characteristics is opposition to modernity. Before going further, we must recognize the perspective lurking behind such a characterization. It presupposes that modernity is (or ought to be) the norm, and that opposition to it constitutes the exception that requires explanation. This is part of the politics of nomenclature—the use of language to pursue the essentially political goal of "normalizing" our approach to life.

I cannot help wondering about the historical basis for claiming (as modernist proponents implicitly or explicitly do) that opposition to changes we currently accept as modern differs from opposition to changes that occurred in earlier times and that contemporaneous opponents would have seen as "modern"—that is, new and different. Why, we should ask, are the Russian Raskolniki not seen as fundamentalists? Did they not emerge from their battle against the reforms of Nikon and Peter I with a self-conscious opposition to change? Why is the Counter-Reformation's insistence on doctrinal orthodoxy different from what we call fundamentalism today? How, for that matter, do Jews who forcefully pursued the Sabbatian heresy in the eighteenth century or who forcefully opposed the Hasidic movements later in that century differ qualitatively from those who condemn modern heresies in the nineteenth and twentieth centuries?

The answer seems to revolve around the question of whose ox is getting gored, and whether that ox has any claim on our progressive concerns. Evidently, when "old believers" fight "new believers" we have no existential stake in the outcome and can achieve the distance necessary for historical comprehension. But when old (or new) believers fight unbelievers, namely "us," we label them "fundamentalists" and pretend that they are some new creature, never before encountered in human history, that cries out for sociological explanation. Perhaps worse, we delude ourselves into believing that, by calling them "fundamentalists" and imagining that this term conveys information rather than judgment, we have actually explained something. Obviously, those who seek to reassert the supremacy of their religion in the modern period must oppose some aspects of modernity, but other "Copernican revolutions" have occurred in human history and have called forth analogous responses from those whose way of life was thereby threatened. Opposing change, even while accommodating oneself to aspects of it, is as old as the human species. While perhaps always futile, such opposition is inevitable.[12]

In any event, let us examine this characteristic more carefully. For opposition to modernity to be a meaningful characteristic of a religious group we must show that such opposition is basic to the group's identity. For, as we all know, modernity itself emerges, at times quite self-consciously, in opposition to tradition. If we understand tradition and modernity as ideal constructs, all traditional patterns naturally oppose any modern counterpart. Were this not so, roughly half the courses in the humanities and social sciences sections of college catalogs would be devoid of foundation. Furthermore, the confrontation between these two constructs naturally creates a higher level of self-consciousness in those who wish to remain "traditional." That this has happened in the Jewish community has been amply demonstrated by Jacob Katz, the premier historian of the confrontation of traditional Jewish life with modernity. But it happened elsewhere and early, as we can observe in Klaus Epstein's description of the attitude of German conservatives in the late eighteenth century:

> They felt, no doubt, that what they had defended had an importance going beyond the immediate case, and that defeat might have far-reaching repercussions. From this feeling it was in theory only a short step toward an explicit conservative *Weltanschauung*—a small though crucial step. . . . It was taken at that time as an inescapable response to the challenge of the *Aufklärung* with its general program of transforming every sector of life. The *Aufklärung* forced men with Conservative inclinations to abandon their unreflective Traditionalism—their instinctive and inarticulate acceptance of the

status quo — in favor of an explicit and self-conscious defense of the *totality* of society.[13]

The rise of modernity pushed conservatives to a level of self-conscious opposition; or in the words of Jacob Katz, it created an Orthodoxy from a traditionalism.[14] This represents a normal and natural reaction to the profound changes, and concomitant disorientation, brought on by the modern revolution; it is to be expected, and it emerged very early in the modernization process.

We need to establish criteria if we are to distinguish today's fundamentalist Jewish opposition to modernity, which ostensibly originated in recent times, from the earlier orthodox opposition. I would suggest that we need to establish something more than self-conscious opposition to modernity. Rather, the criterion should be that the ideology or practices of the group in question *emerge* self-consciously in opposition to modern patterns of thought or behavior, whatever their ostensible resemblance to earlier forms of traditional life. This would contrast with instances of unbroken continuity of traditional patterns into the modern period, which — even if accompanied by heightened self-consciousness of a conflicting system of values — would not qualify as being fundamentalist in any meaningful sense. Of course, there is a middle position, in which traditional patterns are reinforced by the challenge of modernity and are pursued with greater rigor and vigor, with a corresponding shift in one's sense of identity. This is clearly what happened among Hungarian and Lithuanian antimodernist Jews, starting in the middle of the nineteenth century. I do not know what to call this, but *fundamentalist* seems wrong because the term presupposes a fundamental change in religious life, rather than social circumstance, when in fact no such change occurred. To be sure, the Orthodox community of Hungary underwent an enormous social revolution in the 1860s and 1870s, with the creation of *Austrittsgemeinde* — communities that self-consciously separated themselves from the organized Jewish community and developed the ideology we call "ultra-Orthodoxy." But this separatism requires further discussion before we can comfortably categorize it as fundamentalist. It was grounded in a distinct historical reality: the Jewish community structure; the theoretical ability of one group of Jews to exercise religious authority over other segments of the community, depriving them of their religious "rights." The full contours of this story are only now being revealed comprehensively in the research of Jacob Katz and Michael Silber. Its resemblance to the historical experience of other religious groups is nil.

In assessing the opposition of the "ultra-Orthodox" community of Hungary (and Lithuania) to the modern age, we must ask what specifically this opposition entails. To what specifically were they opposed, and how did this opposition manifest itself in their religious and social life? What to them was "modernity"?

The patterns of Jewish modernization varied from one location to another, just as the general pace and direction of modernization varied significantly in Great Britain, France, and Prussia (to take the three most influential models). In revolutionary France, the prevailing political ideology was grounded in a theory of natural right. The logic of this position demanded that participation in the rights and duties of the *citoyen* be extended to Jews as to all others. Thus, in 1791, despite strong opposition, the Jews of France were emancipated. It was, however, made perfectly clear that Jews were expected to earn this emancipation after the fact, by completely recasting their religious and ethnic identities.

In Prussia and the Habsburg lands, the doctrine of natural right remained anathema, except perhaps during the brief reign of the Habsburg monarch Joseph II (1780–1790). Nevertheless, the logic of absolutism demanded that the conventional relationship between the Jewish community and the political authorities be modified. Previously, Jews had exercised autonomy over their internal affairs within the boundaries established by the crown; they were essentially free of interference. The logic of absolutism could not accept the legitimacy of a social and political unit that was not under the direct control of the crown. Therefore, Jewish autonomy had to be curtailed significantly. At the same time, Jews were not granted the rights and duties that applied to all others. Both those who approved of this discrimination, and those who did not, agreed that the Jews as they were were not acceptable.

The debate, particularly in Prussia, revolved around the question of what would make them acceptable. Was emancipation, as the granting of equal rights to Jews became known, the *sine qua non* for reforming Judaism? Or should emancipation be seen as the prize to be rewarded when and if the Jews ever made themselves acceptable? In Prussia, the second position carried the day. As a result, Jews there were pressured to change their ways to suit the tastes of the majority. Thus, the most significant early modern movements within the Jewish community were self-consciously devoted to acculturation, some would say assimilation; to a very substantial degree the changes they effected in religious life, education, social life, vocational choice, and so on were directed toward satisfying the demands of non-Jews.[15]

They were not the product of an organic growth of new values and concerns out of the older culture, a luxury that was afforded Prussia's Protestant elites.[16] Of course, to a large extent, the attempt to satisfy the demands of the general society was quite hopeless. As Johann David Michaelis, the famous orientalist from Göttingen, put it, the Jew who eats pork is to be trusted even less than the Jew who does not. Nevertheless, Berlin's Jews were tireless in their efforts to appease the majority culture.

One strategy employed was to fantasize about a neutral society—a society in which one's humanity overrode considerations of class and ethnic community. As Jacob Katz described this imagined realm, "The common element in all society's categories is that the individual stood as a human being in direct relationship to it, beyond his belonging to particular traditional associations, beyond his involvement in his class, church or guild."[17] To be sure, such fantasies were not limited to Jews; indeed, most of the Jewish writers drew their inspiration from Lessing and others (such as Christian Wilhelm Dohm). Still, the Jews of Prussia had the greatest stake in realizing the goal of a neutral society; and they pursued it, with all its assimilatory demands, with vigor. Even Moses Mendelssohn, whose Jewish learning and commitment is beyond question, was drawn to what Jacob Katz once viewed as the assimilationist ideology. In an early work in which he still reflected the lessons of his childhood in Hungary, Katz described the situation as follows:

> Another fact stood over against Mendelssohn's rootedness in Judaism, and was sufficient to neutralize it. He confronted the non-Jewish world not in his capacity as a Jew, but rather as a philosopher, author, or simply a human being. This is the fundamentally new stance of the Jews of the Enlightenment, in contrast to the Jewish stance of the pre-assimilatory period. The persona they projected to the outside world was no longer determined by their Judaism.

Katz goes on to note, however, that "this stance is not to be confused with certain consciously assimilatory circles of the 19th and 20th centuries, who sought to veil their Jewish descent in silence."[18]

Among the more self-consciously assimilatory groups Katz has in mind was the "Verein für Cultur und Wissenschaft der Juden," a group of disaffected intellectuals from the University of Berlin, primarily. Their assimilatory program was quite clear. The president of the group, Eduard Gans, the first editor of Hegel's *Lectures on the Philosophy of History*, stated clearly that the Verein's program was one of "die Zerstörung der Rabbinismus," the destruction of rabbinic culture, so as to produce a Judaism more suited to the time. When it became clear (as it soon did) that the group could not bring this about with any rapidity, and that Gans could never advance in Berlin given his religious association, he converted to Christianity—a few weeks after the conversion of a more famous member of the Verein, Heinrich Heine.

Some early attempts to reform Judaism were clearly directed toward assimilating essentially Protestant forms of worship into Judaism. These forms included the introduction of an organ, the introduction of a vernacular sermon, and a curtailed reading from the Torah. This part of the story is well known, and I will not deal with it further now. The important point is that traditionalists knew all about these reforms and understood them as attempts to leave Jewish identity behind. While I certainly cannot endorse this understanding of what motivated the early Reformers, I would not consider it an irresponsible or incoherent reading either. Given the precedents and the vocabulary they had to work with, the traditionalists' reaction could not have been otherwise.

In reviewing the Jewish encounter with modernization, we should not overlook the unique role played by various European governments, particularly the Austrian and Russian emperors. Each government had its own reasons—political and religious—for introducing extensive changes to the Jewish way of life. Michael Silber and Michael Stanislawski have recently written on the state's role in the modernization of the Jews in the Habsburg and Romanov domains, respectively, as has Israel Bartal on both.[19] After Joseph II's death in 1790 the Habsburgs were less intrusive than Nicholas I was to be in Russia, but the reforms Joseph set in motion continued to reverberate within the Jewish educational systems of the empire. The government actively encouraged secular schooling, which the traditional community resisted as best it could—in some places more successfully than in others. And while we, no doubt, consider the establishment of modern schools with state-approved curricula to be an enlightened and progressive development, we should note that no educational policy is devoid of political concerns. States wish their citizens to be educated in certain ways, which rarely coincide with the perceived needs of cultural minorities. Further, this new effort diverged significantly from previous practice. In preabsolutist times, Jews were largely free to develop their educational institutions as they saw fit. In seeking to produce citizens who can serve the rational ends of the modern state (in Max Weber's terms), the modern state has felt entitled to curtail the educational freedoms of its minorities.

Thus, in the modern world, so-called "ultra-Orthodox" Jews are probably far less free to transmit their cultural ideals without adulteration than were their ancestors in premodern times. From the perspective of "fundamentalist" Jews, the modern state has brought less religious freedom, not more.[20]

In Russia, as Stanislawski has argued, the state's educational and other programs, which seemed to correspond to the program of the Jewish "enlighteners," forced on the traditional communities of the Russian empire—Hasidic and anti-Hasidic alike—a very clear sense of lost prerogatives and possibilities. Indeed, Stanislawski claims that the Russian government and its policies should properly be seen as the force that transformed Russia's traditional Jewish communities into a self-conscious Orthodoxy.[21] The program for educational and communal reform came from outside, although it clearly had many proponents within the Jewish community. It was sudden, it was drastic, and (with the establishment of two government-sponsored rabbinical schools) it challenged the basic authority structure that had prevailed throughout the Russian lands. Further, it deprived the community of its previously enjoyed "right" to educate its children as it saw fit. Finally, much of the Jewish community discerned clear conversionist tendencies in other policies implemented during Nicholas's reign, particularly his cruel conscription program. While historians can debate whether this was an accurate perception, it undeniably became an important historical force in its own right. Even if today we judge this perception to be mistaken, we have no basis to question the sincerity and rationality of those who saw contemporaneous events in this light.

No discussion of Jewish modernity would be complete without an evaluation of the reality of Jewish apostasy, and the forces that led so many Jews to it. While there surely were some sincere conversions by Jews, who now had the opportunity to observe and understand Christianity under new circumstances,[22] many Jews converted to Christianity throughout Europe because it was the only basis on which they could fully participate in the modern world.[23] In virtually all the European lands, access to professions and university positions was limited at some time or other during the nineteenth century. Undeniably, many Jews felt that they had to choose between converting to Christianity or watching the modern world pass them by. The fact that so many converts were or became prominent in their chosen fields merely enhanced the sense among nonconverts that conversions were epidemic, even in places where they were not.

I could go on with this litany of problems that modernization brought to Europe's Jews. I make no pretense here of having told the whole story, and certainly there are other models with which we can understand the development of modern Judaism. My intent here is to focus on the many problems that modernization brought to traditional Jewish communities, and to identify from traditional writings the perception that prevailed in these communities; my purpose in doing so is to suggest that this perception was not and is not irrational or devoid of historical foundation. The vision of modernity as unrelentingly hostile to the aspirations of traditional Jews is a plausible way to understand the events, and it represents the vision of modernity that prevailed among the orthodox of the nineteenth century and prevails today among the "fundamentalists" of our time. The modernity that prevailed among the Orthodox of the nineteenth century and prevails today among the "fundamentalists" of our time. The cultures, and to appropriating non-Jewish religious forms for Jewish religious practice. It was a modernity in the context of which Jews took on themselves the impossible task of convincing the French, the Germans, the Russians, and the Hungarians that they were worthy of being considered equals.

For instance, Rabbi Moses Sofer, generally considered the most vociferous opponent of modernization among Hungarian Jews in the early decades of the nineteenth century, understood the modernity he confronted in corrosive and assimilationist terms. In one particularly stirring sermon, delivered in 1838, Sofer pointed to the futility of the assimilationist program, arguing presciently that the more the German Jews tried to be Germans, the more the Germans would come to hate them.[24] It is interesting that Sofer did not invoke this as some kind of theological principle, as many other more moderate voices did, but rather stated simply that experience teaches that this is so. I do not mean to suggest that Sofer, known as the Hatam Sofer, would have been more sympathetic if he had supposed that the assimilatory program could be more successful. I point to this sermon simply to illustrate that Sofer was thoroughly consumed by the assimilatory side of the program of Jewish modernizers, to which he was bitterly opposed, and that he also perceived the efforts as thoroughly futile. In his own mind, his opposition to modernity was nothing less than opposition to the disappearance of Judaism and the Jewish people, which he considered—*not without reason*, although certainly not correctly—to be the goal of Jewish modernizers.

In his lengthy responsum dealing with the various practices Jewish reformers were adopting, written in 1820, Sofer again made clear that the practices he opposed were unacceptable because they originated in the Christian community. He opposed the use of the organ in the synagogue, not so much because it violated traditional Sabbath law, since this issue could be mitigated (although not eliminated); rather, the physical presence of the organ in the synagogue was unacceptable, even on weekdays, because of its centrality in Christian liturgical tradition. In the same responsum, which was written in answer to Eliezer Liebermann's two works, *Or Nogah* and *Nogah Zedek* (which justify Reform practices on rabbinic grounds), Sofer opposed the adoption of hymns in German. He noted that Liebermann wished to retain Hebrew for the central prayer, "the Eighteen Blessings," but wished to do away with it elsewhere, on the grounds that people no longer understood the "holy tongue." Sofer argued that it was indeed unacceptable for people to pray in a language they did not understand, but he urged that the answer was not to diminish the place of Hebrew, but to teach it. If worshipers could be taught the "language of the Gentiles," they could be taught Hebrew.[25] Thus Sofer's objection to the introduction of German hymns was not actually halakhic, but was rather based on his awareness that behind them stood an erosion of support for maintaining a separate language—the hallmark of assimilation. This awareness, in turn, was grounded on a time-honored vision of religious separation that was basic to the continuity of traditional Judiasm, and, indeed, of many religious communities.

Finally, in assessing Sofer's antimodernism, I must say that often *our* perception of what is important shapes how he is read. Thus, modern Jewish historians always quote Sofer's punning adaptation of the rabbinic phrase "the new is prohibited by the Torah" (in its original context, meaning the new grain referred to in Leviticus 23:14) as an example of his visceral antimodernism. Of course, they only quote the usage (in his *Responsa, Orah Hayyim* #28) in which the Ḥatam Sofer opposed the restructuring of the synagogue to move the reader's table to the front. He had insufficient legal grounds to justify his opposition but was unwilling to reconcile himself to the desired change, which he considered totally unnecessary and an effort to imitate Gentiles. Thus, he objected that "the new is prohibited by the Torah," forbidding the restructuring on these rather flimsy grounds. Yet this was not the first time Sofer had used the phrase to object to a change in communal practice. The first time, in 1819 (at *Responsa, Yoreh De'ah* #19), Sofer objected to those who wished to reinstitute certain difficult practices that were halakhically required but had fallen into desuetude. Although he himself observed one of them, he felt that he could not justify reinstating these practices for the community, "for one does not rush to create a prohibition; and even more so, [one does not rush] to permit [new things], for the custom of Israel is Torah, and the principle is that 'the new is prohibited by the Torah everywhere' and the old is far better (*v'hayashan u-m'yushan m'shubah mimenu*)."

This remarkable responsum shows that Sofer cannot be characterized as simply a visceral antimodernist. It rather appears that we, who bring expectations of fealty to modern ideals, are inclined to see Sofer's overall approach this way. Sofer was a highly conservative legal scholar, whose understanding of the history of his legal tradition was akin to what Hans Blumenberg has described as the essentially Darwinistic process of cultural understanding.[26] Although Blumenberg himself seems to feel that his description applies uniquely to myth, the same process might well apply to other areas of human endeavor. As I use the notion here, it means that cultures go through processes of ideational natural selection, in which the bearers of that culture—over time and unconsciously—shape its lasting ideals and practices. This seems to be the position represented by Sofer and by many other halakhists before and since. According to his understanding, the customs of Israel coalesce over time, and these constitute its true ideals ("the custom of Israel is Torah"). No self-conscious change—neither a severer approach nor a more lenient approach—is possible without compromising the basic values that are embodied in the system and that animate it. Our expectation that people should no longer think this way leads us to see in this position nothing more than opposition to modernity. Opposition there was, but Sofer's approach to Jewish sources was scarcely exhausted or defined by it. He had other things on his mind.[27]

Finally, the social history of Hungarian Jewry has yet to be written. From what is known (to me anyway), one could hardly claim that a "movement," fundamentalist or otherwise, ever emerged there specifically to fight modernity. Certain individuals did view this as their task, to be sure. A separatist community existed, sure; a widespread desire to be *insulated* from modernity, sure; but an active desire to commandeer the power of the state and turn back the clock, no. The Hungarian (and to a lesser extent, the Lithuanian) Orthodox community was obsessed with separating from the dangers of modernity, but it had already written off those who were seduced by them. This insulation from the Jews who were already "lost" allowed the rabbinic leaders of these communities to become much more demanding regarding observance of the law, because they no longer had to formulate decisions that the entire community could maintain;

rather, their audience became a much more select group, whose level of observance could be pushed higher.[28] Undoubtedly the Ḥatam Sofer was much venerated, and he exercised considerable influence and power in Pressburg and its environs. From his Yeshivah many students went on to lead a reinvigorated Orthodoxy that strenuously rejected what it understood as assimilatory and conversionist trends, whether spawned within the Jewish community or imposed from without. This is the modernity they rejected, and I would argue that it differs completely from the "modernity" encountered by the majority cultures of Europe. From this example it appears that efforts to level important historical distinctions obscure the historical record and explain nothing.

I have focused on Sofer because he is one of the earliest of the aggressive opponents of Jewish modernization and is often identified as a leading animator of this opposition. Further, his efforts to combat religious change took place more than 150 years ago; they are not the product of any global awakening of fundamentalism in the last two decades. Were the scope of this essay not limited, I could go on to discuss several important voices in the Orthodox camp who vigorously opposed modernization, from the leaders of the Hasidic dynasties of Kock, Gur, Belz, Munkacs and Satmar (extending from central Poland to the Ukraine to Hungary), *inter alia*, to Akiva Yosef Schlesinger of Hungary and Abraham Yeshaya Karelitz, the Hazon Ish, of Lithuania and Bene Brak, for whom moderation in opposing change was most definitely a vice. Each of them assumed a leadership role in the efforts to insulate Jewish life from what they perceived as the corrosive effects of modernity; each is a complex figure, whose thinking draws on different sources and attitudes to Jewish life and history; and each must be brought to life individually to get a full sense of the ideological range of Orthodox opposition to Westernization and modernity.

Beyond questions of ideology, the student of this aspect of Jewish life must go on to look at the variegated socioeconomic, demographic, and political conditions of the Jews throughout Greater Hungary and Eastern Europe in order to appreciate what drew hundreds of thousands of Jews to these distinct Orthodox communities. Once all of this has been done, one would get an appropriately complex picture of Jewish Orthodoxy and its roots in pre–World War II European conditions. Such a portrait would harness our inclination to think that we are dealing with a single phenomenon within the Jewish community, and, *a fortiori*, that we are dealing with a largely overlapping set of worldwide religious phenomena.

We tend to expect Orthodox East European Jews, having survived the Holocaust and having relocated to the United States or Israel, to drop their contemptuous assessment of modernity; but this is again a product of our arrogance. It ignores the unattractive elements in our own culture. It ignores the overwhelming, formative power of the European experience; it ignores the extent to which this community today sees its physical destruction as being a result of the modern age, not as constituting some kind of aberrant temporary derailing of the age's program of progressive advancement.

Thus, when we examine the nature of the Jewish experience in the modern age, we find that it has differed in many respects from the experiences of other religious communities. "Modernity" confronted this often despised minority in a way unparalleled by other groups. Many Jews—ultimately, the majority—embraced this modernity and have emerged as full participants in the wide range of modern options. Others have embraced modernity more cautiously, attempting to walk the narrow path along which tradition and modernity may be partially reconciled. Clearly, Jews have paid a high price for this acceptance of modernity and its demands. Meanwhile, a small group of traditional or "ultra-Orthodox" Jews have refused to pay this price. And however much their refusal may have cost them, one must understand that they emerged in a European environment that they perceived as hostile to their continued existence. Their refusal to adapt to modern values, when viewed historically, scarcely cries out for fanciful explanation.

The matter is somewhat different in the modern state of Israel, in which the ultra-Orthodox community has been far more aggressive in pressing the state to accommodate its needs, and in trying to impose its views on others. This is certainly an important historical phenomenon, but its roots do not lie in the events of the last two decades, during which the alleged "global reawakening" of fundamentalism took place; rather they penetrate to the earliest stages of the Zionist movement.

The very vision of what could justify the Jewish settlement of Palestine in premessianic times, as developed by R. Naftali Zvi Yehudah Berlin, a leading Orthodox voice for such settlement, involved a community true to the ideals of Torah. As he put it in a letter to the leader of the secularist camp, it is one thing for individuals to go their own way religiously within Europe; there one can exercise no control over anyone else. But within the Holy Land, there can be no justification for permitting violations of religious law; such a stance would be a total betrayal of Jewish destiny. I might add that Berlin was one of the most moderate voices within his community. The opposition to religious freedom of choice within the Jewish community of Palestine/Israel is not part of some global awakening of religious conservatism; it was an essential part of the program of most of the Orthodox leaders of Europe and Jerusalem from the 1880s onward. Because many of them recognized that they could not succeed in creating such a society, they opposed the Zionist endeavor.

History—the disintegration of the Ottoman Empire, the British mandate, the rise of the Soviet Union, the Holocaust, and the emergence of the independent state of Israel—has brought these opposing viewpoints into one political arena, and a good old-fashioned *Kulturkampf* (now many decades old) has erupted.[29] To be sure, that *Kulturkampf* has become more heated in recent years, and the demands of the Orthodox have increased. This has been due to an important electoral shift that took place primarily among the non-Orthodox within Israel, and to Israel's byzantine political system, which gives disproportionate power to small minorities. In 1977 the Likud Party ousted the Labor Party from power, and since then neither party has been able to put together a coalition that did not include fringe elements. Enticing these elements to join the coalition involves conceding to them certain areas of authority. The ultra-Orthodox have welcomed this opportunity to implement some of their long-standing goals. A technical term does indeed exist for those who maximize their opportunities to exercise power and achieve goals, but it is *human being*, not *fundamentalist*.

If we now turn to the recent "right-wing Zionist fundamentalists" that Lustick has in mind, the issue becomes much easier to deal with. These people are not opposed to modernity. They are opposed to pluralism and democracy, to the extent that these interfere with the realization of what Lustick has called "transcendental imperatives"; but then again, so was Voltaire. The lines of battle are clear here. For committed democrats, only the democratic process itself can ultimately produce society's goals; indeed, many would argue that maintaining the process is the only "transcendent" goal of social and political life. The Jewish, Zionist "fundamentalists" disagree. For them, the goal of greater Israel transcends the claims of the democratic process and outweighs—perhaps negates—any claims Arabs might make to the possession and exercise of certain civil and human rights. I do not wish to be seen as defending this viewpoint. I simply think that it is historically wrong to see in the uncompromising, transcendent politics of these "fundamentalists" an essential opposition to modernity. After all, totalitarian and authoritarian politics, of which these "fundamentalists" are enamored, while not devoid of earlier roots, are a truly modern phenomenon, as Hannah Arendt has taken considerable pains to demonstrate.[30] We flatter ourselves if we suppose that all instances of ugly politics are premodern or in some other sense nonmodern.

The religious segment of the right-wing "fundamentalists" (and as Lustick reminds us, not all who share the political position are committed to it religiously) strongly oppose the peculiarly modern phenomenon of secularism—by which I mean the recognition of a distinct, secular public realm that is the *sine qua non* for a pluralistic society. In this respect they differ from other religious people who oppose secular values, but who nevertheless, for the sake of public harmony and for their own protection, acknowledge a distinct public realm of human intercourse. In this respect Israel's political "fundamentalists" resemble exponents of more recent American fundamentalism. But the resemblance stops here. Consequently, the term *fundamentalist* does not tell us much about this movement.

Further, intolerance of the more generic value-neutral political arena is not limited to "religious fundamentalists." This is perhaps most easily demonstrated by turning Lustick's definition around. If fundamentalists are those who regard their "tenets as uncompromisable and direct transcendental imperatives to political action oriented toward the rapid and comprehensive reconstruction of society,"[31] the nonfundamentalists must be those who are ready to compromise, are devoid of transcendent purpose, and are opposed in principle to the radical restructuring of society. But under this definition, some of the most important political ideologies and movements of the modern age—starting with the patronizing absolutism of Voltaire—do not qualify as nonfundamentalist.

Lustick's specific ideological concerns here are paramount; after all, how many people would refer to the African National Congress as a fundamentalist organization, even though its adherents seem to fit Lustick's definition nicely? Because we modernists are sympathetic to the goals of the ANC, we are not prepared to stereotype its members as bigoted or simplistic fools. In consequence, we do not label their transcendent and authoritarian politics as fundamentalist. Viewed in historical perspective, the reliance on absolute authority and transcendent purpose to bring about desired goals is as old as humanity itself and will doubtless remain with us. For this reason, we should be suspicious of the nature of our own arrogant assumption that "our" way is self-evidently correct, and equally suspicious of the motives that underlie our appreciation of a term that conflates all other approaches and identifies them as deviant. With a little more respect for history and a lot less ideological posturing, we may come to understand the world in complex terms that defy simplistic description. We will then stop labeling uncompromising, transcendent political movements *that we do not like* as fundamentalist, and we will attempt to come to grips with them in a more serious way — as, indeed, the rest of Lustick's book does quite nicely.

The Study of Texts

Basic to most uses of the term *fundamentalism* is a desire to indicate a particular — again, absolute and unyielding — approach to the interpretation of "sacred" texts. Other parts of this book have already indicated that the fundamentalist approach goes beyond "literalism," and yet the idea of fundamentalism remains intimately tied to some notion of the inerrancy of scripture. It seems to me that, if this concept is to have any meaning, it in fact must encapsulate at least three distinct claims. The first claim is that scripture is the "inerrant" word of God; that is, God as author certifies the correctness of the entire text. Second, the doctrine of scriptural inerrancy, if it is to have any practical meaning, must also be predicated on the assertion that "we" — the interpreting community — are capable of inerrantly ascertaining the inerrant claims of scripture, whether through literalism (where appropriate) or through "common sense" or through the action of divine grace bestowed on the elect. Third, one must presume that scripture constitutes a strictly monosemic text. To grant the possibility of polysemy would undermine the authority of the interpreting community's exegeses.

Now, the first of these claims would be affirmed by virtually all premodern and traditional Jews. The second claim is far more problematic. While traditional Jews would certainly affirm that their system of exegesis works — that they are *the* authoritative community of interpreters — they nevertheless must live with the reality of *maḥloket*, disputes among authoritative interpreters. Ultimately, the means for resolving such disputes is to insist that the majority interpretation should rule, without issuing any claim that this is *the* correct interpretation. Thus, the community of interpreters establishes the authoritative legal interpretation, but it makes no claim that its interpretation is *ipso facto* devoid of error; and indeed, mechanisms are at least theoretically available by which the authoritative interpretation may be overturned.[32] Certainly, one could not necessarily establish the superiority of one interpretation over another by claiming that the said exegesis more closely conformed to the literal or the "commonsensical" meaning. Nor could one establish authority by appeal to grace or even divine intervention. Thus, while there is a claim to inerrancy on the giving end of scripture, there is none on the receiving end; practical questions are resolved authoritatively, but not "inerrantly."

When we turn from practical issues in exegesis to the larger issue of the meaning of the scriptural witness in general, we find that Jewish traditional exegesis is based on commitment to a polysemic text. As a substantial literature has developed in recent years regarding this, I will not deal with the matter further. What is of importance here is that this commitment to polysemy remains intact in the face of the challenges of modernity. That is, the challenges of modernity do not push the "ultra-Orthodox" Jews away from their commitment to polysemy (although among some Lithuanian Jewish scholars it does lead to a reconceptualization of what this polysemy entails), as they might be expected to do if we were right in characterizing these believers as fundamentalists obsessed with fighting modernity.

Let us again look at the Ḥatam Sofer. In a remarkable sermon delivered on the eighth day of the month of Tevet—a day on which, according to *Megillat Ta'anit*, the Torah was translated into Greek— Sofer exclaimed:

> Behold, the translation of the Torah into Greek or any other language is evil and bitter. For the Torah is written in its language, which was communicated from the mouth of the Holy One, blessed be He, to Moses our teacher, may he rest in peace; it is like a hammer shattering a rock,[33] and every verse bears several different interpretations. One can truly not interpret any verse literally, such that it would not bear another interpretation. . . . This is not the case when the Torah is translated into a foreign language; there one must necessarily choose one simple meaning and write it in that language, for the languages of the nations do not so bear [multiple meanings].[34]

This commitment to polysemy does not deny the literal meaning; it simply states that the literal meaning never exhausts scripture as a source. To attempt to render the text monosemic is to strip it of its divinity. The "gates of interpretation" remain open; new interpretations can and will take their place alongside time-honored ones. In no way has the threat of modernity interfered with this commitment.

There have been attempts by Jewish traditionalists to subsume all rabbinic interpretation under the "literal meaning," most notably by Meir Leibush Malbim (1809–1879). By claiming that all legal-midrashic interpretation is actually *peshat* (the plain significance of the biblical text) and that all synonyms and parallelisms actually impart distinct meanings, Malbim asserted the legal monosemy of the legal texts and the absence of poetic and stylistic tropes in the "poetic" sections. Yet not even he denied that the narrative sections impart multiple meanings.[35]

It is noteworthy that Malbim was drawn to this position by his attempt to reconcile traditional Jewish hermeneutics and *modern* textual assumptions that presuppose the supremacy of *peshat*. It was the modernists, starting with Spinoza, who asserted that the text has *one* definitive meaning and that rabbinic and medieval exegesis is defective, owing to its inability to recognize this fact.[36] Spinoza and those who followed him understood perfectly well that asserting a definitive, monosemic exegesis provided a potent weapon in the battle against Jewish tradition—and indeed, all interpretive tradition.[37] In this respect many modern voices share something in common with American fundamentalists, since the latter were fighting against the "tradition" of liberal Protestant exegesis by asserting scripture's inerrancy and definitive meaning.

The commitment to polysemy was equally evident in the approach of Jewish traditionalists to Talmudic texts. Again, the Ḥatam Sofer was an important author of "novellae" on the Talmudic text; and these novellae are by no means content with ascertaining the simple, commonsensical meaning of the text, although Sofer was reputed among his own students to prefer such understandings. The same may be said of the various Lithuanian rabbis who wrote commentaries on the Talmud.

When we turn to our other "fundamentalists"—the more political ones—again we cannot find an attitude toward texts comparable to that held by American fundamentalists. The guru of this group is Rabbi Abraham Isaac Hacohen Kook, whose writings are filled with mystical interpretations of all kinds of texts. Of course, when they find a text they like (such as Genesis 23, which details the purchase of the cave of Makhpelah by Abraham, thus "proving" that "Jews" had established a claim to the land before the later conquests), they readily assert its unquestionable authority. Conversely, they ignore texts they do not like, or they interpret them out of existence. An example of this is the treatment given to the passage toward the end of Genesis 21, in which Abraham presumably cedes a portion of the land to the descendants of Abimelech. Obviously, this text is problematic, since it seems to counter the force of the passage in Genesis

23. Consequently, this text is usually noted in conjunction with the comments of the medieval exegete, Rashbam, who explains that Abraham was punished for this act by having to suffer the pain detailed in Genesis 22, the "Binding of Isaac" story. All of this simply proves the old Belgian proverb cited by Spinoza in his *Theologico-Political Treatise*: "geen ketter ahne letter"—that is, there is no heretic without a text. I do not see anything more substantial than this in the rather eclectic recourse to texts among Israeli "fundamentalists."

The Perception of Besetment

The primary focus of this volume is not on the perception of being beset that we, in our study leading up to this book, considered a basic part of fundamentalism. Nevertheless, it does come up in different places, and a few brief comments about it are in order here.

Before dealing with the Jewish experience, we should once again note the elements of perspective and bias that shape the discussion. We speak of a "perception" of besetment, which not-so-subtly implies that a significant degree of irrationality is involved in seeing oneself as "beset." And indeed, this is sometimes true. Yet many of the groups we routinely identify as fundamentalist have good reason to feel beset: they have had alien ideas and values imposed on them. We who are devoted to modern culture prefer either to ignore this fact, rather than to come to terms with the imperialistic nature of so much of modern culture (not to mention the legacy of imperialism in the narrower sense), or to acknowledge it but maintain that in the end the imposition was for "their own good." The reality is that modernity, on many levels, has been profoundly disorienting for many groups, religious and otherwise; and at times this disorientation has been deliberately imposed on inhospitable cultures. This is besetment.

To turn to the Jewish side of things, the ultra-Orthodox and the right-wing Zionist "fundamentalists" undoubtedly sense that the world as a whole is hostile to them and their needs. What does this demonstrate? One reaction is to say that it merely proves the old line that some paranoids do have enemies, and that sometimes they get them the old-fashioned way: they *earn* them. A less flippant response would be to call immediate attention to the fact that this attitude has been a constant of Jewish thinking—not to mention Jewish reality—for centuries. It was ultimately formulated in overtly theological terms, which were perhaps best summarized by Naḥmanides in the thirteenth century. Having argued that the suffering of the righteous in this world represents recompense for their few sins, while ensuring them eternal happiness, Naḥmanides writes:

> It is according to this measure that most of Israel suffers far greater pain in this world than do the other nations. How can this be? There must be nations in which there are righteousness and fitting deeds; there is certainly sin in Israel. But the nations who worship the stars and heavenly influences are condemned by virtue of their idolatry to Gehenna and oblivion; Israel, which cleaves to the creator of all things, may he be blessed, their lot is [eternal] life. Therefore, judgment is extended against Israel in this world, to cleanse them of the filth of sin; similarly, a good measure is extended to the idolatrous nations as a reward for their righteous and fitting deeds [in this world]. . . .[38]

Thus, in traditional Jewish thinking, part of the divine plan decrees that Jews should suffer in this world at the hands of the nations. Their "besetment" is a natural part of divinely ordained existence. Of course, there is nothing novel in this statement by Naḥmanides; the attitude pervades rabbinic documents. If "a perception of besetment" betokens fundamentalism, than the Jews of virtually all historical ages should be classified as fundamentalists.

I think it is not overly cynical to note that, despite the comforts enjoyed by American Jews, little has occurred in the modern age as a whole to disabuse Jews of the notion that they are beset. Most have rejected the notion that this situation is the product of a divine plan, instead seeking historical, sociological, economic, and psychological explanations of the Jewish condition. For scholars of antisemitism, business has been brisk over the last two or three decades. Somehow, despite this, some believers have continued to conceptualize the etiology of this condition in overtly theological terms. Their rejection (or ignorance) of conflicting and sometimes mutually exclusive academic models is not irrational, and it is not in need of social-scientific explanation; it simply offends our sense of self-importance.

The Ideology of Gender Control

As we take up the issue of gender control and modern fundamentalism, we once again come up against questions of perspective. In most traditional societies, women and men are assigned very different roles in the economic, social, and cultural life of the group. Commonly the sometimes rigid definition of roles deprives women of many of the prerogatives available to men within those societies, and thus of many of the "rights" that we would claim they have. In recent decades we have come to regard this as wrong and unacceptable. Movements to effect change in this area have spread, slowly, throughout much of the globe. These efforts have met with resistance, and their degree of success varies from place to place.

As noted throughout this essay, efforts to bring about change always meet resistance; and often enough we recognize that, when we speak of an ideology of gender control, we are merely talking about people committed to maintaining the social and political status quo. This scarcely constitutes fundamentalism, however, so we insist further that, among fundamentalists, women are uniquely singled out as the targets of anger. They serve as convenient targets of a rage that is actually generated by the fundamentalist groups' inability to exercise control over the world around them. This scapegoating of women supposedly takes place because women are the embodiment of the "other" within a given society. In offering this formulation, we hope to insulate our discussion from the criticism that we are simply judging other groups' behavior by standards—in this case, feminist ideals—that we unreflectingly accept as normative. Yet I do not think that we have actually succeeded in so insulating our claims. Inescapably, we raised the question in the first place because we concurred at the outset that changing the status of women is, or should be, desirable; that is why we treat those who vigorously resist such change as cultural Neanderthals whose existence requires explanation.

Further, we arrogate to ourselves the right to determine the framework within which the issues must be considered. For instance, here we treat the question of abortion as being primarily or exclusively a question of women's rights; thus we feel free to argue that opponents of choice are centrally motivated by their opposition to these rights. But is this the framework within which this issue has been conceptualized in the past? Is it the only framework within which the issue may be viewed?

Karen Brown is sensitive to the question, but she provides a response totally devoid of historical foundation. For centuries, Christian thought on the issue of abortion has revolved around the question of the fetus—and in particular its moment of ensoulment or "formation."[39] The Western inquiry into the morality of abortion never considered the desire of the mother to control her body as morally decisive. We may consider this a substantial flaw in Western moral reasoning; but we must, nevertheless, understand it for the important historical force that it is. Nor was the intention of the condemners of abortion simply to load women up with children so that they could thereby be "controlled." As John Boswell points out, many staunch opponents of abortion throughout the Christian centuries looked on abandonment and exposure in a rather sanguine manner, if not with tacit approval. Both abortion and abandonment are methods of "family planning"; yet abortion is usually characterized as murder in the relevant literature, while abandonment is seen by Augustine (for example) as the "ordinary recourse of parents who have unwanted children."[40] It is not murder because it is possible that the children will be taken in by others. In the end, abandonment puts the matter in God's hands, whereas abortion precludes God's mercy from realization.

Now undoubtedly, insisting that a pregnancy be carried to term, knowing full well that the child is likely to be abandoned, betrays remarkable insouciance about the health hazards of pregnancy and delivery (and the suffering of the child)—although abortion was not without its perils either. Still, the focus of Christian thought has always been the status of the fetus and, as it were, its "right to life." There is nothing innovative in the contemporary articulation of this concern. Consequently, it need not be diagnosed as a product of social stress or a retrograde reaction to the recent advances of women. Whether particular adherents are brought to it by these forces is another matter; I do not pretend to know the answer, but I do know that legitimately providing an answer requires far more than enunciating smug and self-satisfied pronouncements about the inability of such adherents to deal with stress or sexuality. There is something very wrong in our implied accusations of insincerity and misplaced anger, which are themselves grounded in our imperialistic insistence that the issue must fundamentally revolve around women's rights and no other issue. Once again, the question of controlling the perspective and the terms of the debate is critical.

Let us turn then to the Jewish sources. Viewed in an academically respectable manner, it is clear, from the earliest to the most recent traditional sources, that Jewish women have lived in a world defined by men and have occupied a cultural position defined by men. Their status in society is determined by their place within the houses of their fathers and then of their husbands. They are subject to gender-specific limitations on property rights, inheritance rights, their appropriate place within the public life of the community, and on and on. Women do have a claim to independent personhood as it pertains to legal and personal status, but they are generally considered ineligible to learn Torah—the most important religious activity within this traditional world. In short, within Jewish life and law, women are classically anomalous. Therefore, from a modern perspective, the lot of the Jewish woman within the traditional sphere leaves much to be desired. We must note, however, that women who accept the presuppositions of the system see themselves as living within a world defined by God's will, not by a male power structure. While many thinkers, from Machiavelli to Freud, have taught us to interpret such notions as extensions of the dominant power structures, this should not lead us to conclude that women living within the system see themselves as powerless and miserable.

For purposes of determining whether an ideology of gender control has been adopted and pursued by present-day "fundamentalists," it is totally irrelevant that, from a modern perspective informed by feminist scholarship, we can only feel that the lot of the traditional woman leaves much to be desired. The question we must confront is whether among Jewish "fundamentalists" there really is an ideology of gender control (as claimed by my colleagues) or whether the continuity of traditional gender patterns is simply an accepted part of the larger continuity—real or imagined—that govern the lives of traditional Jews. To sustain the first claim, we must identify some intensification of the discriminatory patterns of earlier ages or isolate some novel expression of anger or scorn directed at women. I know of no evidence that points to such an identification.

The laws of Judaism, with their at times disparate impact on men and women, continue to shape the lives of thousands of Jewish women who live within "fundamentalist" communities. We may wish that this was no longer so (although it is not clear to me why it should be our business); but there is no evidence that the lot of women has worsened as a result of the perceived powerlessness of "fundamentalist" Jewish men, who have in turn elected to take out their anger against women. I know of no evidence indicating that Jewish women living within the "fundamentalist" orbit have, as a group, been special targets of the anger and hatred that are hypothesized to be directed against the "other." It seems to me that the anger provoked in Jewish "fundamentalist" males by Jewish reformers, Jewish accommodators, and Gentile harassers is directed squarely against Jewish reformers, Jewish accommodators, and Gentile harassers. To be sure, many of these reforms and accommodations to modernity involve changing—and by our standards, improving—the status of women. But they are part of a much larger pattern of reforms and accommodations, all rejected with equal vigor.

Further, a study of the sources reveals that rabbinic decisors within the "fundamentalist" world continue to take very seriously the enormous existential consequences of their power over the personal status—in respect to marriage and divorce—of Jewish women. Many have engaged in rather dubious casuistry to free a woman from a life of loneliness that might otherwise result from one of their decisions. Their indignation at those who are cavalier in this area may be illustrated by Sofer's letter to an unnamed rabbi, who refused to implement a release issued by other rabbis that would have allowed a woman to remarry. He asked the rabbi if he had any legally relevant counterevidence to offer that could justify his refusal to effect the release. If not, he wrote indignantly, paraphrasing the prophet Micah (2:9), "on what basis do you banish the women of my people from their pleasant homes?"[41] This attitude was by no means unique to Sofer.[42] Have there been horror stories in this area all the same? Absolutely; but they are the result not of a countermodern ideology of gender control, but of a centuries-old legal system that affects men and women differently.

Indeed, we would do well to remember that, as the modern segment of the Jewish community committed itself to modern, middle-class bourgeois values, women were increasingly relegated to the home and were placed in charge of "domestic affairs," including, of course, the rearing of children. Sources recording the bourgeois attitudes of the Jewish middle class from Paris to St. Petersburg reflect this new reality of Jewish family life; they also reflect the extent to which the wives in these modern families bore the brunt of their husbands' anger and disappointment, as the world did not always work according to plan.[43] Thus, for example, Pauline Wengeroff complained bitterly of the extent to which she was precluded by her modern husband's tyranny from enjoying the fruits of modernity.[44] It is only in the most recent of times that liberal forms of Judaism have attempted to include women on the same terms as men in the intellectual and religious life of the community. True, the traditional segments of the Jewish community have not followed suit, but I do not see this as a manifestation of an ideology of gender control. Only by assuming that all rational people will respond positively to the demands of modern feminism can we produce such a picture.

A possible exception may be seen in the hysterical reaction of some rabbis—not all of whom would otherwise be called "fundamentalists"—to the efforts of Orthodox women to create women's prayer groups within the confines of Jewish law, as they and their rabbinic advisers understand it. While there may be room to discuss the halakhic issues here, the reactions of many rabbis have gone well beyond such dispassionate discourse, to charges of licentious and lascivious behavior. Here it is hard to avoid concluding that we are witnessing a reaction fueled by a countermodern ideology of gender control. Even here, though, the reaction must be seen in a larger context within which the "ultra-Orthodox" have always considered the modern Orthodox to be a threat on all the issues that separate them. The issue of women's prayer groups takes its place at the recent end of a long list that includes the question of secular education, Zionism, and the issue of how to relate to liberal Jewish movements, inter alia.

As far as the Israeli "fundamentalists" go, I know of no study that would permit well-grounded analysis of this. All discussion at this point must be impressionistic. My own impression, formed at quite a distance, is again that the thesis is not sustainable. It seems to me that these people have a sufficient outlet for their anger at "otherness" in the Arab population. Further, women serve as spokespersons for the movement, and, indeed, occupy leadership positions, at least among the nonreligious "fundamentalists." The Orthodox element in this group obviously remains firmly committed to the traditional role separation of the sexes, but I do not know of any reason to think that sharpening this separation is a fundamental part of their program. It is a by-product of their Orthodoxy, and not a countermodern anything.

. . .

So there you have it. In answer to the questions with which we began, I do not see *fundamentalism* as a useful term; to the contrary, it draws connections where none ought to be drawn, and it levels distinctions that are crucial to serious understanding. Jewish "fundamentalists" share few of the specific concerns of American fundamentalists; and more important, the historical context from which their ideals and values were generated bears little, if any, resemblance to the one that has given rise to Protestant fundamentalism in America. Judaism as a religion and the history of Jews as a people differ breathtakingly from their supposed Protestant analogue. "Modernity" itself means something quite different in these two contexts, and consequently opposition to it is different. Texts are appropriated differently, and women are treated differently. The sense (and reality) of being beset is grounded in a totally different set of circumstances.[45]

In case anyone missed it, the bonus word here is *different*. Are the superficial resemblances sufficient to justify leveling all this difference? I think not.[46]

Notes

1. An important epistemological problem should already be apparent: we necessarily presuppose that we know what fundamentalism is, and that we know which groups can be identified as fundamentalist. "Knowing" this, we may proceed to enumerate what we consider the common (and essential) characteristics of these groups, so that we can then determine what fundamentalism is. The circularity of this procedure is obvious. For the sake of this paper, I am prepared to accept the operating assumptions of my colleagues—and to discuss the groups that are considered fundamentalist—in order to demonstrate that we have not done justice to the task of identifying the common characteristics in a helpful and illuminating way.

2. There is, actually, a nice symmetry in all this. These groups do not keep their views private out of a commitment to pluralism or out of respect for other points of view. Rather, their isolation from modern society is grounded in contempt for its irreversible decadence. Nevertheless, because they avoid us and so affect us less, they offend us less.

3. Many conservative groups have recognized this and have struck back with the phrase "liberal fundamentalist," which I have seen in a number of articles. This phrase further expands the linguistic efforts of certain conservatives to portray liberals as people who do not think well. It takes its place alongside other terms such as "knee-jerk liberal," "bleeding-heart liberal," and the more recent "politically correct liberal," each of which suggests that liberals do not use their minds intelligently, or at all.

4. Karl von Eckertshausen, *Über die literarische Intoleranz unsers Jahrunderts. Eine akademische Rede abgelesen in einer öffentlichen Versammlung . . . in München den 5. April 1785* (Augsburg, 1789), p. 114, as cited in Klaus Epstein, *The Genesis of German Conservatism* (Princeton: Princeton University Press, 1966), p. 72.

5. See Georg G. Iggers, *The German Conception of History*, 2d ed. (Middletown, Conn.: Wesleyan University Press, 1983), pp. 29–43.

6. Thus, he begins his ultimate chapter with the question, "Wie kam also Europa zu seiner Cultur, und zu dem Range, der ihm damit vor andern Völkern gebühret?"; he answers, "Ort, Zeit, Bedürfniss, die Lage der Umstände, der Strom der Begebenheiten drängte es dahin; vor allem aber verschaffte ihm diesen Rang ein Resultat vieler gemeinschaftlichen Bemühungen, sein eigner Kunstleiss." (J. G. Herder, *Sämmtliche Werke*, ed. B. Suphan [Berlin, 1871], vol. 14, p. 492.)

7. Ian Lustick, *For the Land and the Lord: Jewish Fundamentalism in Israel* (New York: Council on Foreign Relations, 1988), p. 6.

8. Avishai Margalit, "Israel: The Rise of the Ultra-Orthodox," in *New York Review of Books*, Nov. 9, 1989, p. 38.

9. Compare Bruce Lawrence's discussion in *Defenders of God* (San Francisco: Harper & Row, 1989), pp. 120–52, with that of James Davison Hunter in Norman J. Cohen, ed., *The Fundamentalist Phenomenon* (Grand Rapids, Mich.: William B. Eerdmans, 1990), pp. 56–71. The remarks of the British

chief rabbi, Jonathan Sacks, are instructive. He writes, "Of this, I am sure: that every Jew, from Neturei Karta to the most radical Reform, is convinced that he or she is a centrist Jew. Wherever a Jew stands in the spectrum of commitment, those to the right of him are fundamentalists, and those to the left of him are the assimilators. By a miracle of cognitive geometry, the midway point between fanaticism and unacceptable compromise always coincides exactly with wherever the individual happens to stand." (Jonathan Sacks, ed., *Orthodoxy Confronts Modernity* [Hoboken, N.J.: KTAV, 1991], p. 143.)

10. See Pnina Navè Levinson, *Einführung in die rabbinische Theologie* (Darmstadt: Wissenschaftliche Buchgesellschaft, 1982), pp. 11–15. This section of the book is entitled *Fundamentalisten und Progressive*. Guess which group is on the right side of history.

11. All these groups have in turn been shaped by their own particular historical circumstances, which differ significantly in many respects. Similarly, their thinking has been shaped by their distinct intellectual traditions. I have collapsed important distinctions in the interest of keeping this an essay and not a book, but I admit that this is a strange procedure to adopt in an essay that inveighs against leveling important historical distinctions.

12. It is worth noting that, when Yehudah Liebes wished to describe the teachings of R. Asher Zelig Margoliot—a leading voice of the ultra-Orthodox community earlier in this century, who advocated as complete a separation from the modern community as was possible—the historical analogue he chose was the Dead Sea sect. While not claiming influence, of course, he notes the many parallels in views and desired social structure. Further, he notes that Margoliot also drew from the writings of R. Jacob Emden, a leader in the battle against the Sabbatian heresy in the eighteenth century. See his "The Ultra-Orthodox Community and the Dead Sea Sect" (Hebrew) in *Jerusalem Studies in Jewish Thought* 3 (1982): 137–52 (references to Emden on p. 143). For more on antecedent reactions to "heresy," see Elisheva Carlebach, *The Pursuit of Heresy* (New York: Columbia University Press, 1990).

13. Epstein, *Genesis of German Conservatism*, p. 66.

14. In this sense, Hunter's claim that "[f]undamentalism is orthodoxy in confrontation with modernity" (Cohen, *Fundamentalist Phenomenon*, p. 57) begs the conceptual question; all orthodoxy, as the name implies, emerges in conscious opposition to "heterodoxy." The question is whether the modern heresy is so qualitatively distinct that opposing it requires new conceptualization, or whether it is no different in essence from the processes that led to the crystallization of earlier orthodoxies.

15. This is not to say that those who adhered to modern values were insincere; nor does it mean to suggest that they were opportunists or anything else of the kind. I do mean to suggest that *one* critical factor in the shaping of modern Jewish values was the sometimes intense pressure to

conform to the newly emerging patterns of behavior in the various European lands.

16. The claim regarding Prussia's Protestants requires more justification that I can provide here. The following brief remarks should suffice for now. Most students of the German *Aufklärung* have noted that its approach to religious life was far more conservative than was that of its French counterpart. It drew heavily on its Lutheran heritage and transformed this in the process. See Panajotis Kondylis, *Die Aufklärung* (Stuttgart: Klett-Cotta, 1981), pp. 538ff.; Peter Hans Reill, *The German Enlightenment and the Rise of Historicism* (Berkeley: University of California Press, 1975), pp. 5–7, 162–72, and passim. Further, much of the political and social reform in the German states was fueled by the demands emerging from pietistic circles; while, to be sure, the reform involved the secularization of these demands, the organic connection is visible. In addition to Reill, see Laurence Dickey, *Hegel: Religion, Economics, and the Politics of Spirit, 1770–1807* (Cambridge: Cambridge University Press, 1987), chapter 1. Even Hans Blumenberg, who insists that the break between modern and premodern society was greater, acknowledges the firm connection between modernity and Christianity. See his *The Legitimacy of the Modern Age* (Cambridge: MIT Press, 1983), parts one and two. See also E. Troeltsch, *Protestantism and Progress* (Philadelphia: Fortress Press, 1986), passim.

17. Jacob Katz, *Die Entstehung der Judenassimilation und deren Ideologie* in idem, *Zur Assimilation und Emanzipation der Juden* (Darmstadt: Wissenschaftliche Buchgesellschaft, 1982), p. 48.

18. Katz, *Die Entstehung*, p. 50. Later in his career Katz, under the influence of Alexander Altmann's work, repudiated this vision of Mendelssohn, in my view quite correctly. What is interesting here is that, as a young professional historian/sociologist who emerged from the traditional Hungarian religious culture, Katz could see Mendelssohn and his disciples in no other light. Despite his academic training in Germany, the view of Mendelssohn that he imbibed from his native culture prevailed. As histories of the modern period produced by Hungarian traditionalists make clear, the Hungarians could conceptualize what was happening in Germany, Austria, and eventually in Hungary itself in no other terms than as apostasy at worst, and assimilation at best. See, for example, what I believe to be the most recent and comprehensive such work, Benziyon Jakobovics, *Zekhor Yemot Olam*, 2d ed. (Bnei Brak, 1987), throughout. That most professional historians would—rightly, I think—insist that the social forces involved are much more complex than these accounts would suggest does not make the traditionalists' reading of events incoherent or baseless.

19. See Michael K. Silber, "The Roots of the Hungarian Schism" (Ph.D. dissertation, Hebrew University, 1985), as well as his "The Enlightened Absolutist State and the Transformation of Jewish Society: Tradition in Crisis? Toward the Emergence of a Neutral Polity in the Reign of Joseph II," to be

published in the proceedings of the conference *"Tradition and Crisis* Revisited", held at Harvard University, Oct. 11–12, 1988; Michael Stanislawski, *Tsar Nicholas I and the Jews* (Philadelphia: Jewish Publication Society, 1983); Israel Bartal, "'Ost' and 'West': Varieties of Jewish Enlightenment," to be published in the proceedings of the above-mentioned conference.

20. There is certainly some overlap between this aspect of Jewish "fundamentalism" and the efforts of American Protestant fundamentalists to oppose the teaching of evolution and to introduce "creationism" in its stead. Yet there is also one very important distinction. American Protestants hope to influence the curriculum in *public* schools, whereas the Jewish "fundamentalists" were (and are) seeking to create their own network of schools. This difference is no doubt rooted in the different self-perceptions of the two communities, with the Protestant fundamentalists aspiring to majority status. It is of course true that both are subject to the larger curricular authority of the state, and both resent it.

21. There is an element of paradox to all this: the Russian government was ultimately more sympathetic to the relatively conservative elements within the Jewish community than to the liberal ideals of the Jewish "enlightened," which it saw as a source of potential danger. Nevertheless, when the government's absolutism was compromised by such conservatism, the latter had to give, as one sees in the establishment of the "Crown Rabbinate" and the general intrusion of the state into affairs once left to the Jewish community.

22. See Jacob Katz's "Religion as a Uniting and Dividing Force in Modern Jewish History," in Katz, ed., *The Role of Religion in Modern Jewish History* (Cambridge: Association for Jewish Studies, 1975), pp. 6–8.

23. This story has been told often, particularly with regard to famous apostates such as Heinrich Heine. The phenomenon was not limited to the famous. For one memorable account of Jewish apostasy and the pressures that led to it, see Pauline Wengeroff, *Memoiren einer Grossmutter*, vol. 2 (Berlin: Verlag von M. Poppelauer, 1913), pp. 182–99.

24. I do not wish to exaggerate the degree of sociological insight at work here. While Sofer's position is easily verified historically, I have no doubt that his own understanding of the situation was informed (if not shaped) by an array of traditional sources that link assimilation to what we can anachronistically call antisemitism, and redemption to the absence of assimilation. Thus, in *Exodus Rabbah*, the enslavement of the Israelites is linked to their assimilation in Egypt, while in the *Mekilta*, their redemption is linked to the fact that they did not overassimilate, since they kept their own names and did not take on Egyptian ones. In my "What Else Did the Ḥatam Sofer Say?" [in Isadore Twersky, ed., *Aspects of the Modern History of Hungarian Jewry* (Cambridge, Mass.: Harvard University Press, forthcoming)], I develop at much greater length Sofer's view that the assimilatory patterns of Jewish modernizers would lead to grave physical dangers. This same perspective was shared by many rabbinic figures in Europe in the late nineteenth

century. One interesting example is the discussion by R. Naftali Zvi Yehudah Berlin (the head of the Yeshivah in Volozhin) regarding the causes of anti-semitism, written after the ferocious pogroms of 1881. There he develops the notion that, through assimilation, Jews have presented the larger society with a being that fit into no identifiable category. Such an unrecognizable and indigestible anomaly led to the desire for its eradication. (See his "She'ar Yisrael" in his *Rinat Yisrael: Shene Peirushim al Shir-ha-Shirim*.) I will leave it to others to determine how to evaluate this material; I am content to claim only that, while (in Berlin's case) it may suffer from the logical fallacy of *post hoc, ergo propter hoc*, it is not an irrational way to view the events of his decade. As for Sofer, he predicted violence before the fact and was certainly right. Whether he correctly identified the causes, the reader must judge.

25. *Teshubot Ḥatam Sofer*, part 6, resp. #86.

26. See his *Work on Myth*, trans. Robert M. Wallace (Cambridge, Mass.: MIT Press, 1985), pp. 149–73. See also the translator's introduction, pp. xix–xxiii. Blumenberg's discussion of the "distortion of temporal perspective" is also of enormous value in identifying the flaws of modernist triumphalism.

27. I treat this point at length in my "What Else Did the Ḥatam Sofer Say?"

28. I hope at some point to undertake a study of the frequency of certain phrases in the responsa literature that indicate the rabbis' recognition that they have reached the limits of their authority. For example, if a rabbi were faced with a communal practice that, while clearly wrong from a textual point of view, was entrenched and not subject to change by rabbinic fiat, he might fall back on the talmudic principle that one should leave the community alone; it is preferable that they sin unwittingly, rather than purposefully (as they would be doing if the rabbi called attention to the impropriety). My impression (and at the moment it is nothing more) is that reliance on this justification for leniency becomes less frequent among decisors serving the ultra-Orthodox community in the late nineteenth and twentieth centuries.

29. For a discussion of the matter, see Ehud Luz, *Parallels Meet* (Philadelphia: Jewish Publication Society, 1989).

30. See Hannah Arendt, *The Origins of Totalitarianism* (New York: Harcourt, Brace, Jovanovich, 1973); see also Zygmunt Bauman's *Modernity and the Holocaust* (Ithaca, N.Y.: Cornell University Press, 1989), in which the author argues that the Holocaust itself is the logical extension of the rational bureaucratic social order characteristic of the modern state.

31. See note 7.

32. See Mishnah Eduyyot 1:5–6. The interpretation of these mishnah passages has been the source of endless controversy in both the medieval and the modern worlds. While some interpretations imagine change to be more easily achieved than do others, all recognize that *theoretically* change is possible within the system of majority rule.

33. The phrase is from the Babylonian Talmud, Sanhedrin 34a. The Tal-

mud explains, "just as the hammer produces many sparks, so a verse has many meanings."

34. Moses Sofer, *Derashot*, vol. 1, p. 102a.

35. See James Kugel, *The Idea of Biblical Poetry* (New Haven: Yale University Press, 1979), pp. 288–92. For further discussion, see Noah Rosenbloom, *HaMalbim* (Jerusalem: Mossad Harav Kook, 1988).

36. Although this is not the place to develop the point, it seems to me that here we have touched on a fundamental divide between the "literalism" of medieval Jewish exegetes and the modern claim regarding the definitive meaning of the text. For the medievals who were committed to revealing the literal meaning of the text, another source of information that provided yet other meanings was always available—whether that source was unbroken tradition or midrashic exegesis. For many of the early moderns, the definitive meaning, whether literal or not (and usually it was), was the only reference point. No other source of knowledge could uphold traditional practice and understanding.

37. I hope to develop this theme further in a book on the history of Jewish legal interpretation. For now it is sufficient to note that, for many modernizers, asserting that the biblical text in itself can yield definitive interpretation, and that one has no need for a traditional interpretive community, gave them a potent weapon with which to challenge the authority structures of the religious traditions they were combating.

38. Moses Naḥmanides, *Torat ha-Adam*, in C. Chavel, ed., *Kitve Ramban*, vol. 2 (Jerusalem: Mossad Harav Kook, 1962), p. 268.

39. See John T. Noonan, Jr., "An Almost Absolute Value in History" in Noonan, ed., *The Morality of Abortion: Legal and Historical Perspectives* (Cambridge, Mass.: Harvard University Press, 1970), pp. 1–59.

40. John Boswell, *The Kindness of Strangers: The Abandonment of Children in Western Europe from Late Antiquity to the Renaissance* (New York: Pantheon Books, 1988), passim; quotation from p. 170.

41. Solomon Sofer, ed., *Iggerot Soferim* (Tel Aviv: Sinai Publishing, 1970), part 2, p. 38. See Babylonian Talmud, Eruvin, 63b.

42. This was well-understood by Aḥad Ha-am, the Zionist thinker and essayist; see his "Torah she-balev" in Aḥad Ha-am, *Al Parashat Derakhim*, vol. 1 (Berlin: Jüdischer Verlag, 1921), pp. 95–96, which comes out in opposition to the satire of Yehudah Leib Gordon, "Kotzo shel Yud." The latter work did much to energize the view that nineteenth-century rabbis were particularly cruel to women in their application of Jewish law.

43. See Paula Hyman's "The Modern Jewish Family: Image and Reality," in David Kraemer, ed., *The Jewish Family: Metaphor and Memory* (New York: Oxford University Press, 1989), pp. 187–90.

44. Wengeroff complained of modernizing Jewish men: "Manche verlangten von den Frauen nicht nur Zustimmung, sondern auch Unterwerfung,— sie verlangten von ihnen die Abschaffung alles dessen, was gestern noch heilig war. *Alle modernen Ideen, wie Freiheit, Gleichheit, Brüderlichkeit, in*

der Gesellschaft predigend, waren diese jungen Leute zu Hause ihren Frauen gegenüber die grössten Despoten, die rücksichtlos die Erfüllung ihrer Wünsche forderten." Elsewhere she wrote of her husband, ". . . Er ist nie auf den Gedanken gekommen, dass ich meine eigenen Grundsätze, Gewohnheiten habe, dass ich bereits von Haus aus zu ihm mit Erinnerungen, ja sogar mit gewissen Erfahrungen kam; und dass die mannigfachen Lebensumstände meine Standhaftigkeit ausgebildet und gefestigt haben. Er gab sich nicht die Mühe, sich meinem innern Wesen zu nähern und es zu erkennen. Er fordert von mir vor allem Unterwürfigkeit und Verleugnung meiner Grundsätze." Wengeroff, *Memoiren*, vol. 2, pp. 139–40 (emphasis added) and 179, respectively. Lest I convey the impression that only modern women were dissatified with their lot, it should be noted that the first wife of R. Berlin, Raine Batya, apparently complained bitterly about her exclusion from the world of Jewish learning. There is a certain symmetry to the fates of modern and traditional Jewish women in Europe.

45. In this essay, I have focused on aspects of the modern Jewish experience that differ from that of American Protestant fundamentalists. I do not intend to suggest that Judaism is somehow unique in this. In my view, it does not constitute the exception that justifies the extension to other cultures; rather, what has been said here about Jews and Judaism can be applied to all the alleged fundamentalisms, *mutatis mutandis.*

46. As I was putting the finishing touches on this essay, I came across a startling example of the significance of perspective in dealing with the aspects of Jewish modernity. In a review of Paul L. Rose's *Revolutionary Antisemitism in Germany from Kant to Wagner*, Anthony Quinton wrote, "At its mildest, destruction of *Judentum* could mean simply the gradual and *largely painless* cultural absorption of the Jews by the Gentile majorities among whom they lived" (Anthony Quinton, "Idealists Against the Jews" in *New York Review of Books*, November 7, 1991, p. 39, emphasis added). The notion that the cultural absorption of a minority might ever be "largely painless" could only be formulated by the member of a majority culture, who believes that absorption by a majority is ultimately a good thing for minorities. From such a point of view, resistance to absorption no doubt appears obtuse and in need of patronizing explanation. Adopting a different perspective would cast the matter in an entirely different light, to say the least.

Fundamentalism
+ Gender
ed. J. S. Hawley
ny: Oxford, 1994

7

Fundamentalism
and the Control of Women

KAREN McCARTHY BROWN

Religious fundamentalism is very difficult to define; yet many of us—scholars and journalists in particular—think we know it when we see it. For those attuned to gender as a category of analysis, a stab of recognition is often occasioned by the presence of high degrees of religiously sanctioned control of women. In conservative religious movements around the world, women are veiled or otherwise covered; confined to the home or in some other way strictly limited in their access to the public sphere; prohibited from testifying in a court of law, owning property, or initiating divorce; and they are very often denied the authority to make their own reproductive choices.

I propose to take up the thread of the control of women and follow it into the center of the maze of contemporary fundamentalism. Yet I will not argue, as might be expected, that the need to control women is the main motivation for the rise of fundamentalism, but rather that aggravation of this age-old, widespread need is an inevitable side effect of a type of stress peculiar to our age.

I will suggest that the varieties of fundamentalism found throughout the world today are extreme responses to the failed promise of Enlightenment rationalism. Fundamentalism, in my view, is the religion of the stressed and the disoriented, of those for whom the world is overwhelming. More to the point, it is the religion of those at once seduced and betrayed by the promise that we human beings can comprehend and control our world. Bitterly disappointed by the politics of rationalized bureaucracies, the limitations of science, and the perversions of industrialization, fundamentalists seek to reject the modern world, while nevertheless holding onto its habits of mind: clarity, certitude, and control. Given these habits, fundamentalists necessarily operate with a limited view of human activity (including religious activity), one confined largely to consciousness and choice. They deny the power of those parts of the human psyche that are inaccessible to consciousness yet play a central role in orienting us in the world. Most of all they seek to control the fearsome, mute power of the flesh. This characteristic ensures that fundamentalism will always involve the control of women, for women generally carry the greater burden of human fleshliness.

This essay is an exploratory one. Its topic is huge and it ranges widely, crossing over into several academic disciplines other than my own. Occasionally I am forced to paint with a broad stroke and a quick hand. Writing that is preliminary and suggestive can be risky, but the connections I see between religious fundamentalism and other, larger aspects of our contemporary world seem compelling enough to lead me to take that risk. My argument begins close to home, in the United States, with Christian anti-abortion activism.

The Anti-Abortion Movement in the United States

The "pro-life movement" emerged in the 1970s as a new type of religio-political organization. It was a bottom–up movement that used sophisticated, top–down technology. In the early stages of the movement, the organizing work was done around kitchen tables. But the envelopes stuffed at those tables were sent to addresses on computer-generated mailing lists, the product of advanced market-research techniques. This blend of grass-roots organization and advanced technology quickly brought a minority movement[1] to a position of significant political power. The combination of traditional and modern methods also reveals an ambivalence toward the ways of the modern world that I will later argue is characteristic of fundamentalist movements.

Many observers have noted an inconsistency in the pro-life position. The very groups who launch an emotional defense of the fetus's right to life are curiously indifferent to children outside the womb. As a rule pro-lifers do not support social programs focused on issues such as child abuse, day care, foster care, or juvenile drug use. They oppose welfare programs in general and have taken no leadership in educational reform beyond concern with sex education, public school prayer, and the theory of evolution. Furthermore, their so-called pro-life argument is deeply compromised by staunch support for increased military spending and for the death penalty. It seems clear that the pro-life position is not a consistent theological or philosophical stance. A quite different kind of consistency emerges from the full range of this group's social policy positions. Their overriding concern is that of maintaining strong and clear social boundaries— boundaries between nation-states, between law-abiding citizens and criminals, between the righteous and the sinful, between life and death, and not coincidentally, between men and women. This is a group centrally concerned with social order and social control.

Beyond the trigger of the 1973 Supreme Court decision in *Roe* v. *Wade*, stresses with a broader historical range have contributed to a focus on boundary maintenance in the anti-abortion movement. The upheavals of the 1960s created the immediate historical context of the anti-abortion movement of the 1970s. Student activists of the 1960s questioned the authority of parents, educators, and politicians. Black activists challenged the cherished American myths of equal opportunity and equal protection under the law. And the Vietnam War not only raised questions about U.S. military prowess but also planted doubts about the moral valence of the international presence and policy of the United States. These are very specific reasons why Americans in the 1970s might have felt that the social and moral orders were becoming dangerously befuddled.

In the last frantic days of the Vietnam War, when the United States struggled to withdraw from Southeast Asia with some semblance of dignity and control, Operation Babylift hove into view as both a distraction from and a panacea for feelings of defeat and confusion. A heroic military maneuver, it was designed to rescue mixed-race children—the offspring of GIs and Vietnamese women. The American public was told exaggerated stories: the Vietnamese would abandon these children; no one would care for them; they would have to sleep on the streets, and eat from the gutters. Helping the vulnerable, in this context, was an act with complicated motives and messages. Among the latter were reassurances about the power of our technology and of our armed forces. The Vietnamese children, a number of whom turned out not to be orphans at all,[2] became pawns in a larger game of self-assurance and self-justification.

The 1980s have seen other, smaller examples of the kind of self-redemption that Americans find in dramatic rescues of the vulnerable. During the period when the Cold War was winding down and people were beginning to ask what it had been all about, the media became obsessed with a "high-tech" cooperative U.S.–Soviet effort to free blue whales trapped by arctic ice. In the same genre is the 1987 drama in which sophisticated oil-drilling equipment was used to rescue the toddler Jessica McClure from a narrow pipe into which she had fallen in her Odessa, Texas, backyard. Millions of people followed her agonizing story, and images of her triumphant rescue became icons of American technological ingenuity and goodwill. These stories hint at a broader context in which the anti-abortion movement can be seen: it is a continuous Operation Babylift at the local level. Indeed, one of the most active anti-abortion groups has drawn on the same combination of militancy and morality by dubbing itself Operation Rescue. And as with Operation Babylift, involvement with the anti-abortion cause provides activists with an image of self grounded in power, effectiveness, and righteousness.

Yet this kind of dramatic, unambiguous self-affirmation is being sought in the context of a shrinking world defined by complex interconnections that are increasingly difficult to deny, even harder to comprehend, and virtually impossible to control—or so it feels. For us in the United States, each day's news reports bring more reminders of our involvement in violence, poverty, and environmental damage at home and abroad. Our political power and our technology seem to have rapidly outdistanced our intellectual and moral wisdom in applying them. Having cast ourselves in the role of military and moral guardians of the world, we are doubly troubled by these realizations. A deep sense of guilt, even shame—pervasive, if still largely inchoate—colors the lives of Americans in the late twentieth century. With this as background, anti-abortion activity emerges as an emotionally charged denial of complicity. The one who takes a strong and visible stand against abortion, cries out: "Look at me! I am as innocent as the lives I save."

Such deep-seated needs to assert control and claim righteousness are not likely to have been provoked only by the events of the 1960s. The emotional tenor of the anti-abortion movement alone seems to suggest that it is a response to deeper and older sources of stress. Seeing this movement as an event of the late Enlightenment provides clues to the nature of the deeper stress.[3]

A World Suddenly Too Big

From the mid-nineteenth century into the early decades of the twentieth, the writings of travelers, missionaries, and, eventually, anthropologists were popular bedside reading materials in the United States. Americans were fascinated by exotic "others." They were concerned about their own place in this expanding, newly complex world. Most of these books did more than titillate. With their implicit or explicit social Darwinism, they also carried deeply comforting messages of progress and of Western superiority. Such messages, coming from many sources, infused an air of optimism into an otherwise disorienting age. During the same general time span, the seeds of American fundamentalism were sown and came to fruition.

Some of the social forces that shaped this period—expanding knowledge of and contact with the larger world, and increased communication—had emerged over a relatively long period of time. Others, such as the burgeoning of cities, the dramatic increase in immigrant populations, and a series of shifts in women's roles, had occurred more recently.[4] All of these forces came together in the second half of the nineteenth century to contribute to a general sense of vertigo; the world was becoming too big, too complicated, and too chaotic to comprehend. Most important, each individual's own place in it was uncertain. Religion, given its basic orientational role in human life, emerged as a natural arena for dealing with the resulting stress.

From that period until this in the United States, conservative Christians have come under a double attack. On one level, they have had to deal with the general stress of the times; and on the other, with the direct challenge of Enlightenment rationalism in the form of biblical higher criticism and evolutionary theory. The reaction of some groups of Christians has been ironic: they have responded to the threat by mimicking Enlightenment rationalism. The religion-versus-science debate pits against one another groups who share a common intellectual style: each claims to possess the truth. Believers, like rationalists, stress consciousness, clarity, and control.[5] Morality is codified; sacred narratives are taken literally and sometimes attempts are made to support them with "scientific evidence"; all sorts of truths are listed and enumerated; scripture becomes inerrant. Furthermore conscious consent to membership in the community of belief, on the model of "making a decision for Christ," becomes increasingly important.

These are the religious groups we call fundamentalists. Their central aim is to make of their religion an Archimedean point in the midst of a changing world. But to do so, they must limit their religion's responsiveness to its social environment; and as a result they are left with little flexibility to respond to the complexity of their own feelings or to the challenge of a changing world. Sometimes they fall into aggressively defending brittle truths. This is what makes fundamentalism in the contemporary world problematic and, in some cases, dangerous.

When fundamentalism and its anti-abortion activism are set in this very broad context, they seem to be only coincidentally about women, even though the results of such action are likely to have a profound and enduring effect on women's lives. Yet more is involved than has so far met the eye. We must push to an awareness of deeper levels of social stress and come to an appreciation of other sorts of psychosocial processes before we can understand why this late-twentieth-century drama is being inscribed on women's bodies and lives.

Gender Roles and the World of Childhood

Object-relations theory is a branch of neo-Freudian thought that shifts the spotlight on human psychological development from the Oedipal stage backward to the earliest and (the theory asserts) most formative period of human development. A highly vulnerable time of life, much of it is lived through without language and without the contextualizing concepts of time and space. According to object-relations theorists, this causes emotions such as joy and fear, hunger and longing to have an oceanic, engulfing quality to them. Since each of us as an infant endures a protracted period of wordless vulnerability, all of us as adults carry deep preverbal memories in which feelings have this type of resonance. In our adult lives we struggle, mostly without success, to recreate with lovers the pure bliss and profound security of the infant's surrender to its mother's embrace. And in our public lives, we construct elaborate defenses against unnameable longings and swelling fears whose provenance we do not know. The stresses of life, when sufficiently strong, form chains of association that plummet through the strata of memory and reimmerse us in the affect of infancy. At such times, we can easily feel overwhelmed, and everything can feel threatening.

Given the childcare arrangements that prevail in most parts of the world, the great majority of human beings live through this crucial period of development in the exclusive or nearly exclusive company of women.[6] As a result, very strong feelings we have as adults are likely to activate background memories of a woman's presence. In *The Mermaid and the Minotaur*, Dorothy Dinnerstein makes the point in this way:

> The sense of [the mother's] presence—carnally apprehended in rocking and crooning, in cuddling and mutual gazing—is what makes the world feel safe. Separation from the touch, smell, taste, sound, sight of her is the forerunner of all isolation, and it eventually stands as the prototype for our fear of the final isolation. . . . The mother's too tight, rough, or jerky handling of the baby's body, her delay in feeding its mouth or cleaning its skin, are the forerunners of all human insensitivity, callousness, treachery. In the body's pain, which it is up to the mother to prevent, is all the terror of annihilation. The sinking sense of falling—loss of maternal support—is the permanent archetype of catastrophe.[7]

Object-relations theory helps to explain why the disorienting stress described earlier might well come to a focus in a woman-centered issue such as abortion. It is consistent with Dinnerstein's theory to argue that stress from almost any source, if sufficiently strong, will provoke a need to control the dangerous power of women. "The crucial psychological fact is that all of us, female as well as male, fear the will of woman," says Dinnerstein.[8] She adds that male dominion and privilege are social constructs deriving from "a terror that we all feel: the terror of sinking back wholly into the helplessness of infancy."[9] Fear of female will ("the earliest and profoundest prototype of absolute power"[10]), when combined with deep memories of the joy and security found in a woman's presence, produce a powerful ambivalence toward women that is apparent in the myths, religious practices, social structures, and daily interactions of peoples around the world. In one moment woman is a goddess; in the next, she is a voracious, polluting monster. Scratch the surface of the Victorian cult of true womanhood, or its recasting in the idealized image of the 1950s housewife, and this ambivalence pours forth. Women can be idolized only when their sphere of activity is carefully contained and their power scrupulously monitored. If it is true that fundamentalists are more strongly affected by the stresses of modern life than are some other types of Christians in the United States, then it should not be surprising that they exhibit higher levels of this ambivalence toward women. In fundamentalism, women are highly honored as mothers, but they are also forbidden the freedom to refuse this elevated role.

By preventing mothers from "murdering children," anti-abortion-ists are able to act decisively in the cause of restoring moral and social order; at the same time, they can also "save" themselves by demonstrating their righteousness. Furthermore, each successful "res-cue" serves as tangible proof of the power of Christian faith over the forces of sin and death. And when pro-life advocates expand their arena of action to include the heroic medical rescue of newborns with severe birth defects, as in the Baby Jane Doe case of 1983–1984, they reinforce the alliance between technological prowess and moral superiority that we have seen at work elsewhere. The rhetoric of the anti-abortion movement also strengthens the American world view at basic levels. Discussion of the fetus's "right to life" depends on seeing it as an individual in competition with its mother. So in at least one of its voices, the anti-abortion movement reinforces the traditional American values of individualism and competition.

Opposition to abortion is thus a supersaturated symbolic act— one that functions on many different levels. It addresses the troubling questions of social order and moral righteousness raised in the 1960s; it vents the energy of the more amorphous stresses of modernity; it makes the world feel safer at the deepest level by keeping women in their place; it meets a profound need for a personal and collective sense of competency and virtue; and it also reaffirms familiar theolog-ical and cultural tenets. All of this is at stake in the pro-life stance, even though anti-abortion activists claim it is a simple and clearcut matter of preventing murder.

Fundamentalism is a reactive social movement that uses theolog-ical justifications to control what its adherents perceive as threaten-ing in the world and to certify the moral probity of these adherents. Yet because the deeper motivations for feeling threatened are inacces-sible to direct control and even to consciousness, the specific arenas in which fundamentalists try to exercise control, such as the abortion issue, inevitably become overdetermined. The strong emotions raised in fundamentalists by issues like abortion, prayer in the public schools, and homosexuality—to mention only a few—indicate that much more is going on than meets the eye.

One great strength of religious systems is their ability to articu-late meaning in both verbal and nonverbal codes and thus to work in an integrated way with the full range of the conscious–unconscious spectrum that makes human beings what we are. While fundamental-ists naturally operate across this spectrum like everyone else, funda-mentalism implicitly claims that this need not be the case. Uncon-scious motives, deep longings, and fears are denied, and responsibility for them is abandoned, as fundamentalism makes a pretense of being all about cut-and-dried truth and clear and recognizable feelings. The magic and the mystery are gone from fundamentalist religion.

The repressed does not, however, disappear. It simply goes underground and emerges through oblique channels. This contributes to the high emotional charge on issues such as abortion and to the overdetermined nature of these religio-political issues in the contemporary scene. At the root of fundamentalism are a failure of nerve in the face of the complexity of life and a decision to make things cleaner and clearer, no matter what the cost. A general look at religion and how it functions in human life will offer greater insight into the impetus for religious fundamentalism, as well as into the convolutions to which it leads.

The Psychosocial Functions of Religion

"Our most important assets," according to Susanne Langer, "are always the symbols of our general *orientation* in nature, on the earth, in society, and in what we are doing: the symbols of our *Weltanschauung* and *Lebensanschauung*."[11] It is religion that provides us with these models of our world so that we may comprehend it, see it whole, and place ourselves within it. Langer speaks of such symbols as providing us with "safe unconscious orientation."[12]

The enormity of the task that religious symbols perform for us mandates that, to a significant extent, their mechanisms remain inaccessible to consciousness. Should reason be able to plumb the depths of our basic orienting symbols, we would feel the burden of responsibility for conscious choice in the smallest social exchange, the most seemingly insignificant interaction with our environment. Thus religion is somewhat like the inner ear: we need it for balance, but conscious control of its operations would rob us of the possibility of spontaneous and graceful movement. We would not, for example, be able to dance.

Clifford Geertz takes this point a step further, by suggesting that religion works in a way that is innately contrary to reason. Religions, says Geertz, have the unique characteristic of being not only models of reality, but also models for it:[13]

> Religion is never merely metaphysics. For all peoples the forms, vehicles, and objects of worship are suffused with an aura of deep moral seriousness. . . . Never merely metaphysics, religion is never merely ethics either. The source of its moral vitality is conceived to

lie in the fidelity with which it expresses the fundamental nature of reality. The powerfully coercive "ought" is felt to grow out of a comprehensive factual "is," and in such a way religion grounds the most specific requirements of human action in the most general contexts of human experience.[14]

In other words, Geertz suggests that "religious symbols formulate a basic congruence between a particular style of life and a specific . . . metaphysic, and in so doing sustain each with the borrowed authority of the other."[15]

Since the process by which an ethic and a world view authenticate one another does not take place in a vacuum, but in the midst of the push and pull of history, it inevitably results in an unending cycle of mutual readjustment between the "is" and the "ought"—the known and the felt. Current values are adjusted to reflect the authority of The Story; but the formative story can also be reinterpreted to reflect current values. To take a contemporary example, some Christians point to the creation narrative of Genesis 1 as proof that women ought to be subservient to men. Meanwhile other Christians, who support the equality of women, argue that the text has been mistranslated or misinterpreted.[16]

The whole of the maneuver Geertz describes by which religion generates meaning could be called an instance of "circular reasoning," and its two constituent steps also offend the standard rules of logic: in one, an "ought" is derived from an "is" (the so-called naturalistic fallacy); and in the other, the authority of the "is" is reinforced by the emotional energy of the "ought" (what some would call thinking contaminated by feeling). But religion is precisely not logical. The task of orienting us in the world compels religion toward symbols rather than rational constructs. Only symbolic forms of expression—narratives, images, rituals—are condensed enough to tie up worlds in small bundles and flexible enough to sustain myriad interpretations, thus holding together diverse peoples and enduring over long periods of time through processes of continual change. Religious symbol systems can thus direct human history without determining it. And while religions can be said to have enduring truths and values, neither remain exactly the same.

Geertz[17] and others have argued that, because human beings have only very generalized genetic programming, our symbol-making has come to play a central role in the survival of our species. As a species we have relatively few instincts or physical characteristics geared to survival. Human beings do not have claws, fangs, venom, or camouflage; nor do we have bodies covered in fur, scales, or feathers. And unlike other animals, we are born without genetic programming that tells us who our enemies are. It takes us years of experience and socialization to learn to recognize (or create) them—usually among our fellow human beings. *Homo sapiens* survives as a species only because some adults engage in long-term child care and because enough of us can, usually collectively, outsmart our enemies and the elements. We human beings endure because we are masters at making tools and symbols. Thus the creation of culture—and especially of rich religious symbol systems, through which particular groups communicate their views and values to the young while reinforcing them in people of all ages—can be understood as a human response to a lack of genetic programming. Geertz has suggested that we think of religion as something like external DNA.[18]

We human animals are furthermore engaged in constant, organically based exchange with our environment, and much of this process is simply unavailable to rational control. In the broader context of what Gregory Bateson calls "an ecology of mind," even the general category of consciousness shows itself to be only one, rather limited way in which human beings interact with the world. As has often been argued, we humans do create our own reality. But this is not because there is nothing out there beyond our minds; it is rather because we tend to focus on the world with a kind of purposive attention that gives back to us only information that speaks to our intentions and hypotheses. This problem has become particularly acute in an age mesmerized by scientism, the offspring of Enlightenment rationalism.

Bateson's criticism of Western medicine is instructive for what it says about the typical operation of consciousness. He says our medical knowledge is deeply flawed because it lacks a systemic understanding of the body in relation to its larger context. Medical researchers, he argues, have usually focused on particular diseases; and when they have found ways to cure them, they have taken their attention elsewhere. The result is a fragmented and distorted view of the body's functioning. Bateson concludes his discussion with this comment:

> The point . . . which I am trying to make . . . is not an attack on medical science but a demonstration of an inevitable fact: that mere purposive rationality unaided by such phenomena as art, religion, dream and the like, is necessarily pathogenic and destructive of life; and that its virulence springs specifically from the circumstance

that life depends upon interlocking *circuits* of contingency, while consciousness can see only such short arcs of such circuits as human purpose may direct.[19]

In the face of a chaotic, expanding world that traditional religions fail to comprehend adequately,[20] Enlightenment rationalism holds out the promise that reason can provide us with a model of the world that will allow us to see the meaning of the whole of things and, what is more, will allow us to direct our own fate within it. But this promise cannot be kept, because reason necessarily fails to appreciate the complexity of the task. Enlightenment rationalism posits a human being who is little more than a cerebral cortex separated from the rest of the brain, from the body as a whole, and from the environment in which it exists. Using reason alone to negotiate life fragments our sense of self and seriously limits our ability to engage fully with the world.

Fundamentalists sense the inadequacy of such a rationalistic view and fiercely defend their stake in religion. But they too misunderstand the task. Feeling out of control in the contemporary world, fundamentalists reject Enlightenment rationalism while continuing to imitate its drive for clarity and control. As a result they end up with religions whose form more nearly resembles constructs of reason than the multileveled, flexible symbol systems that both Geertz and Langer describe. Missing in fundamentalism is precisely the dimension of religion that appeals to our embodied selves and to aspects of mind that we share with other members of the animal kingdom.

What is at stake here is one of the most basic questions we can ask about ourselves as human beings: who are we? Are we cerebral masters of our environment, or are we embodied creatures enmeshed within it? This is a profound theological question, but for the moment we can respond to it most efficiently by looking at something quite tangible—the human brain.

Our brain did not evolve so much as it grew by a process of accretion. The reptilian brain is still with us, functioning as the human brain stem. In it is located the fight-flight response, a response that can be triggered by the claustrophobia of a traffic jam, as well as by a snarling predator. And it is not unlikely that, in the contemporary world, our reptilian brains sound their alarm repeatedly in the course of a more or less normal day. This is the deepest, most inchoate level at which we can feel the kind of stress that is characteristic of the contemporary age. This stress is inaccessible to reason,[21] but religious symbols, when functioning fully, can address such basic feelings of insecurity in the world. Exploring the power of the nonverbal dimensions of religious communication requires looking at the next oldest segment of the brain.

The limbic lobe (formerly called the "smell brain") is wrapped around the reptilian stem; in it is located a complex series of olfactory responses and sexual and feeding behaviors, as well as the capacities to nurture and to play. The well-known aural and visual richness of religious rituals is frequently augmented by the less differentiated, more primal experiences of touch,[22] taste, and smell associated with the limbic lobe. Laying on of hands, bathing, embracing; wine, honey, milk; hot pepper, incense, flowers—all become communicative in religious contexts. This gives us some rudimentary insight into the power of religion to make contact with the whole person, including deeper nonverbal aspects of ourselves.[23]

Consider this example from my own field research: a distraught client seeking healing from a Haitian Vodou priestess was given a bath of milk and herbs. The client was told to leave the infusion on her skin for a number of days. The woman later reported that, when she fell asleep with her head cradled on her arm, the crease in her elbow reeked of sour milk. She said she smelled "like a baby." For a long time, she could not get out of bed. She lay there, her body in a fetal position, and she cried. The Vodou healer did not seek through rational discourse to convince the woman that her world was not as precarious as it felt. Instead, through smell-memory, the healer took her client directly to a place of deep security so she could experience and ultimately contain her grief. A psychologist would call this regression in the service of the ego. A neurologist might call it the olfactory activation of infantile memories held in the part of our brains that we humans share with all other mammals—the limbic lobe. We can identify it as an example of the nonrational powers of religious communication.

Atop the limbic and reptilian brains rests the cerebral cortex with its massive, differentiated right and left lobes, the seats of various sorts of associations that we speak of as higher intelligence. This brain of ours, with its evolutionary strata, can also operate in integrated ways. For example, the limbic system is said to provide the "emotional drive" for activity in the cerebral cortex.[24] So the point is not that human beings are merely (or even primarily) animals responding to danger, while searching for sex, food, and security; it is that, whatever else we have added to ourselves as a species in the evolutionary process—and that is a lot—we have not left our embodied, animal selves behind.

Fundamentalism is characterized by the repression of these nonverbal and nonrational dimensions of human interaction with the environment. The moral code of fundamentalists tends to emphasize control of the body and its appetites, and particularly control of sexuality. Its theologies promise transcendence of various human limitations, including death. Fundamentalism characteristically distances and disguises human mortality. This tendency provides us with strong clues about the depth of the stress that occasions these religious movements, as well as the extent of the control exercised in an attempt to contain the stress. Fundamentalists' fear of mortality, and of the flesh in general, also directly fuels the need to control women.

Throughout most of the world, women play the role of designated "other" in sociocultural contexts defined by men, and thus they tend to carry the projections of all that is undesirable or threatening in human existence: sexuality, emotion, pollution, sin, and mortality.[25] All of these share a connection to the flesh, yet it is not immediately clear why our flesh should be such a threat. Since the physical body decays and finally dies, we might think that all negative attitudes toward the body boil down to fear of death. But this answer is too cerebral, according to Dinnerstein. She suggests that what we learn about the flesh in infancy is "incomparably deeper and denser, more immediate and vivid, than the abstract notion of nonexistence will ever be."[26]

The time of infancy is one of powerful bodily exchange between mother and infant. Solace, security, joy, pain, frustration, failure, and loss of control are all experiences encoded in the flesh—the flesh of the mother, of the child, and of the two in interaction. Dinnerstein argues that, since the ability to conceptualize our mortality comes later in life, by the time we begin to come to terms with it, what we learned about the flesh while "in the cradle" has already set the emotional tone for our encounter with death.[27] At some level we never forget what we learned about the flesh as infants: it can provide us with the deepest contentment we will ever know, but it can also betray us in the most profound way.

When the body proves unable to do what we want it to do (here the experiences of old age echo those of infancy), we come up hard against human limitation. And through the discipline of the mother, however gentle, we come face to face with the body's vulnerability to the tyranny of another.[28] Thus the same deep ambivalence that we saw at work in relation to women is also characteristic of our attitudes toward the flesh. But in the contemporary world, control issues loom so large that many of us have been willing to strike a fearsome bargain. We have chosen to deny and control the flesh. We have given up the contentment that is possible through the acceptance of our embodied selves, in order to preserve the appearance that we can master our world and contain our vulnerability. This is true of all of us to some extent and of fundamentalists to a great extent.

Yet even those who have struck this bargain must do something with the lingering fears and promises of the flesh, lest they disrupt our adult act. Since "it is the hand on the cradle that in fact shapes our feeling for the mortal flesh,"[29] our ambivalence about the flesh is already surrounded with the aura of a woman's presence. So we project this ambivalence about the flesh, with all its permutations, onto women in general; and then we carefully circumscribe the arena in which women's power operates. But again the price we pay for the gain in security is considerable: we severely limit women's freedom; and worse, we cut ourselves off from our bodies, from other embodied selves, and from our natural environment, while posturing as the masters of all three. The issue in the denial of the flesh, and in the control of women who bear the burden of human fleshliness for the entire species, is not death per se, but the larger issue that encompasses it: control.

Gender roles are the most basic building blocks of social organization. Gender roles, along with the important distinction between child and adult, are the social categories that the child learns first and that loom largest in the child's world. Firming up the boundaries by stressing the differences between these social domains thus re-creates the security and manageability of a child's world. Keeping women, about whom we have such deeply ambivalent feelings, clearly under the control of men makes the world seem more orderly and more comprehensible. With men at the helm, the power of the flesh is kept in its place. The clean, daylight powers of reason and spirit are in charge, and we all—men and women alike—at some level, feel safer. It should not be surprising, then, that so much of the fundamentalist agenda focuses on defining the roles and monitoring the behavior of women and children.

Fundamentalism Cross-culturally

Up to this point, I have been concerned with Christian fundamentalism in the United States, but in the process I have focused on dimensions of the story that serve, without denying the significance of local variations, to characterize fundamentalism around the globe. Religious fundamentalism is born in times and places where, for a variety of reasons, the world suddenly seems too complex to comprehend; and one's place in it, too precarious to provide genuine security.

One example is modern India, where the cult that developed around the recent immolation of a young woman on her husband's funeral pyre has been described as an instance of fundamentalism. In this volume John Hawley demonstrates that the background for the *sati* of Roop Kanwar was emerging Hindu nationalism in India augmented by a multitude of local destabilizing forces in Deorala, the site of the immolation. Furthermore, as Hawley and other authors have pointed out, Deorala is not a truly deprived area, and its residents are not traditionalists out of contact with the larger realities of modern India. I would therefore suggest, along with Hawley, that fundamentalism is not primarily a religion of the marginalized, as some have argued. Its more salient feature is that it develops among people caught off balance. Hence, fundamentalist groups often arise in situations where social, cultural, and economic power is up for grabs; many, like these groups now being referred to as Hindu fundamentalists, arise in postcolonial situations. Far from being essentially marginal to the societies in which they exist, fundamentalists are often directly involved in the political and economic issues of their time and place. And they often have a significant, if precarious, stake in them.

For the Rajputs in Deorala, traditional sources of pride and authority are being challenged by increasing contact with the cities of Jaipur and Delhi, and through them, all of India. These Rajputs are experiencing the disorientation of having to depend on economic and political systems beyond their control. Marwari merchants and industrialists, financial backers of the cult of the goddess Sati, are destabilized in another way. As their economic role expands throughout India, they risk their livelihood in a wider, less familiar, and less predictable world than the one in which earlier generations operated. The Marwari focus on the district around Jhunjhunu with its important Sati shrine gives them their emotionally saturated Archimedean point. The case of the Marwari businessmen suggests, even more directly than does that of the Rajputs, that fundamentalism is not a religion of the marginalized, but of the disoriented.

In the contemporary Indian context, rallying around the *sati* of Roop Kanwar (like anti-abortion activity in the United States) reasserts social control and demonstrates moral worth. It strengthens gender boundaries and provides an example of undiluted, innocent virtue that vicariously underwrites the virtue of Rajputs and Marwaris in general. Furthermore, as in the United States, insecurity about social control and moral rectitude is displaced onto the body of a woman. But in the *sati* ritual described by Hawley, the drive to kill the devouring, fleshly goddess and to enshrine the pure, spiritual one is much more painfully literal.

Both men and women attended the *sati* of Roop Kanwar, and both men and women subsequently revere her. At first glance this may seem difficult to understand, but the complicity of Indian women in the practice of *sati* has to be considered on more than one level. At the deepest level its explanation lies in the fear of women's will and women's flesh that men and women share, and in the relief that both feel when these forces are kept in check. But on another level there are explanations of a much more practical nature. Most Indian women's economic security heavily depends on marriage. A woman doing homage at a Sati shrine thus signals to her husband and to the world at large, as well as to herself, that she intends to be good and to do good, according to her society's standards. Thus she chooses to ignore any anger or fear she might feel about the practice, in the name of living a secure and ordered life. It is a herculean task for women to try to define the meaning and worth of their lives in terms different from those that prevail in their community. So some security can always be found in surrendering to, and even helping to strengthen, the accepted gender norms.

The situation of women in the New Religions of Japan is more complex. All the Japanese New Religions, regardless of when they began, exist now in a post-occupation context. Allied occupation forces rewrote the Japanese civil code, granting women more autonomy and removing any legal significance from the traditional *ie* or household. Thus all of the New Religions are dealing with significant and rapid social change, including changes in gender roles. Many of the leaders in the New Religions are women, and these women—like the men who have power in the same arenas—argue for renewed emphasis on the patriarchal *ie* and on women's submission to male power in general. Ironically, women leaders speak thus while profiting from a degree of personal and economic independence that would have been unthinkable when the *ie* reigned as the normative social unit. Helen Hardacre, in her essay in this volume, suggests that such women, like some of their American Christian fundamentalist counterparts, are unprepared to deal with the new freedoms women have in these two countries. Hardacre once remarked that these women engage in a denial of "the reality of fundamental social change . . . [and] seek to win at the old game by sacralizing the rules and playing them harder and harder."[30] Women's deep ambivalence about their own power makes this possible. These women may look like contortionists, but in some ways they have managed to construct a no-lose situation. Women leaders in fundamentalism get to exercise their power and their passion, while defining themselves as safe and submissive women.

In Japan and in the United States, unlike in India, fundamentalism has arisen in the context of recent and dramatic changes in gender roles. These changes have undoubtedly raised the general stress level in society, but they probably have not, in themselves, been responsible for the appearance of fundamentalism in either place. More important, both Japan and the United States have operated as international superpowers within the last century. Militarism speeds the process of encounter with the larger world and raises expectations about the possibility of controlling that world. Even though Japan experienced defeat and occupation, it now manages to exercise wide-ranging power through business and industry. Both Japan and the United States are enmeshed in a recently expanded world too complex to negotiate with moral certainty. Many Americans and Japanese have apparently found the moral questions of the contemporary age too troubling to let lie. Fundamentalists in both places resist the view that amorphous forces, such as those of the market or of politics, control their lives. And in both places fundamentalists tend to make a strong argument for the individual's control over his or her own salvation—an argument that receives less stress among Indian fundamentalists. Yet in all three countries, people seem to be turning to religion to get their bearings in the world, hopeful that religion can tell them who they are within it.

If fundamentalism were no more than a religious response to profoundly disorienting stress, examples of it could be found throughout human history. But the attempt to control this stress through various strategies of rationalization—including technological ones—makes fundamentalism a child of the late Enlightenment.

Outside the Western world, the enemy is most often Euro-American political and cultural hegemony, an isomorph of Enlightenment rationalism. Scholars sought to comprehend a disorderly and threatening world by classifying and systematizing its contents. Imperialist and other occupying armies, as well as colonial administrators, did the same. Individualism, liberal values, sophisticated technology, rapid communication, and rationalized and centralized bureaucracies have reached much of the world through the agency of a hovering Western presence from which they cannot be separated. This makes for a complex situation. "Modernity" is despised because it is Western, but simultaneously it is embraced because it is powerful. Its power resides not only in technological competence and bureaucratic efficiency but also in the *Weltanschauung* and *Lebensanschauung* that underlie them. In the midst of an expanding and confusing world, the promise of this degree of clarity and control is difficult to renounce.

So when it is expedient or even necessary to reject things Western, the form in which their promise is conveyed can be retained and transformed in local, directly religious terms. Then begins the process of defining the whole and placing the self within it. Again, this is an operation central to all religions; what is distinctive about fundamentalist forms of religion is the powerful need adherents exhibit to possess an unchanging truth and to control their fate within the whole of which they are a part.[31]

It has often been suggested that reverting to the authority of the past and emphasizing the centrality of scripture are defining characteristics of fundamentalist religion. I would prefer to point to a broader category. The need for an Archimedean point is definitive of fundamentalism. Divine revelation is one way of establishing that point, and the existence of sacred texts nails it down nicely, but revelation of a more recent and even nontextual form can meet the same need.

In this vein let me suggest the Rastafarian movement in Jamaica as an example of fundamentalism. The Rastafarians have no sacred text, except insofar as certain very select passages of the Bible are used to authenticate the movement. But divine revelation occurs through dream, vision, and trance (the latter assisted by the use of marijuana). The control of women—the covering of their bodies, the limitation of their activity to the domestic sphere, and the prohibition against birth control—is also present. The Rastafarians are currently significant players in postcolonial Jamaican politics, a situation in which power is clearly "up for grabs." Rastafarians furthermore claim a moral high ground that is set in contrast to the immorality of "Babylon," their term for Western-style modernity. Yet their participation in the visual arts, music, and politics makes them consumers of technology and information on a scale only possible in the modern world.[32] In all these respects the Rastafarians look very much like other fundamentalists we have been surveying, especially in their attitudes toward women. The relative absence of an appeal to "the fundamentals" of a prominent text does not disqualify them from belonging to the wider set. Rather, it points to the fact that the doctrine of scriptural inerrancy among "book-oriented" fundamentalist groups is really only a particular expression of the Archimedean instinct shared by all.

The Seductive Promise of Enlightenment Rationalism

We scholars have trouble thinking clearly about fundamentalists because we often fail to recognize that we swim in the same ideological stew they do. We are all creatures of the late Enlightenment. These last decades of the millennium are an especially confusing period, one in which a major shift in consciousness is taking place; and from where we sit, the outcome appears uncertain. Scholarly circles entertain increasing doubt about the usefulness, or even the possibility, of operating out of pure reason and objectivity. Academics are no longer confident that thought can be neatly separated from feeling or from the social location of the thinker. In the larger world, moreover, we are coming to doubt that the science and technology born of these revered mental operations can solve the human problems we once thought they could. So on the one hand we are beginning to question profoundly the assumptions of the Enlightenment, while on the other the very products of Enlightenment attitudes—technology, bureaucratic organization, and fundamentalist religions—are asserting their control over our lives more strongly than ever. We scholars are threatened by the loss of our own Archimedean point, although we usually reject the artificial reassertion of that unchanging point of truth that fundamentalists embrace. So we tend to stress the differences between ourselves and the fundamentalists[33] and to suppress the similarities. Considering these similarities helps significantly in clarifying the situation.

While fundamentalism was taking shape in the United States, intellectuals throughout the Western world were becoming increasingly professionalized and specialized. During this period, scholars tried to dispel the felt disorder of the world in a manner not unrelated to the maneuverings of fundamentalists. They tried to control the chaos by showing it to be the result of forces that could be described systematically and analyzed rationally.

This was the era of megatheory—the time of thinkers such as Durkheim and Freud, as well as the period during which Marxist thinkers were making their ideology a major force in the world political arena. These particular heirs of Enlightenment rationalism are especially relevant to our discussion because each felt it necessary, in the process of constructing his theory, to expose a grand deception at the heart of religion.

Marx, Durkheim, and Freud all saw themselves as building rational models of the world that could, in principle, replace religion. Each offered a comprehensive theory intended to function as a system of basic orientation in the world. Their writings are thus good examples of the seductive power of Enlightenment rationalism.

Scholars such as Marx, Durkheim, and Freud felt certain that they could construct (to adopt Geertz's language) an adequate "model of" life. The more troubling issue was the "model for" dimension— morality. To their credit, all three of these master theoreticians recognized the significance of the issue. Each was concerned, in his own way, with social order and with the way in which values would be generated and protected once societies had outgrown religion, a development they thought inevitable. Their solutions to this dilemma share a common feature. Not surprisingly, all three men wanted to raise value negotiation to the level of consciousness and to exercise more control over it. For Marx, false consciousness was the instrument of oppression, and justice could not prevail until, through a combination of thinking and acting, people became clear—that is, conscious—about the real nature of the economic relations that determined their lives. Freud conceptualized the unconscious and recognized its power in shaping behavior (and in that way made a great contribution to our understanding of ourselves), but he defined its contents as repressed materials and devised a therapeutic model that depended on bringing them to consciousness. Durkheim, who advocated a system of education in values that amounted to straightforward social indoctrination, was perhaps the least insightful on this issue.[34] These three thinkers stand here as examples—and to a great extent determiners—of the Enlightenment intellectual tradition in which we contemporary scholars work. It is a tradition that naively trusts in the capacity of reason to deal with the full range of human life.

For contemporary scholars, trying to think about fundamentalism is a bit like being lost in a hall of mirrors. The process is confusing because, at least in the contemporary Western world, scholars of religion and religious fundamentalists often adopt the same epistemological style, one that claims access to universal, ahistorical truths. Scholars share with many fundamentalists a tendency to invest texts with great authority. Furthermore, in both the Religious

Studies classroom and the fundamentalist pulpit, things religious tend to be enumerated, codified and, above all, made clear. Thus both groups engage in the pretense of being fully in control of what we deal with. Scholars and fundamentalists both operate with a view of self that stresses consciousness and discipline, while denying that deep hungers, fears, and needs influence our search for meaning. We also have other, more subtle matters in common: we are both hierarchically organized; we jealously guard our boundaries; we quibble over whom we will admit to membership; and we make neophytes go through more or less elaborate initiation rites. Most important, scholars and fundamentalists alike are currently threatened by the potential breakdown of their hegemonic world views.

A recent sign of such a threat in the academy is the postmodernist critique. By deconstructing texts and situating subjects, postmodernists expose the power plays behind claims to transcendent reason. Yet even these intrepid critics can fail to escape the scholarly imperialism they criticize. For some, the very absoluteness of their naysaying reveals a last-gasp bid for an intellectual Archimedean point and thus for transcendence of the human condition.

Just as reason has failed to provide us with a single coherent and authoritative view of the world, so Western cultural and technological dominance has failed to bring prosperity and to transcend diversity on either a domestic or a global scale. And around the globe religious fundamentalists, like some postmodernist critics, reach for absolutes and thereby unwittingly imitate what they seek to discredit. This is emphasized here to call attention to the crossfire of projections that occurs when scholars and fundamentalists describe one another. But stress in scholarly and religious circles is only part of a much larger picture.

The Failed Promise of Enlightenment Rationalism

Modern communications, transnational economic pressures, and wars waged from the opposite side of the globe have brought many populations intimate knowledge of the vastness and complexity of their worlds. In the late twentieth century, the others in relation to whom we must define ourselves are more available to our experience and imagination than ever before; yet few if any of us have a satisfactory model for understanding ourselves within this complex, stressful world.

We all live in and are defined by a world too big and unstable for intellect or belief to comprehend, and we all react to intimations—as well as a few pieces of hard evidence[35]—of the failed promise of the Enlightenment. Academics, politicians, and ordinary folk the world over are immersed in this challenge and most commonly react to it (as fundamentalists do) by assuming that, with sufficient effort, the chaos can be first comprehended and then managed. In this way fundamentalists are simply extreme versions of the rest of us.

An emphasis on the control of women is characteristic of fundamentalism, but there is some of it everywhere in the world. The anti-abortion movement in the United States arises out of a much broader context in which, among other signals of misogyny, public power and authority have been denied to women for centuries. And the Sati cult could not have become an issue in Indian nationalism if in general Indian women were not seen as sources of pollution as well as of blessing—as a result of which they have been subject to a variety of social controls through the ages. When the mind and the spirit are cut off from the body, women become magnets for the fear raised by everything in life that seems out of control. The degree to which control is exercised over women is therefore a key to the profundity of stresses felt by most persons and groups. Fundamentalism is a product of extreme social stress.

Religion, whose primary function is to provide a comprehensible model of the world and to locate the individual safely and meaningfully within it, is an obvious place for this type of stress to express itself and seek redress. But as long as religions deal with this stress by positing a world that can be directly known, and in which it is possible to determine one's own fate, they only reinforce the controlling tendencies of Enlightenment rationalism and do nothing to move us beyond it to whatever comes next. We should be suspicious of any religion that claims too much certainty or draws the social boundaries too firmly. In this period marked by the gradual breakdown of Enlightenment rationalism and Euro-American hegemony in the world, something more is necessary. We need help in accepting ourselves as organic creatures enmeshed in our world rather that continuing to posture as cerebral masters granted dominion over it. This requires that we learn to trust the wisdom of our mute flesh and accept the limitations inherent in our humanity. If we could do this, it would radically diminish our scapegoating of women and all the other "others" who provide a convenient screen on which to project fears.

The resurgence of religion that we are experiencing at the turn of this millennium should not be viewed in an entirely negative light. If any system of orientation in the world can help us now, it seems likely to be a religious one. There is no small comfort in knowing that, as the grand ambitions spawned by the Enlightenment falter in the present age, what is likely to emerge is not what several generations of social scientists predicted. It is not civilization marching toward increasing secularization and rationalization. What is slowly being revealed is the hubris of reason's pretense in trying to take over religion's role.

Notes

1. From the beginning of the anti-abortion movement to the present, opinion polls have consistently shown that the majority of people in the United States favor a woman's right to have an abortion.

2. Some Vietnamese mothers later admitted that they claimed their own children were orphans so that they would be taken on the rescue flights and have a chance for a better life in the United States.

3. In the United States before the mid-nineteenth century, anti-abortion sentiment, in any sense of concern for the life of the fetus, was not an issue of any significant import, in either the public or the religious arena. Before that it was ignored in the law. In the Christian tradition, furthermore, abortion was until recently opposed primarily because it was a means of birth control that could disguise women's infidelity.

National anti-abortion laws came into being in the United States in the middle of the nineteenth century as a result of agitation from the newly founded American Medical Association, a group that sought to professionalize the practice of medicine and make it the province of men only. Part of this effort involved delegitimating the competition—midwives. This challenge to midwives prompted national laws against abortion.

An epidemic of German measles in the years 1962–1965, during which thousands of pregnant women who contracted the disease were unable to obtain abortions, resulted in the birth of approximately 15,000 deformed infants and helped create the context of public opinion that underlay the 1973 *Roe* v. *Wade* Supreme Court decision that legalized abortion. Shortly after that, the anti-abortion movement began. See Beverly Wildung Harrison, *Our Right to Choose: Toward a New Ethic of Abortion* (Boston: Beacon Press, 1983), especially pp. 232–33; also Barbara Ehrenreich and Deirdre English, *Witches, Midwives and Nurses: A History of Women Healers* (Old Westbury, N.Y.: Feminist Press, 1973).

4. Betty A. DeBerg, *Ungodly Women: Gender and the First Wave of American Fundamentalism* (Minneapolis: Fortress Press, 1990), has an excellent discussion of the general changes—and particularly the changes in women's roles—attendant to the formation of fundamentalism in the United States. See also Randall Balmer's essay in this volume.

5. Often the only kind of control that fundamentalists can exercise

over a chaotic and threatening world rests in their claim to have a privileged understanding of the deeper meaning of the chaos. Fundamentalists who engage in "end-time" thinking thus sometimes find themselves in the position of welcoming the signs of modern social decay because these signal the approach of the time when God will call home the chosen few.

6. Dorothy Dinnerstein, in *The Mermaid and the Minotaur: Sexual Arrangements and the Human Malaise* (New York: Harper & Row, 1976), argues that many of the ills of the world could be addressed most directly by increasing the participation of men in childrearing. This, she says, would not do away with the vulnerability of infancy, but it would have the effect of spreading the resulting adult vulnerabilities more evenly across the two genders.

7. Dinnerstein, *The Mermaid and the Minotaur*, p. 131.

8. Ibid., p. 161.

9. Ibid.

10. Ibid.

11. Susanne Langer, *Philosophy in a New Key* (New York: New American Library, 1951), pp. 241–42. Emphasis in original.

12. Ibid.

13. Clifford Geertz, "Religion as a Cultural System," in Geertz, *The Interpretation of Cultures* (New York: Basic Books, 1973), pp. 87ff.

14. Geertz, "Ethos, World View, and the Analysis of Sacred Symbols," in Geertz, *The Interpretation of Cultures*, p. 126.

15. Geertz, "Religion as a Cultural System," p. 90.

16. This is what contemporary biblical scholars call the hermeneutical circle.

17. Geertz, "Religion as a Cultural System," pp. 92–93.

18. "As the order of bases in a strand of DNA forms a coded program, a set of instructions, or a recipe, for the synthesis of the structurally complex proteins which shape organic functioning, so culture patterns provide such programs for the institution of the social and psychological processes which shape public behavior." Geertz, "Religion as a Cultural System," p. 92.

19. Gregory Bateson, *Steps to an Ecology of Mind* (New York: Ballentine Books, 1972), p. 146. Emphasis in original.

20. Western imperialism led the way to global awareness and thus laid the groundwork for the greatest spiritual challenge the human species has faced so far. Without denying the economic and political motives behind the Christian missionary enterprise, I want to note the significance of the theological task it faced. If religion is the repository of the symbols that orient us within the world, then, as our world expands, so must our religions' ability to comprehend that world and to place us—individuals and communities—meaningfully within it. But Western Christianity, arguably the first religion to face the challenge of developing a truly global world view, proved unequal to the task.

Backed by the imperial apparatus of the countries that sent them, Christian missionaries dealt with the expanding world by claiming the universal truth of their own particular perspective, and they naturally turned to Enlightenment scholarship to authenticate their claims to racial, cultural, and moral superiority. Throughout Africa, Asia, and the Pacific islands, conversion became the issue, as it did among African slaves and Native Americans. Conversion is not an expansion, but simply a change of world view. Rather than locating individuals and groups within a more complex global context, Christian missionaries demanded that converts choose sides. And thus the challenge of comprehension slid easily into one of domination.

21. "The data suggest that the brain is arranged so key aspects of emotional life, like primitive fears, can operate largely independent of thought. This arrangement may explain why certain emotional reactions, like phobias, are so tenacious despite their obvious irrationality. It may also explain other baffling facts of emotional life, such as why troubling experiences from life's earliest years can have such powerful effects decades later." Daniel Goleman, "Brain's Design Emerges as a Key to Emotions," *New York Times*, August 15, 1989.

22. While "passing the peace," Christians shake hands, embrace, and sometimes kiss. The sense of touch that human beings find so meaningful in these contexts is as widely shared among living creatures as anything we humans can experience.

"Traditionally, feeling is our fifth sense; it should be counted as first. It has come down to us, little changed, from remote, primitive ancestors—coelenterates and low worms—who relied on it almost entirely. It is the last form of awareness to fade in the twilight of sleep or anesthesia and the first to reemerge. It is indeed primal." H. Chandler Elliot, *The Shape of Intelligence* (New York: Charles Scribner's Sons, 1969), p. 100.

23. A concise, accessible introduction to the functioning of the brain is found in Gary G. Tunnell, *Culture and Biology: Becoming Human*, Basic Concepts in Anthropology Series (Minneapolis: Burgess Publishing, 1973).

24. Elliot, *The Shape of Intelligence*, p. 232. Only recently have researchers begun to appreciate the interdependency of thought and feeling. See also "'Emotional-Perceptive Cycling' a Link Between Limbic System and New Brain," in Marilyn Ferguson (ed. and pub.), *Brain/Mind Bulletin* 7(6) (March 8, 1982).

25. Simone de Beauvoir made this point first and, perhaps still, most eloquently. See *The Second Sex* (New York: Alfred A. Knopf, 1952), pp. xvi–xviii.

26. Dinnerstein, *The Mermaid and the Minotaur*, p. 128.

27. Ibid., p. 136.

28. Cf. Dinnerstein, *The Mermaid and the Minotaur*, p. 166.

29. Dinnerstein, *The Mermaid and the Minotaur*, p. 128.

30. Helen Hardacre, "Japanese Fundamentalism," paper presented to the Barnard and Columbia Religion Departments' faculty seminar on fundamentalism, New York, April 17, 1989, p. 33.

31. Perceiving this depends on understanding that different groups draw the circumference of their operative "world" in different ways. For Rajputs and Marwaris who support the Sati cult, the whole is "Hindu India"; for the protesters of the Shah Bano verdict, the whole is more likely to be worldwide Islam.

32. Cf. Maureen Rowe, "The Woman in Rastafari," *Caribbean Quarterly*, monograph (Kingston, Jamaica: University of the West Indies, 1985); and Diane J. Austin-Broos, "Pentecostals and Rastafarians: Cultural, Political and Gender Relations of Two Religious Movements," *Social and Economic Studies* 36(4)(1987): 1–38.

33. In their introduction to this volume, John Hawley and Wayne Proudfoot refer to this characteristic as "them" and "us" thinking.

34. See Emile Durkheim, *On Morality and Society* (Chicago: University of Chicago Press, 1973).

35. The growing ecological crisis is one of the most tangible pieces of this evidence; it also reinforces the point that reason alone is an insufficient problem-solving tool, because we are incapable of holding in consciousness the full range of the interconnectedness of things.

Bibliography

Abedi, Mehdi, tr. *Zendigi-Nameh Imam Khomeini*. Tehran: Fifteenth of Khordad Publishers, n.d.

Aḥad Ha-am. "Torah she-balev." *Al Parashat Derakhim*. Berlin: Jüdischer Verlag, 1921.

Arendt, Hannah. *The Origins of Totalitarianism*. New York: Harcourt, Brace, Jovanovich, 1973.

Arjomand, Said Amir. "Iran's Islamic Revolution in Comparative Perspective." *World Politics* 38(3) (1986): 383–414.

Austin-Broos, Diane J. "Pentecostals and Rastafarians: Cultural, Political and Gender Relations of Two Religious Movements." *Social and Economic Studies* 36(4) (1987): 1–38.

Balmer, Randall. *Mine Eyes Have Seen the Glory: A Journey into the Evangelical Subculture in America*. New York: Oxford University Press, 1989.

Banwari. "*Nar-nārī Saṁbandh* [The Connection between Man and Woman]." *Jansattā*, September 29 to October 1, 1987.

Barr, James. *Fundamentalism*. London: SCM Press, 1977.

Bartal, Israel. "'Ost' and 'West': Varieties of Jewish Enlightenment." Paper presented to the conference "*Tradition and Crisis* Revisited." Harvard University, October 11–12, 1988.

Bateson, Gregory. *Steps to an Ecology of Mind*. New York: Ballentine Books, 1972.

Bauman, Zygmunt. *Modernity and the Holocaust*. Ithaca, N.Y.: Cornell University Press, 1989.

Beecher, Catharine E. *A Treatise on Domestic Economy, for the Use of Young Ladies at Home, and at School*. Boston: March, Capen, Lyon, and Webb, 1841.

Beecher, Catharine E., and Harriet Beecher Stowe. *The American Woman's*

*Home; or, Principles of Domestic Science; Being a Guide to the Forma-
tion and Maintenance of Economical Healthful Beautiful and Christian
Homes.* New York: J. B. Ford, 1869.

Bhasin, Kamla, and Ritu Menon. "The Problem." *Seminar* 342 (February
1988): 12–13.

Bhushan, Shashi. *Fundamentalism, a Weapon Against Human Aspirations.*
New Delhi: National Convention of Secularism, 1986.

Bjorkman, James Warner, ed. *Fundamentalism, Revivalists, and Violence in
South Asia.* Riverdale, Md.: Riverdale, 1988.

Blumenberg, Hans. *The Legitimacy of the Modern Age.* Cambridge, Mass.:
MIT Press, 1983.

_____. *Work on Myth.* Translated by Robert M. Wallace. Cambridge, Mass.:
MIT Press, 1985.

Boone, Kathleen. *The Bible Tells Them So.* Albany, N.Y.: SUNY Press, 1989.

Boswell, John. *The Kindness of Strangers: The Abandonment of Children in
Western Europe from Late Antiquity to the Renaissance.* New York:
Pantheon Books, 1988.

Brandt, Edward M. "Mother." *The Way of Truth* 47 (May 1989): [ii]–1.

Bumiller, Elisabeth. *May You Be the Mother of a Hundred Sons: A Journey
Among the Women of India.* New York: Random House, 1990.

Bynum, Caroline Walker; Stevan Harrell; and Paula Richman, eds. *Gender
and Religion: On the Complexity of Symbols.* Boston: Beacon Press,
1986.

Candland, Christopher, ed. *The Spirit of Violence: An Annotated Interdisci-
plinary Bibliography on Religion and Violence.* New York: Harry Frank
Guggenheim Foundation, 1992.

Caplan, Lionel, ed. *Studies in Religious Fundamentalism.* Albany, N.Y.:
SUNY Press, 1987.

Carlebach, Elisheva. *The Pursuit of Heresy.* New York: Columbia University
Press, 1990.

Carstairs, Morris. *The Twice-Born.* Bloomington, Ind.: Indiana University
Press, 1967.

Chavel, C., ed. *Kitve Ramban.* Jerusalem: Mossad Harav Kook, 1965.

Chodorow, Nancy. *The Reproduction of Mothering: Psychoanalysis and the
Sociology of Gender.* Berkeley: University of California Press, 1978.

Cohen, Norman J., ed. *The Fundamentalist Phenomenon.* Grand Rapids,
Mich.: William B. Eerdmans, 1990.

Coleridge, Samuel T. *Confessions of an Inquiring Spirit.* Ed. by H. S. Hart.
Stanford, Calif.: Stanford University Press, 1957.

de Beauvoir, Simone. *The Second Sex.* Translated and edited by H. M. Parshley. New York: Alfred A. Knopf, 1957.

DeBerg, Betty A. *Ungodly Women: Gender and the First Wave of American
Fundamentalism.* Minneapolis: Fortress Press, 1990.

Dessouki, Ali E., ed. *Islamic Resurgence in the Arab World.* New York:
Praeger, 1982.

de Tocqueville, Alexis. *Democracy in America*. Trans. by Henry Reeve; ed. by Henry Steele Commager. New York: Oxford University Press, 1947.

Deville, Tammy. "Praying Mothers." *The Way of Truth* 47 (May 1989): 2.

Dhagamvar, Vasudha. "Saint, Victim or Criminal." *Seminar* 342 (February 1988): 34–39.

Dickey, Laurence. *Hegel: Religion, Economics, and the Politics of Spirit, 1770–1807*. Cambridge: Cambridge University Press, 1987.

Dinnerstein, Dorothy. *The Mermaid and the Minotaur: Sexual Arrangements and the Human Malaise*. New York: Harper & Row, 1976.

Dobson, James. "Dr. Dobson Answers Your Questions." *Focus on the Family* 13 (May 1989): 8.

Dodd, Peter C. "Family Honor and the Forces of Change in Arab Society." *Middle East Studies* 4 (1973): 40–54.

Douglas, Ann. *The Feminization of American Culture*. New York: Alfred A. Knopf, 1977.

Dowey, Edward, Jr. *The Knowledge of God in Calvin's Theology*. New York: Columbia University Press, 1952.

Durkheim, Emile. *On Morality and Society*. Chicago: University of Chicago Press, 1973.

Ehrenreich, Barbara, and Deidre English. *Witches, Midwives and Nurses: A History of Women Healers*. Old Westbury, N.Y.: Feminist Press, 1973.

Elliot, H. Chandler. *The Shape of Intelligence*. New York: Charles Scribner's Sons, 1969.

Engineer, Asghar Ali. *The Shah Bano Controversy*. Bombay: Orient Longman, 1987.

_____. *Status of Women in Islam*. New Delhi: Ajanta Publications, 1987.

Epstein, Klaus. *The Genesis of German Conservatism*. Princeton, N.J.: Princeton University Press, 1966.

Esposito, John L., ed. *Voices of Resurgent Islam*. New York: Oxford University Press, 1983.

Ferguson, Marilyn. "'Emotional-Perceptive Cycling' a Link Between Limbic System and New Brain." *Brain/Mind Bulletin* 7(6) (1982).

FitzGerald, Frances. "A Disciplined, Charging Army." *New Yorker* (May 18, 1981): 53–141.

Flake, Carol. *Redemptorama: Culture, Politics, and the New Evangelicalism*. Garden City, N.Y.: Anchor Press, 1984.

Geertz, Clifford. *The Interpretation of Cultures*. New York: Basic Books, 1973.

Goleman, Daniel. "Brain's Design Emerges as a Key to Emotions." *New York Times*. August 15, 1989, C1.

Graham, Sylvester. *A Treatise on Bread, and Bread-Making*. Boston: Light & Stearns, 1837.

Guha, Ranajit, ed. *Subaltern Studies II*. Delhi: Oxford University Press, 1983.

Gupta, Sanjukta, and Richard Gombrich. "Another View of Widow-Burning and Womanliness in India." *Journal of Commonwealth and Comparative Politics* 22(3) (1984): 252–58.

Haddad, Yvonne, and Ellison Banks Findly, eds. *Women, Religion, and Social Change.* Albany, N.Y.: SUNY Press, 1985.

Hardacre, Helen. *Kurozumikyô and the New Religions of Japan.* Princeton, N.J.: Princeton University Press, 1986.

Harlan, Lindsey. *Religion and Rajput Women: The Ethic of Protection in Contemporary Narratives.* Berkeley: University of California Press, 1992.

Harrison, Beverly. *Our Right to Choose: Toward a New Ethic of Abortion.* Boston: Beacon Press, 1983.

Hawley, John Stratton, ed. *Sati, the Blessing and the Curse: The Burning of Wives in India.* New York: Oxford University Press, 1994.

———, ed. *Saints and Virtues.* Berkeley: University of California Press, 1987.

Hawley, John Stratton, and Donna Marie Wulff, eds. *The Divine Consort: Rādhā and the Goddesses of India.* Boston: Beacon Press, 1986.

Herder, J. G. *Sämmtliche Werke.* Edited by B. Suphan. Berlin: Weichmannsche Buchhandlung, 1871.

Hobsbawm, Eric, and Terence Ranger, eds. *The Invention of Tradition.* Cambridge: Cambridge University Press, 1983.

Iggers, Georg G. *The German Conception of History.* Middletown, Conn.: Wesleyan University Press, 1983.

Jai, Janak Raj. *Shah Bano.* New Delhi: Rajiv Publications, 1986.

Jakobovics, Benziyon. *Zekhor Yemot Olam.* Bnei Brak: Yeshivat Ohel Yosef, 1987.

Joshi, V. C., ed. *Rammohun Roy and the Process of Modernization in India.* Delhi: Vikas, 1975.

Jones, Kenneth W. "*Ham Hindū Nahīn*: Arya–Sikh Relations, 1877–1905," *Journal of Asian Studies* 32(3) (1973): 457–75.

Juergensmeyer, Mark. *The New Cold War?: Religious Nationalism Confronts the Secular State.* Berkeley: University of California Press, 1993.

———. *Religion as Social Vision.* Berkeley: University of California Press, 1982.

Juster, Susan. "'In a Different Voice': Male and Female Narratives of Religious Conversion in Post-Revolutionary America." *American Quarterly* 41 (March 1989): 34–62.

Kakar, Sudhir. *The Inner World.* Delhi: Oxford University Press, 1981.

Kane, P. V. *History of Dharmaśāstra.* Vol. 2. Pune: Bhandarkar Oriental Research Institute, 1974.

Katz, Jacob. "Die Entstehung der Judenassimilation und deren Ideologie." *Zur Assimilation und Emanzipation der Jüden.* Darmstadt: Wissenschaftliche Buchgesellschaft, 1982.

———. "Religion as a Uniting and Dividing Force in Modern Jewish History." In Katz, ed., *The Role of Religion in Modern Jewish History* (Cambridge, Mass.: Association for Jewish Studies, 1975), pp. 1–17.

Kaushik, Susheela, ed. *Women's Oppression: Patterns and Perspectives*. New Delhi: Shakti Books, 1985.

Keller, Bill. "Soviet Muslims Seek Leader's Ouster." *New York Times*, February 6, 1989, A3.

Kishwar, Madhu, and Ruth Vanita. "The Burning of Roop Kanwar." *Manushi* 42–43 (1987): 15–25.

Kondylis, Panajotis. *Die Aufklärung*. Stuttgart: Klett-Cotta, 1981.

Kraemer, David, ed. *The Jewish Family: Metaphor and Memory*. New York: Oxford University Press, 1989.

Krishna Iyer, V. R. *Justice V. R. Krishna Iyer on the Muslim Woman (Protection of Rights on Divorce) Act, 1986*. Lucknow: Eastern Book Co., 1987.

Kugel, James. *The Idea of Biblical Poetry*. New Haven, Conn.: Yale University Press, 1979.

Kurtz, Stanley N. *All the Mothers Are One: Hindu India and the Cultural Reshaping of Psychoanalysis*. New York: Columbia University Press, 1992.

Langer, Suzanne. *Philosophy in a New Key*. New York: New American Library, 1951.

Laqueur, Thomas. *Making Sex: Body and Gender from the Greeks through Freud*. Cambridge, Mass.: Harvard University Press, 1990.

Lateef, Shahida. *Muslim Women in India: Political and Private Realities 1890s–1980s*. London and Atlantic Highlands, N.J.: Zed Books, 1990.

Lawrence, Bruce B. *Defenders of God: The Fundamentalist Revolt Against the Modern Age*. San Francisco: Harper & Row, 1989.

Lazarus-Yafeh, Hava. "Contemporary Fundamentalism—Judaism, Christianity, Islam." *The Jerusalem Quarterly* 47 (1988): 27–39.

Leslie, I. Julia. "Suttee or *Satī*: Victim or Victor?" *Bulletin of the Center for the Study of World Religions, Harvard University* 14(2) (1988): 13–20. Reprinted in Leslie, ed., *Roles and Rituals for Hindu Women* (Rutherford, N.J.: Fairleigh Dickinson Press, 1991), pp. 175–91.

Levinson, Pnina Nave. *Einführung in die rabbinische Theologie*. Darmstadt: Wissenschaftliche Buchgesellschaft, 1982.

Lewis, Jan. "The Republican Wife: Virtue and Seduction in the Early Republic." *William & Mary Quarterly* 3d series, 44 (October 1987): 689–721.

Liebes, Yehudah. "The Ultra-Orthodox Community and the Dead Sea Sect." *Jerusalem Studies in Jewish Thought* 3 (1982): 137–52.

Lustick, Ian. *For the Land and the Lord: Jewish Fundamentalism in Israel*. New York: Council on Foreign Relations, 1988.

———. "Israel's Dangerous Fundamentalists." *Foreign Policy* 68 (1987): 118–39.

Lutgendorf, Philip. *The Life of a Text: Performing the Rāmcaritmānas of Tulsidas*. Berkeley: University of California Press, 1991.

Luz, Ehud. *Parallels Meet*. Philadelphia: Jewish Publication Society, 1989.

Maitra, Sunil. *Muslim Women's Act: Deathknell of Secularism*. New Delhi: Natural Book Centre, 1986.

Majumdar, Ranjani, et al. "Burning Embers" [videotape]. New Delhi: Media-storm, 1987.

Mani, Lata. "Contentious Traditions: The Debate on SATI in Colonial India." *Cultural Critique* (Fall 1987): 119–56. Reprinted in K. Sangari and S. Vaid, eds., *Recasting Women: Essays in Colonial History* (New Delhi: Kali for Women, 1988), pp. 88–126.

———. "Multiple Mediations: Feminist Scholarship in the Age of Multinational Reception." *Feminist Review* 35 (1990): 24–41.

Marsden, George. *Fundamentalism and American Culture*. New York: Oxford University Press, 1980.

Marty, Martin E., and R. Scott Appleby, eds. *Accounting for Fundamentalisms: The Dynamic Character of Movements*. Chicago: University of Chicago Press, forthcoming.

———, eds. *Fundamentalisms and Society: Reclaiming the Sciences, the Family, and Education*. Chicago: University of Chicago Press, 1993.

———. *Fundamentalisms and the State: Remaking Polities, Economies, and Militance*. Chicago: University of Chicago Press, 1993.

McDannell, Colleen. *The Christian Home in Victorian America, 1840–1900*. Bloomington, Ind.: Indiana University Press, 1986.

McGee, Mary. "Desired Fruits: Motives and Intention in the Votive Rites of Hindu Women." In I. Julia Leslie, ed., *Roles and Rituals for Hindu Women* (Rutherford, N.J.: Fairleigh Dickinson University Press, 1991), pp. 71–88.

———. "Feasting and Fasting: The Vrata Tradition and Its Significance for Hindu Women." Th. D. dissertation, Harvard Divinity School, 1987.

McGloughlin, William, Jr. *Billy Sunday Was His Real Name*. Chicago: University of Chicago Press, 1955.

Menon, Meena; Geeta Seshu; and Sujata Anandan. *Trial by Fire: A Report on Roop Kanwar's Death*. Bombay: Bombay Union of Journalists, 1987.

Meyer, Thomas. *Fundamentalismus*. Hamburg: Rowohlt, 1989.

Miller, Barbara Stoler. *The Bhagavad-gita: Krishna's Counsel in Time of War*. New York: Columbia University Press, 1986.

Mojumdar, Modhumita. "A Visit to Deorala 'Peeth'." *Mainstream* (December 26, 1987): 20–22.

Morgan, Marabel. *The Total Woman*. Old Tappan, N.J.: Fleming H. Revell, 1973.

Mujahid, Abdul Malik. *Conversion to Islam: Untouchables' Strategy for Protest in India*. Chambersburg, Penn.: Anima, 1989.

Nandy, Ashis. "An Anti-Secularist Manifesto." *Seminar* 314 (October 1985): 14–24.

———. *At the Edge of Psychology: Essays in Politics and Culture*. Delhi: Oxford University Press, 1980.

———. *The Intimate Enemy: Loss and Recovery of Self under Colonialism*. Delhi: Oxford University Press, 1983.

Narasimhan, Sakuntala. *Sati: Widow Burning in India*. New York: Anchor Books, 1992.

Naseem, Mohammad Farogh. *The Shah Bano Case: X-Rayed*. Karachi: Karachi Legal Research Center, 1988.

Newman, D. "Gush Emunim Between Fundamentalism and Pragmatism." *Jerusalem Quarterly* 39 (1986): 33–44.

Noonan, John T., Jr. "An Almost Absolute Value in History." In Noonan, ed., *The Morality of Abortion: Legal and Historical Perspectives* (Cambridge, Mass.: Harvard University Press, 1970), pp. 1–59.

Oberoi, Harjot Singh. "Sikh Fundamentalism: Translating History into Theory." Unpublished paper.

Patel, Sujata, and Krishna Kumar. "Defenders of Sati." *Economic and Political Weekly* 23(4) (January 23, 1988): 129–30.

Peil, Barbara A. "A Seasoned Approach." *Kindred Spirit* 11 (Spring 1987): 6–7, 12–13.

Perlez, Jane. "A Fundamentalist Finds a Fulcrum in Sudan." *New York Times*, January 29, 1992, A3.

Pettigrew, Joyce. "In Search of a New Kingdom of Lahore." *Asian Affairs* 60(1) (1987): 1–25.

Qadeer, Imrana. "Roop Kanwar and Shah Bano." *Seminar* 342 (February 1988): 31–33.

Quinton, Anthony. "Idealists Against the Jews." *New York Review of Books*, November 7, 1991, pp. 38–40.

Rapoport, David C., ed. *Inside Terrorist Organizations*. New York: Columbia University Press, 1988.

Reill, Peter Hans. *The German Enlightenment and the Rise of Historicism*. Berkeley: University of California Press, 1975.

Riesebrodt, Martin. *Fundamentalismus als patriarchalische Protestbewegung: Amerikanische Protestanten (1910–28) und iranische Schiiten (1967–79) im Vergleich*. Tubingen: J.C.B. Mohr (Paul Siebeck), 1990.

Rose, Paul L. *Revolutionary Antisemitism in Germany from Kant to Wagner*. Princeton, N.J.: Princeton University Press, 1990.

Rosenbloom, Noah. *HaMalbim*. Jerusalem: Mossad Harav Kook, 1988.

Rowe, Maureen. "The Woman in Rastafari." *Caribbean Quarterly*. Monograph (Kingston, Jamaica: University of the West Indies, 1985).

Ruether, Rosemary Radford, and Rosemary Skinner Keller, eds. *Women and Religion in America*. 3 vols. San Francisco: Harper & Row, 1981.

Ryan, Patrick J. "Islamic Fundamentalism: A Questionable Category." *America* 151(21) (1984): 437–40.

Sahliyeh, Emile, ed. *Religious Resurgence and Politics in the Contemporary World*. Albany, N.Y.: SUNY Press, 1990.

Sangari, Kumkum. "Perpetuating the Myth." *Seminar* 342 (February 1988): 24–30.

———. "There is No Such Thing as Voluntary Sati." *Times of India Sunday Review*, October 25, 1987, p. 3.

Sangari, Kumkum, and Sudesh Vaid. "Sati in Modern India: A Report." *Economic and Political Weekly* 16(31) (August 1981), pp. 1284–88.

Sharot, Stephen. *Messianism, Mysticism, and Magic: A Sociological Analysis of Jewish Religious Movements.* Chapel Hill: University of North Carolina Press, 1982.

Shourie, Arun. "The Shariat." *Illustrated Weekly of India* (January 5, 12, and 19, 1986).

Shweder, Richard. *Thinking Through Cultures: Expeditions in Cultural Psychology.* Cambridge, Mass.: Harvard University Press, 1991.

Siddiqui, H. Y. *Muslim Women in Transition: A Social Profile.* New Delhi: Harnam Publications, 1987.

Silber, Michael K. "The Enlightened Absolutist State and the Transformation of Jewish Society: Tradition in Crisis? Toward the Emergence of a Neutral Polity in the Reign of Joseph II." Paper presented to the conference "*Tradition and Crisis* Revisited." Harvard University, October 11–12, 1988.

_____. "The Roots of the Hungarian Schism." Ph.D. dissertation, Hebrew University, 1985.

Singh, Indu Prakash. *Indian Women: The Captured Beings.* New Delhi: Intellectual Publishing House, 1990.

Singh, Joginder. "Bhai Kahan Singh's Ham Hindu Nahin." *Journal of Sikh Studies* 14(1) (1987): 65–74.

Sivan, Emmanual, and Menachem Friedman, eds. *Religious Radicalism and Politics in the Middle East.* Albany, N.Y.: SUNY Press, 1990.

Sizer, Sandra S. *Gospel Hymns and Social Religion: The Rhetoric of Nineteenth-Century Revivalism.* Philadelphia: Temple University Press, 1978.

Sofer, Moses. *Derashot*, ed. by Joseph Stern. Vol 1. New York (no publisher), 1961.

Sofer, Solomon, ed. *Iggerot Soferim.* Tel Aviv: Sinai Publishing, 1970.

Sprinzak, Ehud. "*Gush Emunim*: The Tip of the Iceberg." *Jerusalem Quarterly* 21 (1981): 28–47.

Stanislawski, Michael. *Tsar Nicholas I and the Jews.* Philadelphia: Jewish Publication Society, 1983.

Sunder Rajan, Rajeswari. "The Subject of Sati: Pain and Death in the Contemporary Discourse on Sati." *Yale Journal of Criticism* 3(2) (1990): 1–23.

Thaiss, Gustav. "The Conceptualization of Social Change Through Metaphor." *Journal of Asian and African Studies* 13(1–2) (1978): 1–13.

Troeltsch, E. *Protestantism and Progress.* Philadelphia: Fortress Press, 1986.

Tully, Mark. *The Defeat of a Congressman and Other Parables of Modern India.* New York: Alfred A. Knopf, 1992.

Tunnell, Gary G. *Culture and Biology: Becoming Human.* Basic Concepts in Anthropology Series. Minneapolis: Burgess Publishing, 1973.

Twersky, Isadore, ed. *Aspects of the Modern History of Hungarian Jewry.* Cambridge, Mass.: Harvard University Press, forthcoming.

Vaid, Sudesh. "Politics of Widow Immolation." *Seminar* 342 (February 1988): 20–23.

Vaid, Sudesh, and Kumkum Sangari, "Institutions, Beliefs, Ideologies: Widow

Immolation in Contemporary Rajasthan," *Economic and Political Weekly* 26(17) (April 27, 1991): WS-2–18.

Wallace, Anthony F. C. "Revitalization Movements." *American Anthropologist* 58 (1956): 264–81.

Watt, W. Montgomery. *Islamic Fundamentalism and Modernity*. London: Routledge, 1988.

Wengeroff, Pauline. *Memoiren einer Grossmutter*. Vol. 2. Berlin: Verlag von M. Poppelauer, 1913.

Williams, Michael A. "Religious Innovation: Towards an Introductory Essay." Working paper, University of Washington, January, 1988.

Yang, Anand A. "Whose Sati?: Widow Burning in Early 19th Century India." *Journal of Women's History* 1(2) (1989): 8–33.

Zakaria, Rafiq. "In Defence of the Shariat." *Illustrated Weekly of India* (March 2 and 9, 1986).

Contributors

Peter J. Awn is professor of Islamic Religion and Comparative Religion at Columbia University. He recently completed a term as Chair of the Department of Religion. Professor Awn received his Ph.D in Islamic Religion and Comparative Religion from Harvard University in 1978. Previously he earned degrees in Philosophy, Classical Languages, and Christian Theology. Professor Awn's book, *Satan's Tragedy and Redemption: Iblīs in Sufi Psychology* (Leiden: E. J. Brill, 1983), a study of the devil in Islamic mysticism, received a book award from the American Council of Learned Societies. He was also the first recipient of the Phillip and Ruth Hettleman Award for distinguished teaching and research at Columbia University.

Karen McCarthy Brown is professor of the Sociology and Anthropology of Religion in the Graduate and Theological Schools at Drew University. Since 1973, she has carried out research on Haitian culture and traditional religion, both in Haiti and in the Haitian immigrant community in Brooklyn. Her written work includes numerous articles on women and on Vodou, as well as the book *Mama Lola: A Vodou Priestess in Brooklyn* (Berkeley: University of California Press, 1991), which was awarded the Victor Turner Prize in Ethnographic Writing by the Society for Humanistic Anthropology of the American Anthropological Association.

Randall Balmer, an associate professor of Religion at Barnard College, Columbia University, is the author of *A Perfect Babel of Confusion: Dutch Religion and English Culture in the Middle Colonies* (New York: Oxford University Press, 1989) and *Mine Eyes Have Seen the Glory: A Journey into the Evangelical Subculture in America* (New York: Oxford University Press, 1989). He has published widely in scholarly and academic journals, and his weekly commentaries on American religion are distributed by the New York Times

Syndicate. His three-part documentary on American evangelicalism, *Mine Eyes Have Seen the Glory,* aired on national television in the spring of 1993.

Helen Hardacre is Reischauer Institute Professor of Japanese Religions and Society, Harvard University. She earned her Ph.D. from the University of Chicago in History of Religions in 1980 and is the author of *Shintō and the State, 1868–1988* (Princeton, N.J.: Princeton University Press, 1989), *Kurozumikyō and the New Religions of Japan* (Princeton, N.J.: Princeton University Press, 1986), *The Religion of Japan's Korean Minority* (Berkeley: University of California Korean Studies Monograph, 1984), and *Lay Buddhism in Contemporary Japan: Reiyūkai Kyōdan* (Princeton, N.J.: Princeton University Press, 1984).

Jay M. Harris is the Harris K. Weston Associate Professor of the Humanities at Harvard University. He is the author of *Nachman Krochmal: Guiding the Perplexed of the Modern Age* (New York: New York University Press, 1991) and *"How Do We Know This?": The Exegetical Foundations of Jewish Law and the Fragmentation of Modern Judaism* (Albany, N.Y.: SUNY Press, 1994).

John S. Hawley is Director of the Southern Asian Institute at Columbia University and Professor and Chair in the Department of Religion at Barnard College. His published works include several books on the devotional literature of Krishna; a co-edited study of Indian goddesses, *The Divine Consort* (Boston: Beacon Press, 1986); and an introductory survey of the major poet-saints of North India, *Songs of the Saints of India,* with Mark Juergensmeyer (New York: Oxford University Press, 1988). A recently edited collection, *Sati, the Blessing and the Curse* (New York: Oxford University Press, 1994), explores matters directly relevant to *Fundamentalism and Gender.*

Wayne Proudfoot is Professor of Religion at Columbia University. His interests include philosophy of religion, modern European and American religious thought, and religious ethics. He is the author of *Religious Experience* (Berkeley: University of California Press, 1985) and is currently working on a book on pragmatism and American religious thought.

Index